# Resurrection of the Body in Early Judaism and Early Christianity

*Doctrine, Community, and Self-Definition*

BY

CLAUDIA SETZER

BRILL ACADEMIC PUBLISHERS, INC.
BOSTON • LEIDEN
2004

Library of Congress Cataloging-in-Publication Data

Setzer, Claudia
    Resurrection of the body in early Judaism and early Christianity / Claudia
    Setzer.
        p. cm.
    Includes bibliographical references (p.   ) and index.
    ISBN 0–391–04175–4
    1. Resurrection—History of doctrines. I. Title.

BT873.S48  2004
236'.8'09015—dc22

2004009982

ISBN 0–391–04175–4
Paperback ISBN 0–391–04243–2

PRINTED IN THE UNITED STATES OF AMERICA

# RESURRECTION OF THE BODY IN
# EARLY JUDAISM AND EARLY CHRISTIANITY

For Michael

# CONTENTS

# ACKNOWLEDGEMENTS

I wish to thank the many people who contributed to this work by their encouragement, advice, and bibliographic suggestions, including Andrea Berlin, Debra Reed Blank, Thomas Ferguson, Martin Goodman, Timothy Horner, Robin Jensen, Richard Kalmin, Nita Krevans, Steve Mason, Byron McKane, Seth Schwartz, Alan Segal, Stephen Shoemaker, Burton Visotzky, and Azzan Yadin. Thanks also to Seth Kasten, the reference librarian at Union Theological Seminary, who has graciously fielded my nit-picking requests for many years. John J. Collins read a portion of an early draft and offered helpful advice. Colleagues Celia Deutsch and Donald Gray read the entire manuscript and critiqued it carefully, eliminating many errors and much fuzzy thinking. The beginning stages of this project were supported by the Spalding Trust (UK) and a sabbatical from Manhattan College.

It is a source of pleasure and trepidation that two distinguished scholars have written ambitious works on resurrection at approximately the same time as I. N. T. Wright's book was published after the bulk of this work was finished, but I found much of his material helpful and congenial to mine. Alan Segal's work is not yet published as this goes to press, but I have profited from conversations with him, a public presentation, and his friendly encouragement.

Thanks to Oxford University Press for permission to publish portions of my article, "Resurrection as Symbol and Strategy," originally published in *JAAR*.

A special thanks to my editor, Patrick Alexander, who has always made me feel this was a joint project. His high standards have greatly improved the quality of this work, and his steady support has made it possible.

My deep thanks to my colleagues at Manhattan College, who provide a warm atmosphere of scholarly energy and collegiality, and also to my sister scholars and supportive friends Celia Deutsch and Diane Sharon. My children, Leora and Alexander, keep me centered and whole. My husband, Michael Greenwald, is at the heart of my life and work. The daily blessings of their presence have helped me bring this work to completion.

# ABBREVIATIONS

| | |
|---|---|
| *ABD* | *Anchor Bible Dictionary* |
| *ANF* | *Ante-Nicene Fathers* |
| *ANRW* | *Aufstieg und Niedergang des römischen Welt: Geschichte und Kultur Roms im Spiegel der neueren Forschung.* **Edited by H. Temporini and W. Haase. Berlin. 1972–** |
| *AnSt* | *Anatolian Studies* |
| *BA* | *Biblical Archaeologist* |
| *BJS* | *Brown Judaic Studies* |
| *BRev* | *Bible Review* |
| *BS* | *Beth She'arim II: The Greek Inscriptions.* **Edited by M. Schwabe and B. Lifshitz. Jerusalem. 1974** |
| *CCSL* | *Corpus Christianorum: Series latinae.* **Turnhout. 1953–** |
| *CIA* | *Corpus inscriptionum atticarum* |
| *CIG* | *Corpus inscriptionum graecarum.* **Edited by A. Boeckh. 4 vols. Berlin. 1828–1877** |
| *CIJ* | *Corpus inscriptionum judaicarum* |
| *FRLANT* | *Forschungen zur Religion und Literatur des Alten und Neuen Testaments* |
| *HR* | *History of Religions* |
| *HSM* | *Harvard Semitic Monographs* |
| *HTR* | *Harvard Theological Review* |
| *HTS* | *Harvard Theological Studies* |
| *HUCA* | *Hebrew Union College Annual* |
| *Int* | *Interpretation* |
| *JAAR* | *Journal of the American Academy of Religion* |
| *JBL* | *Journal of Biblical Literature* |
| *JECS* | *Journal of Early Christian Studies* |
| *JJS* | *Journal of Jewish Studies* |
| *JQR* | *Jewish Quarterly Review* |
| *JR* | *Journal of Religion* |
| *JRH* | *Journal of Religious History* |
| *JSJSup* | *Journal for the Study of Judaism in the Persian, Hellenistic, and Roman Periods: Supplement Series* |
| *JSNT* | *Journal for the Study of the New Testament* |
| *JSNTSup* | *Journal for the Study of the New Testament: Supplement Series* |

| | |
|---|---|
| *JSOTSup* | *Journal for the Study of the Old Testament: Supplement Series* |
| *JSPSup* | *Journal for the Study of the Pseudepigrapha: Supplement Series* |
| *JTS* | *Journal of Theological Studies* |
| *LCL* | *Loeb Classical Library* |
| *MAMA* | *Monumenta Asiae Minoris Antiqua.* Manchester and London. 1928–1993 |
| *NAPSMS* | *North American Patristic Society Monograph Series* |
| *NHC* | *Nag Hammadi Codices* |
| *NovT* | *Novum Testamentum* |
| *NTS* | *New Testament Studies* |
| *PEQ* | *Palestine Exploration Quarterly* |
| *PTS* | *Patristiche Texte und Studien* |
| *RHR* | *Revue de l'histoire des religions* |
| *RSLR* | *Rivista di Storia e Letteratura Religiosa* |
| *SBLDS* | *Society of Biblical Literature Dissertation Series* |
| *SBLMS* | *Society of Biblical Literature Monograph Series* |
| *SBT* | *Studies in Biblical Theology* |
| *SecCent* | *Second Century* |
| *VC* | *Vigiliae christianae* |
| *WUNT* | *Wissenschaftliche Untersuchungen zum Neuen Testament* |
| *ZDPV* | *Zeitschrift des deutschen Palästina-Vereins* |
| *ZNW* | *Zeitschrift für die neutestamentliche Wissenschaft und die Kunde der älteren Kirche* |

# CHAPTER ONE

# INTRODUCTION

"Your doubts, I believe, would be about the power of God?" Tertullian accuses critics who ridicule the idea that the body can be resurrected after death. He reminds them that God created the world and the human being, feats that overshadow resurrection, the mere re-creation of bodies that have already existed (*Apol.* 48.7).

Tertullian's argument illustrates an essential point: early Jews and Christians who believed in bodily resurrection did not accept it as an isolated tenet, but as part of a constellation of beliefs. Belief in resurrection carried with it a set of other tenets, some explicit, some implicit. The most common corollary is the one Tertullian points to here, the power of God.[1] Other ideas that frequently accompany resurrection are ultimate justice, reward for the righteous and punishment for the wicked, confidence in the election of those who hold this belief, and the legitimacy of those who preach and teach resurrection. Drawing multiple ideas in its tow, resurrection possessed a peculiar utility for groups struggling to define themselves. In this book I will show that the way certain groups understood the rich hope in resurrection sheds light on how these groups saw themselves, how they saw others, and how they coped with political and social realities. The assertion of resurrection is ultimately about human dignity and autonomy in the face of hostility. Frederick Douglass chose it as his metaphor when he described how he fought back and beat a brutal master: "A man, without force, is without the essential dignity of humanity. . . . After resisting him, I felt as I had never felt before. It was a *resurrection* from the dark and pestiferous tomb of slavery to the heaven of comparative freedom. . . . This spirit made me a freeman in *fact*, while I remained a slave in *form*."[2] For early

---

[1] This is illustrated in the history of the idea of resurrection through the medieval period. See Caroline Walker Bynum, *The Resurrection of the Body in Western Christianity 200–1336* (New York: Columbia University Press, 1995) 2.

[2] *My Bondage and My Freedom* (New York: Arno and New York Times, 1969) 246–47.

Jews and Christians too, belief in resurrection seemed to say outward forms did not tell the whole truth about deeper realities.

While ideas of some form of afterlife were common in the ancient world, those who believed in resurrection of the body were a minority. Some rejected any idea of afterlife. Many, like the pagan Celsus, thought along Platonic lines,[3] seeing the body as a hindrance whose resurrection would be neither possible nor desirable. He says, "As for the flesh, which is full of things it is not even nice to mention, God would neither desire nor be able to make it everlasting contrary to reason," or more graphically, "What sort of human soul would have any further desire for a body that has rotted?" (*Against Celsus* 5.14). The immortal soul is simply liberated from the impediment of the body at death and continues its existence, according to its deathless nature. No break in existence or divine intervention is necessary. Resurrection, on the other hand, which assumes the death of the body and its restoration after a period of being dead, can only happen through divine action.

Between the two poles of resurrection of the body and immortality of the soul is a range of ideas of the afterlife, many of them not fully articulated.[4] In the materials we will look at, the term "resurrection" does not always say bodily resurrection, nor does it necessarily clarify what kind of body will be raised. Within one set of materials, or even the writings of a single author, divergent beliefs about the afterlife appear.[5]

---

[3] The classic notions of the body as the prison of the immortal soul and death as the liberator of the soul are usually associated with Plato's *Phaedo*, but are probably Plato's reworking of earlier Orphic or Pythagorean ideas, according to Helen North, "Death and Afterlife in Greco-Roman Tragedy and Plato," in Hiroshi Obayashi, ed., *Death and Afterlife: Perspectives of World Religions* (New York: Greenwood, 1992) 49–64. Werner Jaeger shows that earliest Greek poetry shows no sign of belief in immortality of the soul either, but counts on names and the memory of their deeds to save the deceased from oblivion. He also believes that evolution of the concept of an immortal soul preceded Plato: "The Greek Ideas of Immortality," in Krister Stendahl, ed., *Immortality and Resurrection* (New York: Macmillan, 1965) 97–114.

[4] John J. Collins warns against drawing a simple dichotomy between Greek belief in immortality of the soul versus Jewish belief in the resurrection of the body ("The Afterlife in Apocalyptic Literature," in Alan Avery-Peck and Jacob Neusner, eds., *Judaism in Late Antiquity. Part 4. Death, Life after Death, Resurrection, and the World to Come in the Judaisms of Antiquity* [Leiden: Brill, 2000] 129). The popularity of this dichotomy is partly the result of the influential article of Oscar Cullmann, "Immortality of the Soul or Resurrection of the Dead?" in Stendahl, *Immortality and Resurrection*, 9–53 and Cullmann's *Christ and Time* (Philadelphia: Westminster, 1950).

[5] Josephus, for one, expresses a range of beliefs. See Joseph Sievers, "Josephus on the Afterlife," in Steve Mason, ed., *Understanding Josephus* (*JSPSup* 32; Sheffield:

I will briefly review the emergence of some different beliefs in resurrection in this chapter, but that is not the purpose of this book.[6]
In this study I will focus on instances in the first and second century
where the belief in resurrection is crucial to the self-definition of
community. In a striking number of cases people who claim authority

Sheffield Academic Press, 1998) 20–34. Tertullian cites Plato in one instance, claiming every soul is immortal (*Res. Mort.* 3.2, *CCSL* 2.924), but in another case he
maintains people will be raised with all their body parts, including those that will
no longer be needed, such as mouth, teeth, and sex organs.

[6] Numerous books and articles trace the early history of the belief in forms of
the afterlife in earliest Judaism and Christianity. For the Ancient Near East and
the Hebrew Bible, see Richard Friedman and Shawna Overton, "Death and Afterlife:
The Biblical Silence," in Avery-Peck and Neusner, *Death, Life after Death*, 35–59;
Edwin Yamauchi, "Life, Death, and Afterlife in the Ancient Near East," in Richard
Longenecker, ed., *Life in the Face of Death* (Grand Rapids: Eerdmans, 1998) 21–50;
J. A. Scurlock, "Death and Afterlife in Ancient Mesopotamian Thought," in Jack
Sasson, ed., *Civilizations of the Ancient Near East* (New York: Scribner's, 1995) 4.1883–93;
J. Cooper, "The Fate of Mankind: Death and Afterlife in Ancient Mesopotamia"
in Obayashi, *Death and Afterlife*, 19–33. For Egypt specifically, see William Murnane,
"Taking It with You: The Problem of Death and Afterlife in Ancient Egypt," in
Obayashi, *Death and Afterlife*, 35–48. For the Hebrew Bible, sometimes extending
into the Hellenistic period, see George Mendenhall, "From Witchcraft to Justice:
Death and Afterlife in the Old Testament," in Obayashi, *Death and Afterlife*, 67–81;
Robert Martin-Achard, *From Death to Life* (Edinburgh: Oliver and Boyd, 1960); idem,
"Resurrection (Old Testament)," *ABD* 5.680–84; Aimo Nikolainen, *Der Auferstehungsglaube
in der Bibel und ihrer Umwelt* (2 vols.; Helsinki, 1944–46); Robert Grant, "The
Resurrection of the Body," *JR* 28.2 (1948) 120–30 and 28.3 (1948) 188–208. For
works that emphasize the later, Hellenistic period, see Neil Gillman, *The Death of
Death* (Woodstock, VT: Jewish Lights, 1997); George Nickelsburg, *Resurrection, Immortality
and Eternal Life in Intertestamental Judaism* (HTS 26; Cambridge, Mass.: Harvard
University, 1972; idem, "Resurrection (Early Judaism and Christianity)," *ABD* 5.684–
91; Hans Cavallin, *Life after Death* (Gleerup: CWK, 1974); Stendahl, *Immortality and
Resurrection* (New York: Macmillan, 1965); Jon Davies, *Death, Reburial, and Rebirth in
Religions of Antiquity* (New York: Routledge, 1999); Avery-Peck and Neusner, *Death,
Life after Death*; Alan Segal, "Life after Death: The Social Sources," in Stephen Davis,
Daniel Kendall, and Gerald O'Collins, eds., *The Resurrection* (Oxford and New York:
Oxford University, 1997) 90–125; idem, *Life after Death: A History of the Afterlife in
Western Religion* (New York: Doubleday, 2004); Simcha Raphael, *Jewish Views of the
Afterlife* (Northvale and London: Jason Aronson, 1994); Nissan Rubin, "The Sages'
Conception of Body and Soul," in Simcha Fishbane, Jack Lightstone, eds., *Essays
in the Social Scientific Study of Judaism* (Montreal: Concordia University, 1990); idem,
*Kets ha-hayim* (Heb.) (Tel Aviv: ha-kibuts ha-me'uhad, 1997) 47–103; David Kraemer,
*The Meanings of Death in Rabbinic Judaism* (London and New York: Routledge, 2000);
Robert Goldenberg, "Bound Up in the Bond of Life: Death and Afterlife in Jewish
Tradition," in Obayashi, *Death and Afterlife*, 97–108. For the New Testament, see
N. T. Wright, *The Resurrection of the Son of God* (Minneapolis: Fortress, 2003);
Pheme Perkins, *Resurrection* (Garden City, N.Y.: Doubleday, 1984); Leander Keck,
"Death and Afterlife in the New Testament," in Obayashi, *Death and Afterlife*, 83–96;
Bruce Chilton, "Resurrection in the Gospels," in Avery-Peck and Neusner, *Death,
Life after Death*, 215–39; Gerd Luedemann, *The Resurrection of Jesus* (Minneapolis:
Fortress, 1994); Craig Evans, *Resurrection and the New Testament* (SBT 2.12; Napier,

declare others do not belong because they do not believe in resurrection. For these authors it stands as a boundary marker between
authentic representatives of the faith and those who only claim to
belong.[7]

Despite the presence of resurrection in Jewish liturgy and its centrality in Christian theology, in many of today's churches and synagogues we can hardly imagine declaring someone an outsider who
admitted she or he did not expect personal resurrection or even any
kind of afterlife. The issue is not as highly charged for today's believers. Why did it excite people so in these early centuries? Why did
it contribute to the popularity of the Pharisees, who were distinguished by their teaching of it? Why are the Sadducees "written
off " as ignoramuses for their rejection of it? Why does Paul tell the
Corinthians that if there is no general resurrection, then Christ himself was not raised, and the whole of their lives is a waste? Why
does Justin declare that those who reject resurrection do not deserve
to be called Christians? Why do the rabbis name those who reject
resurrection as one of three types who will be denied the next world,
a privilege extended to all Israel, thus reading them out of "Israel?"
What makes resurrection the touchstone?

The answer, I will argue, lies in the peculiar utility of resurrection as a symbol in the construction of community. A classic symbol, it reaches beyond itself.[8] Other ideas coalesce around it. But a
symbol is a not a static entity: rather, it is a tool to make meaning.
As Anthony Cohen observes, it supplies part of the meaning itself,
but is mediated by the experience of the people using it. "Symbols,"
he says, "do not so much express meaning as give us the capacity
to make meaning."[9] In his work on modern communities, he sees

---

Ill.: Allenson, 1970); Henry Joel Cadbury, "Intimations of Immortality in the Thought
of Jesus," in Stendahl, *Immortality and Resurrection*, 115–49; Jürgen Moltmann, *Is There
Life after Death?* (Milwaukee: Marquette University, 1998).

[7] I have not included Origen in this study because I am primarily interested in
the first two centuries. He inherits the developing Christian resurrection apologetic,
but his argument turns away from a material understanding of resurrection to a
more complex notion of spiritual transformation.

[8] Ernst Cassirer calls humans unique as "the symbolizing animal." Humans live
in a different world from other animals by virtue of their ability to think in symbols. Not only do symbols render human experience broader, but they also endow
it with another dimension. See *An Essay on Man* (New Haven: Yale University,
1944), especially pp. 23–41.

[9] Anthony Cohen, *The Symbolic Construction of Community* (London and New York:
Tavistock, 1985). Clifford Geertz's discussion of a symbol as a "vehicle for con-

that it is particularly at boundaries between groups that symbols become charged with importance. In the material we will consider, the belief in resurrection of the dead is part of the forging of community, and is part of a strategy of coping with the distance between what is and what ought to be.

Work in the social sciences and the discipline of rhetoric can supply us with language and categories that help us understand how the idea worked. While no single paradigm explains every use of the belief in resurrection, a family resemblance emerges in the way resurrection functions across communities. Some useful works that train new light on old evidence are Anthony Cohen's discussion of the use of symbols in the construction of community, Ann Swidler's theory of culture as a "tool-kit," and the social-political interpretations of Richard Horsley and Neil Elliott. The work of Chaim Perelman and Lucie Olbrechts-Tyteca and of Averil Cameron focus on rhetoric and rhetorical strategies. While these theories differ on the degree they deem human behavior is conscious or voluntary, they bear a loose similarity in that they all circle around problems of struggle and opposition, group identity, and self-respect. The religions of late antiquity have not left us the kind of evidence that allows a simple importation of modern theories like Cohen's and Swidler's.[10] Horsley, for example, in his critique of functionalism, warns that we run the danger of being ahistorical, and dealing only in abstractions, substituting modern, social-scientific ones for ancient ones, bringing us no closer to the people we hope to understand. Looking so closely at a single belief, resurrection, also risks reductionism, hanging everything on this belief that is part of a larger constellation of values.

─────────

ception" is behind our discussion here. He notes, "Cultural acts, the construction, apprehension, and utilization of symbolic forms, are social forms like any other; they are as public as marriage and as observable as agriculture." See Geertz, "Religion as a Cultural System," *The Interpretation of Cultures* (New York: Basic Books, 1973) 87–125. Cohen shows the plastic, multiform quality of symbols. Both writers emphasize that humans use symbols to make meaning.

[10] Horsley aptly describes the problems of using the social sciences to study early Judaism and Christianity in *Sociology and the Jesus Movement* (New York: Crossroad, 1989) 4–9. The problems are, roughly, the nature of the evidence as fragmentary and indirect, commensurability, and the danger of substituting a new form of abstraction for the old. The term "commensurability," an appropriate match between models and the thing studied, or between modern and ancient contexts, belongs to Stanley Stowers, who also summarizes the problems inherent in the use of social sciences to study ancient religion. See "The Social Sciences and the Study of Early Christianity," in William Scott Green, ed., *Approaches to Ancient Judaism* (BJS 32; Atlanta: Scholars, 1985) 149–81.

I have chosen to focus on resurrection, first, for its intriguing strangeness. Bynum calls it "a notion of stunning oddness." Though it runs counter to what can be demonstrated empirically, it remains a hardy expression of human hope and worth, a response to the apparent isolation and hopelessness of death.[11] Furthermore, I have chosen resurrection because it is the belief that the ancient writers themselves chose as definitive. They point to other people and declare them in or out of their communities based on their attitudes about resurrection. While multiple ideas may be embedded in it, belief in resurrection itself is claimed as the crucial test.

In using the language of strategy, I am not suggesting that its adherents did not genuinely believe in resurrection, nor that their strategy was necessarily conscious or intentional. Beliefs perdure because they work. People use ideas, consciously or unconsciously, because they allow them to live in the world as it is. I do not think the idea worked in identical ways for all individuals or communities. Writers vary, audiences vary, and symbols have multiple meanings. We will look at individual moments in early Judaism and Christianity where belief in bodily resurrection highlights questions of identity and belonging.

### Historical Overview

When did Jews begin to believe in some form of afterlife, and in resurrection in particular? While it is a maxim that the Hebrew Bible contains little mention of the afterlife, and some conclude that ancient Israel must have rejected such beliefs, the picture is murkier. As Friedman and Overton[12] put it, the biblical silence on the afterlife is really more of a whisper. Several bodies of evidence, material and literary, suggest that ancient Israel did not think of life after death as personal oblivion: (1) archaeological finds from the Iron Age suggest the existence of ancestor cults, or at least the belief in some

---

[11] See Julia Kristeva's reflections on Hans Holbein's "Body of the Dead Christ in the Tomb" and its unflinching realism, which she suggests renders it close to contemporary sensibilities, in "Holbein's Dead Christ," Michel Feher, ed., *Zone 3. Fragments for a History of the Human Body: Part One* (3 vols.; New York: Zone, 1989) 238–69.

[12] Friedman and Overton, "Biblical Silence," in Avery-Peck and Neusner, *Death, Life after Death*, 36.

form of afterlife for the deceased. Tombs in Judah containing storage jars, vessels for eating and drinking, jewelry, and amulets imply the dead were seen as in need of sustenance and protection.[13] These goods parallel grave goods from Egypt and Ugarit, where they were clearly linked to the afterlife. Herbert Brichto made a case for ancestor worship in ancient Israel more than thirty years ago, marshalling a broad range of early and late biblical evidence, alluding to land-ownership and family claims on the land. If the dead relied on the living to perform rites to insure a pleasant afterlife, it necessitated continuing possession of ancestral land.[14] Friedman reminds us that the oldest fragment of biblical text, Num 6:24–26, inscribed on two tiny silver scrolls probably worn on the body (for protection after death?), was found in burial caves outside Jerusalem.[15] (2) Terms appear in the Hebrew Bible whose etymologies in the Ancient Near East suggest afterlife. "Sheol" may relate to an Akkadian word that means a place of interrogation, or a place reward or punishment is meted out (e.g., Deut 32:22; Isa 5:14, 14:9). "Rephaim" may mean patrons of the underworld, similar to Ugaritic and Phoenician terms for those in the underworld who can affect the living (e.g., Isa 14:9, 26:14; Ps 88:11). "Teraphim" may indicate ancestral figures used for divination, connected to the Hittite word for "spirit-ancestors" (e.g., Gen 31:34; 1 Sam 19:13, 2 Kings 23:24).[16] (3) Necromancy and divination are regularly condemned, but no one declares them ineffective. The need to suppress these practices testifies to their presence in Israel (Lev 19:26; 20:6; Deut 18:11; 1 Sam 28; 2 Kings 23:24; Isa 8:19). (4) Three resuscitation stories show that death can be overcome, if only temporarily (1 Kings 17; 2 Kings 4; 2 Kings 13:20–21). (5) Most significant for our study, the image of resurrection appears

---

[13] Elizabeth Bloch-Smith, *Judahite Burial Practices and Beliefs about the Dead* (*JSOTSup* 123; Sheffield: Sheffield Academic Press, 1992).

[14] Herbert C. Brichto, "Kin, Cult, and Afterlife," *HUCA* 44 (1973) 1–54. One recent reappraisal of this material is negative about the existence of a cult of the dead in ancient Israel: Brian Schmidt, *Israel's Beneficent Dead* (Tübingen: Mohr Siebeck, 1994); idem, "Memory as Immortality: Countering the Dreaded 'Death after Death' in Ancient Israelite Society," in Avery-Peck and Neusner, *Death, Life after Death*, 87–100.

[15] These scrolls are approximately mid-seventh century B.C.E. See Gabriel Barkay, *Ketef Hinnom: A Treasure Facing Jerusalem's Walls* (Jerusalem: The Israel Museum, 1986) 29–31.

[16] See Friedman and Overton's discussion of these terms, and more examples in "Biblical Silence," 41–45.

in several places. Ezekiel 37:1–15 presents the striking tableau of the
valley of the dry bones, where the bones are knit back together,
flesh covers them, breath enters them, and they return to life. Writing
in the sixth century B.C.E. after the destruction of the First Temple,
Ezekiel faces the uncertain future of exile. Most scholars understand
the vision of resurrection here to be a metaphor for national and
political restoration, not about the resurrection of the individual.
Similarly, the image of resurrection and overcoming of death occurs
in conjunction with hopes of political restoration in Isa 25:8: "He
will swallow up death forever, then the Lord God will wipe away
the tears from every face, and throughout the world remove the
indignities from his people. The Lord has spoken."[17] In contrast to
the dead of the enemy, the dead of Israel will revive: "But your
dead will live, their bodies will rise again. Those who sleep in the
earth will arise and shout for joy; for your dew is a dew of sparkling
light, and the earth will bring those long dead to life again" (Isa
26:19). This passage from the Isaian apocalypse is of disputed date.[18]
But it is clearly also in the context of national vindication.[19] Many
pass this off too as metaphor and not evidence of any belief in resurrection.[20] But metaphors cannot communicate if they have nothing to do with the way people think and live. These images in Ezekiel
and Isaiah likely are metaphorical, and not literal, but would be
meaningless in a context where afterlife is seen as an absurdity.[21]

---

[17] The imagery here parallels the myth of the Canaanite god Mot (death) who
swallows the fertility god Baal at the beginning of the dry season, and is defeated
in the spring by Baal.

[18] See the discussion of the wide range of proposals for dating in William Millar,
*Isaiah 24:27 and the Origin of Apocalyptic* (HSM 11; Missoula: Scholars, 1976). Millar
puts these chapters in the last half of the sixth century B.C.E.

[19] Some suggest Hos 6:1–3 is also about resurrection; however, it is not necessarily about resurrection from the dead, but rather revival of the downtrodden and
near-dead.

[20] An exception is Joseph Blenkinsopp, who questions the consensus that Israelite
religion lacked any sense of an afterlife. He cites Daniel as the first clear attesta-
tion, but argues that these earlier passages show "a less clearly delineated conviction of survival after death was emerging long before that time" *Isaiah* (AB; Garden
City: Doubleday, 2000) 371.

[21] This point is also made by Gillman, *Death of Death*, 74–75. N. T. Wright, for
example, understands a movement from the idea of the restoration of Israel as a
nation to the restoration of bodies (*Resurrection of the Son of God*, 204). He does not
explain why the early examples chose this particular metaphor.

The final passage, one most scholars see as the clearest testimony to resurrection in the Hebrew Bible, is Dan 12:1–3, a prediction that at the end of history Michael will appear and the people be delivered: ". . . Many of those who sleep in the dust of the earth will awake, some to everlasting life, and some to the reproach of eternal abhorrence" (v. 2). From 165–164 B.C.E., the text coincides with the time of the persecution under Antiochus Epiphanes. Unlike many others, I do not see the Daniel passage as so much more explicit than the Isaiah passage, or even the graphic Ezekiel passage. All three references emerge from situations of political turmoil and persecution. All use the image of resurrection of the physical body. All three passages could be metaphorical *or* literal. Furthermore, the continuation of the Daniel passage invokes an image of astral immortality, quite different from bodily resurrection: "The wise leaders will shine like the bright vault of heaven, and those who have guided the people in the true path will be like the stars forever and ever" (v. 3). The search for a chronological development does not succeed. An increasingly specific idea of resurrection does not seem to emerge as the texts get later. Rather, occasional glimpses of resurrection as a powerful image occur at different junctures.

The evidence for the afterlife in the Hebrew Bible is certainly sparse compared to the surrounding cultures in Egypt and Mesopotamia. How do we explain the odd combination of a dearth of explicit references to the afterlife in the Hebrew Bible, the shadowy suggestions of ancestor veneration and burial practices that imply an afterlife, and the live quality of resurrection, whether as poetic metaphor or literal hope, in texts of different date and provenance? Several scholars suggest a deliberate and only partially successful suppression of a cult of the dead in Israel, though they proffer different reasons for it. Mendenhall proposes that the emerging Yahwism sought to unify the people and discourage tribal and clan loyalties,[22] loyalties that would be strengthened by ancestor veneration. Friedman and Overton suggest that landless priests wanted to suppress local forms of worship (such as ancestor veneration) that would compete with a centralized priesthood. They also discouraged practices like necromancy that were not priestly skills. Perhaps there was simply a sense

---

[22] Mendenhall, "Witchcraft to Justice."

that preoccupation with death and afterlife was too "Egyptian,"[23] or
as Segal suggests, too "foreign."[24]

Some have argued that because resurrection appears in late sources
like Ezekiel, Daniel, and the Isaian Apocalypse,[25] the idea is a Zoro-
astrian one that entered Israel from its time in exile.[26] Edwin Yamauchi
has noted some difficulties with this thesis, including the lack of texts
from the Parthian period, the relative lateness of the idea in Zoro-
astrian texts, and its dissimilarity to the idea of resurrection in the
Hebrew Bible.[27] Jewish dead are buried and arise from the earth
through the power of Yahweh. Persian dead are exposed and recreated from the elements through a fiery ordeal. The evidence brought
above shows, Friedman and Overton note, that Israel entertained
the idea of an afterlife in practice, metaphor, and law at different
times in its history. Martin Achard's judgment of forty years ago
seems right, that, while Persian and Canaanite thought might have
played a role, "the essential element is nevertheless found in Israel
itself."[28] More recently, he reaffirms the idea: "the resurrection of
the dead, that is, of the body, is etched within the logic of Old
Testament concepts."[29] The idea of resurrection is implicit in both
the Hebrew Bible's notion of God as the creator of life and as the
ultimate victor over death, as well as the unified nature of the human
being as a body enlivened by breath. No idea is ever borrowed as
an undifferentiated whole. Even if an idea is foreign in origin, to
become popular, it must speak to historical exigencies and resonate
with the internal developments and deeper convictions of a people.

We do not know exactly when Israel translated the use of resurrection as a metaphor for national restoration into the hope of res-

---

[23] Friedman and Overton, "Biblical Silence," 49–56.

[24] Segal, "Life after Death," 91–92.

[25] The dating of Isaiah 25–26 is controversial, but many consider it post-exilic.

[26] Mary Boyce, *Zoroastrians* (London: Routledge, 1979); Bernhard Lang, "Afterlife:
Ancient Israel's Changing Vision of the World Beyond," *BRev* 4 (1988) 19. Discussion
of a foreign origin for Israel's notion of afterlife began early in the twentieth century. See Martin Achard, *From Death to Life*, 186–205, regarding the possible Persian
or Canaanite provenance of the idea. For a judicious assessment of the emergence
of resurrection as a response to external influence, internal development, and historical circumstances, see Gillman, *Death of Death*, 96–98.

[27] Yamauchi, "Life, Death," 47–49.

[28] "Death to Life," 221. Martin-Achard describes a gradual movement towards
the belief in bodily resurrection that comes to fruition in the encounter with Hellenism.
I am not convinced it was a steady development.

[29] "Resurrection (Old Testament)," *ABD* 5.683–84.

urrection of the body, nor exactly how much foreign elements were part of the mix. The essential ingredients for the hope were always present in the affirmation of God's power, his favor towards Israel, and the image of death as God's enemy. Because it appears explicitly in 2 Macc 7 and 12:43–45 and in Daniel, we can safely say it is apparent by the time of the Maccabean revolt and the confrontation with Hellenism.[30]

### The Hellenistic Period

The theme of the reward of the righteous at some future time is implanted in Israel's consciousness, while the expression of that reward is a mix of images of bodily and spiritual survival and revivification. From the second century B.C.E., *The Testament of Judah* describes the messianic age: "And after this Abraham, Isaac, and Jacob will be resurrected to life and I and my brothers will be chiefs (wielding) one scepter in Israel (25.1) . . . those who died in sorrow shall be raised in joy and those who died in poverty for the Lord's sake shall be made rich; and those who died on account of the Lord shall be wakened to life" (25.4).[31] In The Book of the Watchers (chs. 1–36, second–third century B.C.E.) in 1 Enoch, a heavenly journey allows Enoch to see secrets of the future, including the assembling for judgment and reward for the souls of the righteous: "Here shall they be gathered together, and here shall be their judgment in the last days. There will be upon them the spectacle of the righteous judgment, in the presence of the righteous forever" (27:3).[32] A portion of I Enoch a century later, approximately contemporary with 2 Maccabees and Daniel, conveys at least two different things: resurrection ("then the righteous one shall arise from his sleep, and the wise one shall

---

[30] Jan Willem van Henten sees the martyrs' death in 2 Maccabees as patriotic-political expressions. The deaths of Elazar, the seven sons, and Razis are turning-points in history, inaugurating the rescue of the Jews and re-establishment of a Jewish way of life (*The Maccabean Martyrs as Saviors of the Jewish People* [*JSJSup* 57; Leiden: Brill, 1997] 57, 297–301).

[31] Translated by Howard Clark Kee, in James Charlesworth, ed., *The OTP* (2 vols.; Garden City: Doubleday, 1983) 1:782–828.

[32] For a summary of afterlife in the apocrypha and pseudepigrapha, see J. J. Collins, "The Afterlife in Apocalyptic Literature," in Avery-Peck and Neusner, *Death, Life after Death*, 119–39; George Nickelsburg, "Judgment, Life after Death and Resurrection in the Apocrypha and Non-Apocalyptic Pseudepigrapha," in Avery-Peck and Neusner, *Death, Life after Death*, 141–62.

arise" [91:10–11]); and that the spirits of the righteous will come to
life ("the spirits of those who died in righteousness shall live; their
spirits shall not perish, nor their memorial from before the face of
the Great One unto all the generations of the world. Therefore do
not worry about their humiliation" [103:4]).[33] Jubilees, also from the
second century B.C.E., expresses similar ideas: the separation of righteous and the sinners and the wait for reward and punishment. The
bones of the righteous will rest, while their spirits will have joy:
". . . and the righteous ones will see and give praise, and rejoice forever and ever with joy; they will see all of their judgments and all
of their curses among their enemies, and their bones will rest in the
earth, and their spirits will increase joy" (23:30–31).[34]

Also from the second century B.C.E., the persecution under Antiochus
Epiphanes, 2 Maccabees 7 articulates the reward of the righteous
specifically as the reward for martyrs. The second son speaks under
torture: "With his final breath he said: 'Fiend though you are, you
are setting us free from this present life, and the King of the Universe
will raise us up to a life everlastingly made new, since it is for his
laws that we are dying'" (v. 9). The third son, holding out his hands
and tongue, says, "the God of heaven gave these to me, but his laws
mean far more to me than they do, and it is from him that I trust
to receive them again" (v. 11). The fourth son taunts the king: "For
you there will be no resurrection" (v. 14). The mother of the seven
brothers encourages them: "The Creator of the universe, who designed
the beginning of mankind and devised the origin of all, will in his
mercy give you back again breath and life, since now you put his
laws above every thought of self" (v. 23). The resurrection of physical bodies becomes explicit here, since it is the bodies that suffered.
Nickelsburg observes, "Bodily resurrection is the counterpart to bodily destruction; vindication is in kind."[35] Resurrection is explicitly
linked to the God of creation in 2 Macc 7:22–23 and generally to
the restoration of Israel.[36] In 2 Macc 12:43–45, the custom of a collection for a sin-offering for the dead affirms the expectation that
the bodies of the righteous will be raised up.

---

[33] Translation by E. Isaac, in Charlesworth, *OTP*, 1:5–89.
[34] Translation by O. S. Wintermute, in Charlesworth, *OTP*, 2:35–142.
[35] Nickelsburg, "Resurrection," *ABD* 5.686.
[36] Van Henten, *Maccabean Martyrs*.

Many ideas of the afterlife are not fully spelled out. We should not expect explicit definitions in materials that are poetic and often apocalyptic. Many fall somewhere between the options of immortality of the soul or resurrection of the body. Many refer to some kind of recompense and assume some necessary afterlife, but do not clarify the form it will take. Texts that refer to the afterlife in Judaism multiply after the second century B.C.E., producing a rich collection around the turn of the era.

The *Psalms of Solomon*, dated to the end of the first century B.C.E., is a response to the Roman annexation of Judea. Like Enoch, it speaks of heavenly ascents and displays strong themes of judgment: separation of the righteous and wicked according to their deeds. It introduces the theme of the "raising up" of the righteous after death and their enjoyment of eternal life in God's presence (2:31–34), versus the permanent oblivion of the wicked: "The destruction of the sinner is forever, and he will not be remembered when God looks after the righteous. This is the share of sinners forever, but those who fear the Lord will rise up to eternal life, and their life shall be in the Lord's light, and it shall never end" (3:11–12). In this text the wicked are punished by extinction and are erased from memory (13:11; 14:3; 15:3, 12). The writer describes a dramatic close call, where he is jabbed awake at the last moment: "For a moment my soul was poured out to death; (I was) near the gates of Hades with the sinner, thus my soul was drawn away from the Lord God of Israel, unless the Lord had come to my aid with his everlasting mercy. He jabbed me as a horse is goaded to keep it awake; my savior and protector at all times saved me" (16:2–4). While this work employs classic themes of temporary suffering as discipline and eventual extinction of the wicked, it introduces the idea that the eternal life of the holy ones comes with their being "raised up." It implies the resurrection of the body, but is hardly specific. How, when, and in what form the body will be resurrected are left to the imagination.

The Dead Sea Scrolls do not yield a single or sharply-defined picture of life after death, but rather a mosaic of many of the themes apparent in earlier Jewish materials.[37] Philip Davies describes the

---

[37] Davies argues that given the broad variety of materials, the search for a consistent view of the afterlife at Qumran is unpromising, but he sees Qumran as "direct descendants of the Judaism that gave rise to Daniel and Enoch." See "Death, Resurrection, and Life after Death in the Qumran Scrolls," Avery-Peck and Neusner, *Death, Life after Death*, 189–211.

recently published wisdom texts from Qumran Cave 4 as the most explicit about post-mortem survival. They exhibit the usual motifs of separation of the righteous and wicked for judgment, but with a heavy dose of determinism and a concept of saving knowledge. Unlike *Psalms of Solomon* or 2 Maccabees, where the evildoers richly earn their extinction, and the righteous through faithfulness and suffering earn eternal life, divine election determines who shall cling to Wisdom and enjoy "everlasting glory and eternal peace and the spirit of life" (4Q416 frag. 2, col. 15). Wisdom is described as an esoteric, secret knowledge, which God reveals to his elect. In CD 2:7–8, those who depart from the way and merit destruction were destined to stray from the beginning, while the chosen ones are atoned for by God himself: "From the beginning God did not choose them; before they were established he knew their works . . . those whom he hated he caused to stray" (2:13). But regarding the righteous, "[God] raised up for himself those called by name so as to leave a remnant from the land and to fill the face of the world with their seed" (2:11–12). Whether this raised-up remnant enjoys eternity through resurrection, translation to immortality, or in another form is unclear.

Similarly, the Rule of the Community proclaims that God determines humans and their works, creating in them the two spirits (1QS 3:15–20; 4:15–16). They will be set apart at the end of time (1QS 4:25–26). At that time God will purify humans and destroy the ways of deceit and darkness: "Then God will purify by his truth all the works of man and purge for himself the sons of man. He will utterly destroy the spirit of deceit from the veins of his flesh" (1QS 4.20–21). Although the notion of the purification of the body raises the question of afterlife, this document does not really speculate on life after death, but visualizes a satisfying climax to history in this world.

In the Hodayoth, the scroll of hymns, the body is in need of purification. It denigrates the "spirit of flesh" as made of dust, ruled by a spirit of waywardness, incapable of understanding the nature of God (1QH 5.19–24). But God can intervene to bestow upon the just person eternal salvation, "To bestow upon him your abundant compassion, and open the narrowness of his soul to eternal salvation, and endless, perfect peace. You raise up glory from flesh" (1QH 7.19). Later in the work resurrection becomes quite explicit: "Hoist a banner, O you who lie in the dust, Raise a standard, O you eaten by worms" (1QH 14.34). The purification of humanity from falsehood and the renewal of the holy ones requires resurrection, ". . . that bodies eaten by worms may be raised from the dust, to the counsel of your truth" (19.9–12).

According to Emile Puech, 4Q521 is the passage that affirms the belief in resurrection most explicitly in the DSS: "In his mercy he will judge, and the reward of good deeds shall be withheld from no one. The Lord will perform wonderful deeds such as have never been, as he said: for he will heal the wounded, make the dead live, proclaim good news to the meek, give generously to the needy, lead out the captive and feed the hungry . . . (frag. 2, col. 2, lines 9–13).[38] Davies submits that it may be a paraphrase of 1 Sam 2:6: "Yahweh causes to die and causes to live; he sends down to Sheol and brings up," and may simply refer to God's holding the power of life and death. It also echoes the prophets and psalms, referring to Yahweh's rescuing the downtrodden or the near-dead. In another fragment, as Puech reconstructs it, ". . . and they shall be for death, [when] the Reviver (hamechayeh) [makes] the dead of his people [ri]se. And we shall give thanks and declare to you the righteous deeds of the Lord, who [raises] the dead . . ." (frag. 5, col. 2, lines 5–8). Puech's reconstruction is not accepted by all. As in the other materials from this period, the nature of the afterlife in the Dead Sea Scrolls is not carefully delineated nor uniform across the documents.

In portions of Enoch that date to the first century C.E., the image of final judgment includes a transformation of the righteous into angel-like beings: "And I saw a dwelling place underneath the wings of the Lord of the Spirits, and all the righteous and the elect before him shall be as intense as the light of fire. Their mouth shall be full of blessing; and their lips will praise the name of the Lord of Spirits, and righteousness before him will have no end; and uprightness before him will not cease" (39:7). Resurrection is hinted at later in the text when Sheol will give back everything entrusted to it (51:1), including the dead.

A literal resurrection of the body appears in Sibylline Oracle 4, redacted around 80 C.E., "God himself will again fashion the bones and ashes of men . . . and he will raise up mortals then as they were before, and then there will be a judgment over which God himself

---

[38] Emile Puech, *La croyance des Esséniens en la vie future: immortalité, resurrection, vie éternelle? Histoire d'une croyance dans le judaïsme ancien* (Etudes Bibliques Nouvelle 22; Paris: Gabalda, 1993).

will preside" (lines 181–83). The impious remain buried, while the pious see the sun again (lines 187–93).[39]

Fourth Ezra and Second Baruch, from the late first century C.E., continue the theme of recompense and judgment, but continue to present a mixed picture of resurrection of the righteous, transformation to a luminous state, and immortality. The earth will yield up its dead, a messianic age will ensue, and the earth will return to its primordial state for seven days. The process of history will run backwards. "And after seven days the world, which is not yet awake, shall be roused, and that which is corruptible shall perish. And the earth shall give up those who are asleep in it; and the chambers shall give up the souls which have been committed to them" (*4 Ezra* 7.31–32). This will be followed by judgment: "Compassion shall pass away." Paradise and Gehenna are to be revealed, and a condemnation awaits "the nations that have not been raised from the dead" (7.37). Ezra asked what happens after death, when the soul has been yielded up (7.75). There is a period of seven days when, separated from the mortal body, some wander in torment seven ways (7.79–87). The faithful, also separated from their bodies, see seven ways, or orders, but never return to their mortal bodies: "The fifth order, they rejoice that they have escaped what is mortal, and shall inherit what is to come; and besides they see the straits and toil from which they have been delivered, and the spacious liberty which they are to receive and enjoy in immortality" (7.96). In the next stage, they pass into astral immortality: "The sixth order, when it is shown to them how their face is to shine like the sun, and how they are to be made like the light of the stars, being incorruptible from then on" (7.97).

In 2 Baruch, a work from the same period, the righteous are expected to rise after the messianic age: "When the time of the appearance of the Anointed One has been fulfilled and he returns with glory, then all who sleep in hope of him will rise, the righteous to enjoyment, the wicked to torment (30.1–2)." Whether the body is restored is not certain. When Baruch asks in what form they will return (49.2), it appears to be in the same form they had while on earth (50.2–3): "For the earth will surely give back the dead at that time; it receives them now in order to keep them, not chang-

---

[39] Translated by John J. Collins, in Charlesworth, *OTP*, 1:381–89.

ing anything in their form. But as it has received them so shall it give them back. And as I have delivered them to it, so it will raise them." It matters that those still alive recognize their revived dead (50.3–4). But then a transformation takes place: "The shape of those who are found to be guilty as also the glory of those who have proved to be righteous will be changed" (51.1). They will be glorified in their transformation: "Their splendor will then be glorified by transformations, and the shape of their face will be changed into the light of their beauty so that they may acquire and receive the undying world which is promised to them" (51.3). Collins suggests that this combination of resurrection and transformation to a luminous, deathless state may be similar to Paul's image of the raised spiritual body in 1 Corinthians 15.[40]

Pseudo-Phocylides, a Jewish wisdom text from the beginning of the era in Alexandria,[41] similarly juxtaposes an expectation of bodily resurrection and a claim of immortality of the soul (lines 103–15). It warns against disturbing or exposing the dead: "It is not good to dissolve the human frame. For in fact we hope that the remains of the departed will soon come to the light again out of the earth" (lines 103–5). But an apparent denial of resurrection appears: "For we have a body out of earth, and when afterwards we are resolved again into earth we are but dust; but the air has received our spirit" (line 107). Later, "We humans live not a long time but for a season. But our soul is immortal and lives ageless forever" (line 114).

As images of resurrection surfaced in varied texts, the concept of immortality of the soul apart from the body appeared in other Jewish materials as the reward of the righteous. The Wisdom of Solomon, from early first-century Alexandria, makes clear the body does not return (2.5), but for souls of the righteous, "their hope is full of immortality" (3.1–4); "the righteous live forever" (5.15), as opposed to the wicked, who are punished by extinction (4.19). Philo, from the same time and place, does not address the fate of the wicked, but says the souls of those who give themselves to philosophy await "a higher existence immortal and incorporeal in the presence of him who is himself immortal" (*Gig.* 14). Soul is too subtle for the body

---

[40] Collins, "Afterlife in Apocalyptic Literature," 130–31.
[41] See Pieter van der Horst, *The Sentences of Pseudo-Phocylides* (Leiden: Brill, 1978). That the author is a Jew is clear, says van der Horst, but his audience and purpose are less so.

to hold (*Cherub.* 115). *Fourth Maccabees* retells parts of 2 Maccabees, presenting the martyrdom of the seven youths and their mother as a triumph of reason, rewarded by immortality: ". . . but as though transformed by fire into immortality, he nobly endured the rackings" (9.2), and ". . . the prize was immortality in endless life" (17:12; also 13:17; 16:13, 25). Josephus reports a variety of views, some attributable to his sources, but seems most at ease with the Platonic idea that the soul is freed from the body at death.[42] He presents ideas of resurrection in language more suited to immortality. The Sadducees, according to non-Sadducean sources we have, do not believe in resurrection. They may have rejected afterlife altogether, or believed in the immortality of the soul.

### *Resurrection and Belonging*

Our quick survey shows that Jewish materials from the second century B.C.E. through the first century C.E. exhibit a range of understandings of afterlife. Fairly explicit claims of bodily resurrection appear in texts like *1 Enoch* (51), 2 Maccabees, 4Q521, and *Sibylline Oracle 4*. A mix of concepts of resurrection of the body and immortality of the soul appear in *1 Enoch* (91, 103), 1QH, *4 Ezra, 2 Baruch*, and Pseudo-Phocylides. Ambiguity prevails in works that nevertheless imply resurrection, such as "The Book of the Watchers" in *1 Enoch, The Testament of Judah, Psalms of Solomon*, and CD 2:7–12. Immortality of the soul awaits the just in *Jubilees*, 4 Maccabees, Wisdom of Solomon, and Philo's works. Within these broad categories certain sub-themes emerge, such as translation into angelic beings (*Enoch* 39), determinism and saving knowledge (4Q416, CD 2:7–8), and resurrection as reward for martyrdom (2 Maccabees 7).

The first time resurrection occurs as a doctrine by which others identify a certain group is the case of the Pharisees, reported by three sets of sources as a group that upholds resurrection. Resurrection appears in later rabbinic circles in the liturgy, law, and lore, also drawing a circle around who is in and who is out. We will examine both cases at length, instances where belief in resurrection marks a

---

[42] Sievers promotes criteria for separating Josephus's own beliefs from his sources, similar to the criteria of authenticity in New Testament studies. He argues that the idea of the body as a prison for the soul, which Josephus attributes to the Essenes, is congenial to his own views ("Josephus on the Afterlife," 31).

boundary between the groups. In later rabbinic materials a more dualistic conception of body and soul appears, as well as affirmation of the immortality of the soul. Both doctrines of resurrection of the body and immortality of the soul appear in tandem in *b. San.* 91a–b.[43] Later rabbinic literature and the targums contain material about resurrection and include some early statements. These documents, however, evolved over long periods and are redacted after the first century, so are not covered in this survey, but will be dealt with in the body of this work.[44]

Early Christian belief inherits and amplifies the Jewish themes attached to resurrection in its understanding of Jesus' resurrection and the corresponding guarantee of resurrection for believers. God's power is manifested by Jesus' resurrection, as he is so often referred to as "the God who raised Jesus."[45] The suffering ones are raised up and the righteous rewarded. Interestingly, although Jesus' own resurrection is at the heart of earliest Christian belief in general resurrection for the righteous, New Testament texts sometimes take pains to link their belief to broader Jewish belief in resurrection, minimizing the vast difference between a hope in general resurrection of the righteous in the future and the belief that Jesus had already risen from the dead. Jesus rebuffs the Sadducees for their lack of faith in it (Mark 12:24–27 and parallels); Martha replies to Jesus about her recently dead brother, "I know that he will rise again at the resurrection on the last day" (John 11:24); and Acts depicts Paul as a harmless Pharisee preaching general resurrection. The belief in Jesus' resurrection, in its intensified, apocalyptic version, is understood in different ways in the New Testament, but springs from the fertile soil of resurrection belief in first century Judaism.[46]

---

[43] Rubin argues that dualism of body and soul is a later development in rabbinic literature, corresponding to the rabbis' increasing alienation and powerlessness ("The Sages' Conception of Body and Soul"), in Fishbane and Lightstone, *Essays in the Social Scientific Study of Judaism,* 47–99.

[44] For an attempt to extract a "proto-Palestinian Targum," see Paul Flesher, "The Resurrection of the Dead and the Sources of the Palestinian Targums to the Pentateuch," in Avery-Peck and Neusner, *Death, Life after Death,* 311–31.

[45] Nickelsburg suggests this corresponds to the formula "the God who brought you out of Egypt." See "Resurrection," *ABD* 5.684; and Pamela Eisenbaum, "A Speech Act of Faith: The Early Proclamation of the Resurrection of Jesus," in Virginia Wiles, Alexandra Brown, and Graydon Snyder, eds., *Putting Body and Soul Together: Essays in Honor of Robin Scroggs* (Valley Forge, Penn.: Trinity Press International, 1997) 24–45.

[46] See Keck, "Death and Afterlife," in Obayashi, *Death and Afterlife*; Nickelsburg, "Resurrection," *ABD* 5.684; and Pheme Perkins, *Resurrection*, for a summary of the

Even this brief overview reveals several things: First, that there is
no direct and steady unfolding of the doctrine of resurrection over
time, without detours. Rather, it was a conviction that took shape
in different times and places, in confrontation with other cultures,
in response to outside events, and as a result of internal developments. Streams of belief in resurrection of the body and immortality of the soul as rewards for the righteous ran side by side and
often mingled. One did not replace the other over time.

Second, between the idea of immortality of the soul and resurrection of the body is a variety of differing conceptions. It is too
simple to say that Greeks believed in one and Jews the other. The
conceptions vary according to the kind of literature (apocalypse, ser-
mon, law, etc.) and the relative weight given to recompense.

Third, sometimes the mention of the afterlife tells only half of the
story, and does not spell out all the ramifications. The exact details
of how the afterlife will be enjoyed might be sacrificed to make
another point. If, for example, recompense is the main point, then
whether it is bodily resurrection, translation to an astral body or the
like might not be explained. Or the fate of the wicked might be
ignored when the point is to laud the righteous.

Fourth, often we cannot classify documents as holding a single
view of the afterlife. Within a single group of documents there may
be a selection of views, as in the Dead Sea Scrolls. Within the writing of one author, like Josephus, Paul, or Tertullian, multiple views
do appear.[47]

Last, resurrection is not an isolated concept, but part of an ever-
shifting constellation of ideas. Many ideas seem to emerge in tandem with it. It functioned in various contexts in various ways. For
this reason I am not writing a history of the idea of resurrection,
but am looking specifically at how it was used, limiting myself to
contexts of self-definition, boundary-marking, and polemic.

---

range of understandings of resurrection in the New Testament. See also N. T.
Wright, *Resurrection of the Son of God*; and John Carroll and Joel Green, *The Resurrection
of Jesus in Early Christianity* (Peabody: Hendrickson, forthcoming).

[47] See the chart of Cavallin, who classifies all the different elements of belief in
the afterlife and where they appear (*Life after Death*, 197). While one might disagree
with some of his classifications, it clearly demonstrates the variety, complexity, and
non-chronological nature of the belief.

# CHAPTER TWO

# RESURRECTION IN EARLY JUDAISM[1]

## Pharisees and Sadducees

Since an article by Morton Smith in 1959 on the variety of messianic figures and diverse eschatologies in first-century Judaism,[2] most scholars have downplayed the role of belief in differentiating Jewish groups and argued that practices were what articulated group identity, drawing boundaries between "us" and "them." In light of this trend, it is surprising how often the belief in resurrection of the dead appears as a boundary marker between groups like the Pharisees and the Sadducees. Resurrection of the dead is recalled by three independent sets of sources as a distinguishing feature of the Pharisees and a denial of resurrection or the afterlife is remembered by these same sources as a distinguishing feature of the Sadducees.[3] As Smith points out, belief in resurrection is not the sole possession of the Pharisees, nor its rejection unique to the Sadducees; rather, the belief in resurrection emerges as a development in Second Temple Judaism,[4] so it is surprising that these groups are identified this way. If these ideas are so widespread across groups, then mentioning them as defining features *should* be meaningless. Yet the belief in resurrection is cited as a distinguishing marker for Jewish groups in several sets

---

[1] A version of this chapter appeared as "Resurrection of the Dead as Symbol and Strategy," *JAAR* 69 (2001) 65–101.

[2] Morton Smith, "What is implied by the Variety of Messianic Figures?" *JBL* 78 (1959) 66–72. A more recent example is William Scott Green, who says the Messiah is "all signifier with no signified" "Messiah in Judaism: Rethinking the Question," Jacob Neusner, William Scott Green, and Ernest Frerichs, eds., *Judaisms and their Messiahs* (Cambridge: Cambridge University, 1987) 1–13.

[3] The Essenes, too, believed in a form of afterlife, but it is less clearly articulated. Josephus's description implies a belief closer to the more common belief in the immortality of the soul apart from the body (*J.W.* 2.153–54). The Dead Sea Scrolls show a pastiche of themes on afterlife similar to earlier apocalyptic materials. See above, pp. 13–15.

[4] Most summaries of afterlife in Judaism trace the first appearance of resurrection to the Maccabean era, specifically Dan 12:1–3 and 2 Maccabees 7.

of sources. A dichotomy of belief versus practice in group self-definition does not hold.

## Who are the Pharisees?

The problems of talking about the Pharisees and Sadducees are well-rehearsed. We have no direct sources from either group. The sources we do have are generally later and tendentious.[5] By the time the three relevant sets of sources, the New Testament, Josephus, and early rabbinic literature are written or redacted, the Pharisees and Sadducees as such have disappeared. The one exception, Paul, brings up his Pharisaic past to contrast it with his present life or to testify to his own legitimacy. Josephus, who also claims to have been a Pharisee but is no longer, seems to be promoting them to Rome.[6] The gospel presentation of the Pharisees is often typological, casting them as troublesome opponents to Jesus or his followers. The Sadducees appear as straw men, holding the wrong positions, bringing an absurd example of resurrection, only to be soundly trounced by Jesus. Acts' presentation of the Pharisees is designed to underscore Paul's legitimacy.

The Rabbis, though they claim pedigree from their connection to the Pharisees, do not seem to know much about them.[7] The earliest rabbinic literature is redacted at least 130 years after the Pharisees cease to exist as a visible group. Nor do they use the terms *perushim* or *saddukim* consistently.

---

[5] For a summary of the sources on the Pharisees, see Shaye Cohen, *From the Maccabees to the Mishnah* (Philadelphia: Westminster, 1987) 143–64; Anthony Saldarini, *Pharisees, Scribes, and Sadducees in Palestinian Society* (Grand Rapids: Eerdmans, 2001) 77–237; idem, "The Pharisees," *ABD* 5.289–303; or Gunther Stemberger, *Pharisees, Sadducees, Essenes* (Minneapolis: Augsburg Fortress, 1995) 1–66.

[6] Morton Smith, "Palestinian Judaism in the First Century," in Moshe Davis, ed., *Israel: Its Role in Civilization* (New York: The Jewish Theological Seminary, 1956) 67–81; Jacob Neusner, "Josephus's Pharisees," *Ex Orbe Religionum: Studia Geo Widengren* (Leiden: Brill, 1972) 224–53. Steve Mason argues the Pharisees were dominant, but that Josephus laments their power: "Pharisaic Dominance before 70 C.E. and the Gospels' Hypocrisy Charge (Matt 23:2–3)," *HTR* 83 (1990) 363–81. Mason also doubts Josephus's claim to have been a Pharisee: "Was Josephus a Pharisee? A Reexamination of *Life* 10–12," *JJS* 40 (1989) 30–45.

[7] The Rabbis are linked to the Pharisees because the rabbinic position on legal matters matches the Pharisaic one, and because of the prominence of Gamaliel and his son, the former identified as a Pharisee in Acts, and the latter as such by Josephus. Albert Baumgarten suggests the list of ancestors in *m.Avot* 1:1 is Pharisaic because the terms *msr* and *qbl* are technical terms for Pharisaic transmission: "The Pharisaic *Paradosis*," *HTR* 80 (1987) 68–69.

Given all these problems, the striking agreement of these varied sources that the Pharisees promoted resurrection of the dead and the Sadducees denied it suggests its reliability and provokes the question why these matters of belief were crucial to group definition. Scholarship on the Pharisees has centered on questions of power, status, and social function. Saldarini, Baumgarten, Neusner, Mason, and Ellis Rivkin have put forth different definitions of the Pharisees, but agree on their being an intellectual elite, living within society, but committed to a particular way of life, possessing some independent power and influence, but nevertheless dependent on a more powerful group.[8] Saldarini's use of the categories of Gerhard Lenski and Samuel Eisenstadt renders the Pharisees as a politically organized, literate retainer class, seeking power from the governing class.[9] The governing class, however, relies on the retainers to retain their power and prestige. All these proposals point to a group still within society, neither powerfully independent, nor utterly dominated. After reviewing the statements about the Pharisees and Sadducees, I will consider how the belief in resurrection might have served the Pharisees in negotiating their intermediate place in the pyramid of power in Palestinian society.

## Josephus

Although Josephus's statements about the Pharisees vary, perhaps because he is using sources, a certain constellation of characteristics recurs in his reports. The Pharisees are experts and meticulous observers of the Law, and of the extra-Scriptural traditions attributed to their elders. They exhibit power and authority with the people, espouse a certain theology of fate and God, and preach an afterlife of reward and punishment that includes resurrection. Josephus presents this constellation of elements about the Pharisees:

---

[8] Saldarini, *Pharisees*; Albert Baumgarten, *The Flourishing of Sects in the Maccabean Era: An Interpretation* (Leiden: Brill, 1987); Jacob Neusner, *From Politics to Piety* (New York: Ktav, 1979); idem, *Rabbinic Traditions about the Pharisees before 70* (Leiden: Brill, 1971), abbreviated as *The Pharisees: Rabbinic Perspectives* (Leiden: Brill, 1973); Mason, "Pharisaic Dominance;" Ellis Rivkin, *A Hidden Revolution* (Nashville: Abingdon, 1978; idem, "Defining the Pharisees: The Tannaitic Sources," *HUCA* 40–41 (1969–70) 205–49.

[9] Saldarini, *Pharisees*, 120.

(1) Power, prestige, and influence with the people (*J.W.* 1.111–12;
    5.162; 2.411; 2.418; *Ant.* 13.288; 13.298; 13.400–1; 13.408–9;
    13.424; 17.41–44; 18.12–15).
(2) Punctiliousness in observance (*J.W.* 1.110; *Ant.* 13.408–9; 17.41;
    18.12–15).
(3) Devotion to their traditions handed down from their fathers (*Life*
    38.191; 39.198; *Ant.* 13.297; 13.408–9; 17.41; 18.12–15).
(4) Knowledge of Scripture and accuracy of interpretation (*Life* 38.191;
    39.198; *J.W.* 1.110; 2.162).
(5) Belief in afterlife and/or resurrection from the dead (*J.W.* 2.163;
    *Ant.* 18.12–15).

Often two or three of these elements appear together. The fullest
descriptions of the Pharisees, combining all these elements, appear
in *J.W.* 2.162–63 and *Ant.* 18.12–15, the two references where the
Pharisees are compared to the Sadducees.[10] These attributes match
the attributes attached to the Pharisees in the gospels and Acts.
Josephus's statements that they hold the confidence of the masses,
in particular, is implied by their position as prominent foe to be
refuted in the gospels and the group whose legitimacy Luke wants
to borrow in Acts.

> ... The Pharisees, who are considered the most accurate interpreters
> of the laws and hold the position of the leading sect, attribute every-
> thing to Fate and to God; they hold that to act rightly or otherwise
> rests, indeed for the most part with men, but that in each action Fate
> cooperates. Every soul, they maintain, is imperishable, but the soul of
> the good alone passes into another body, while the souls of the wicked
> suffer eternal punishment (*J.W.* 2.162–63).[11]

Josephus then describes the Sadducees as the antithesis of the Pharisees;
they reject the afterlife and Fate, remove God from human affairs,
and attribute everything to free will (*J.W.* 2.164–65). Similarly, the
negations of these Pharisaic characteristics are the same ones applied
to the Sadducees in Mark 12:24–27 (and its Matthean parallel): that
they do not accept resurrection, do not know Scripture, and do not
recognize God's power. The lack of detail about the process of res-

---

[10] Steve Mason judges the sense of these passages to be the same in spite of the
different purposes of the larger works, which suggests the basic elements are genuine (*Flavius Josephus on the Pharisees* [Leiden: Brill, 1991] 299).
[11] Josephus, *The Jewish War* (Thackeray, LCL). All translations from the Loeb
Classical Library.

urrection and the language of reincarnation are, Mason suggests, Josephus's appropriating Hellenistic language to render a Jewish idea of resurrection more congenial to his Greco-Roman audience.[12] Yet as Wright observes, this is about bodies, not spirits or ghosts.[13]

In *War*, Josephus juxtaposes the Pharisees' accuracy in interpretation with their position as the leading sect and their views on Fate and the afterlife. A causal connection is clearer in *Antiquities*, where he cites Pharisaic popularity with the people as a direct result of their views on God and afterlife.[14] Even the Sadducees, he says, must bow to their popularity (*Ant.* 18.17).

> They (Pharisees) follow the guidance of that which their doctrine has selected and transmitted as good, attaching the chief importance to the observance of those commandments which it has seen fit to dictate to them. They show respect and deference to their elders . . . though they postulate that everything is brought about by Fate, still they do not deprive the human will of the pursuit of what is in man's power, since it was God's good pleasure that there should be a fusion and that the will of man with its virtue and vice should be admitted to the council-chamber of fate. They believe that souls have the power to survive death and that there are rewards and punishments under the earth for those who have led lives of virtue or vice: eternal imprisonment is the lot of evil souls, while the good souls receive an easy passage to a new life. Because of these views they are in fact extremely influential among the townsfolk; and all prayers and sacred rites of divine worship are performed according to their exposition. This is the great tribute that the inhabitants of the cities, by practicing the highest ideals both in their way of living and in their discourse, have paid to the excellence of the Pharisees (*Ant.* 18.12–15).[15]

According to Josephus, then, the Pharisees' preaching of an afterlife is responsible in part for their popularity with the common people,

---

[12] Mason, *Josephus*, 168–70. Mason concludes that the elements of immortality of the soul, eternal punishment of the wicked, and an eventual new body for the righteous accord with Josephus's own view. The idea of a new body, seen as punishment by some Greco-Roman philosophers, is seen by Josephus and the Pharisees as a reward for the righteous. See also Joseph Sievers, "Josephus on the Afterlife," in Steve Mason, ed., *Understanding Josephus* (JSPSS 32; Sheffield: Sheffield Academic Press, 1998) 20–34.

[13] Wright, *Resurrection of the Son of God*, 202–3.

[14] He says something similar about the Essenes: "Such are the theological views of the Essenes concerning the soul, whereby they irresistibly attract all who have once tasted their philosophy" (*J.W.* 2.154–58). The notion of reward and punishment, in particular, seems to make them popular.

[15] Josephus, *Jewish Antiquities* (Feldman, LCL).

at least in the cities. He follows with a description of the Sadducees, who reject any idea of an afterlife and any extra-Scriptural law, and "must submit to the Pharisees, since otherwise the masses would not tolerate them" (*Ant.* 18.17). Essenes, he reports, leave everything in God's hands and regard the soul as immortal. Josephus sees these groups as separated, in part, on the basis of their ideas of the afterlife.

*Pharisees, Sadducees, and Resurrection of the Dead in the Gospels*

In the Synoptics, the Pharisees are not connected to the belief in resurrection from the dead, probably because Jesus and the Pharisees agree. It is a dividing line in Jesus' one encounter with the Sadducees (Mark 12:18–27 and parallels). They are identified solely by their non-belief: ". . . and the Sadducees came to him, who say that there is no resurrection. . . ." They bring the example of the seven brothers, who successively marry the same woman and die without offspring. In the resurrection, they ask, whose wife will she be? Jesus defeats them with a combination of Ex 3:6, "I am the God of Abraham, the God of Isaac, the God of Jacob," and the phrase "He is not God of the dead but of the living." He is harsh and seems to dismiss them altogether: "Is not this why you are wrong, that you know neither the Scriptures nor the power of God? (v. 24)." So their failure to affirm resurrection means they do not know Scripture and hold a wrong view of God and his power. They are written off on the basis of this one issue.[16] Belief in resurrection is a marker for a certain knowledge of the Scriptures and a recognition of God's power. This idea matches Josephus's characterization of Sadducees as people who deny resurrection and see God as removed from human affairs (*J.W.* 2.16.4).

The Pharisees, by contrast, are never accused of not knowing Scripture, but of hypocrisy (Mark 7:16; 12:15) and wrongly elevating their own "tradition of the elders" to the status of divine law (7:7–8).[17] Their differences with Jesus or his disciples are ones of stringency in practice. In Mark (and parallels) they argue over issues of eating with tax collectors and sinners (2:16), failure to fast (2:18),

---

[16] In the *Sifre on Numbers* 112.4, the Sadducees are identified as those who despised the word of the Lord. The later image of them in the Babylonian Talmud is as people who are ignorant of Scripture.

[17] See Baumgarten, "The Pharisaic Paradosis," *HTR* 80 (1987) 63–77.

Sabbath-observance (2:23–4; 3:1–6) and ritual purity (7:5). They query Jesus about divorce (10:2) and paying taxes to Caesar (12:14). Often the Pharisees are more stringent, but in the case of divorce, Jesus is more stringent. In the case of taxes, they probably do not differ at all. Each party's practice is an implicit critique of the other group's life-style.[18]

The complaint about the Pharisees, then, is not that they do not know Scripture, but that they misread and pervert it by their παρά-δοσις and develop misguided practices. Similarly, in the question about divorce, Jesus never says they do not know Scripture, but disagrees with their interpretation. In the question about taxes, Mark implies that they do know Scripture perfectly well, but are trying to trap Jesus. The notion of Pharisees committed to their particularistic interpretation of Scripture, which they attribute to their ancestors, and resultant meticulousness in practice is testified to by Josephus, and by Paul, who says he had been a Pharisee (Phil 3:5) in his former life and had been "extremely zealous for the traditions of my fathers" (Gal 1:14). In Acts and Josephus, these attributes of ἀκρίβεια, "meticulousness" in practice,[19] and interpretation and devotion to ancestral traditions appear alongside the attribute of belief in resurrection of the dead.

Matthew transmits the Marcan material in which Jesus answers the Sadducees's question about resurrection and then dismisses them as ignorant of Scripture and God's power because they deny resurrection. Matthew revises the immediately following section (22:34–40) by putting the question about the Great Commandment in the mouths of the Pharisees. They ask *because* he trounced the Sadducees. Matthew

---

[18] Baumgarten observes that strictness in practice is a means of expressing disapproval of another group's laxity. The boundary mechanisms in ancient Jewish sects, he argues, were around practices of food, dress, marriage, commerce and worship. The walls between the Pharisees and others, at least in the Hasmonean period, were not so high, since they ate at the king's table. Baumgarten calls them a "reformist" sect, integrated into the larger society but in a position to critique it (*Jewish Sects*, 13–17, 46). Similarly, Mark 2:16 and 7:1 show table-fellowship between Jesus and the Pharisees.

[19] Baumgarten notes that the language of ἀκρίβεια and "zeal for the Law" are also used by the Zealots and at Qumran and constitute a common terminology of sectarianism ("Qumran and Jewish Sectarianism during the Second Temple Period," Magen Broshi, Sara Japhet, and Shemaryahu Talmon, eds., *Megillot Midbar-Yehudah: arba'im shenot mehlar* [Heb.] *The Scrolls of the Judean Desert: Forty Years of Research* [Jerusalem: Mosad Bialik, 1992] 139–51). However, the "tradition of the elders" seems distinctly Pharisaic.

increases the stakes: "But when the Pharisees heard that he had silenced the Sadducees, they came together. . . ." Anyone can defeat the Sadducees, those who do not know Scripture or God's power, in argument, he implies, but the Pharisees are more difficult. At the end of this dispute and the following one over who is the Christ, the Pharisees are thoroughly silenced: "And no one was able to answer him a word, nor from that day did anyone dare to ask him any more questions (22:46)." If Jesus can silence the Pharisees he can silence anyone, since they are the most authoritative group in Scriptural matters. Two verses later, Matthew adds the logion, "The scribes and Pharisees sit on Moses' seat, so practice and observe whatever they tell you. . . ."[20] While Matthew passes on unchanged Mark's accusation that the Sadducees do not know Scripture, he emphasizes the Pharisees expertise and authority, characteristics that match Josephus's testimony.[21]

Matthew transmits the Marcan material about Pharisaic stringency, but increases the hostile tone and amplifies the charge of hypocrisy, particularly in chapter 23. He puts the charge of demon-possession against Jesus in their mouths (12:24). He directs the parable of the Vineyard and tenants against them (21:45) and adds woes against them in chapter 23. They emerge as a more powerful group in Matthew, and are part of the delegation to Pilate to seal up the tomb (27:62). But Matthew does not criticize their concept of God or views of the afterlife. He does not portray them as ignorant of Scripture, the charge leveled at the Sadducees for their denial of resurrection. They are authorities in their knowledge of Scripture and recognizable by their stringent practices.

Like Matthew, Luke transmits Mark's material about the Pharisees' disputes over matters of practice and includes his own complaints of

---

[20] The incongruity of this verse with the rest of the gospel has evoked much discussion. Mark Powell argues that the Pharisees controlled access to Scripture. In a society where few could find or read a Torah for themselves, the Pharisees were the ones who literally "spoke Torah." The logion says others must depend on the Pharisees to transmit Torah accurately, but no one should trust their interpretation, "Do and Keep What Moses Says (Matthew 23:2–27)" *JBL* 114 (1995) 419–35. On the question of whether the logion is Matthean or traditional, see Mason, who argues it probably goes back to Jesus: "Pharisaic Dominance," 378.

[21] Matthew confuses matters by referring to the Pharisees and Sadducees together in three places (3:7; 16:1, 6) to emphasize that both are lost and promote dangerous teaching. The human tendency to lump all of one's opponents into a single category is probably at work here, and does not imply they saw themselves as similar.

showiness and hypocrisy (12:1; 18:9–14). He adds that they were "lovers of money" (16:14). He puts forth three of the woes against the Pharisees from Q (11:42–4), but is generally less severe than Matthew.

Luke includes the question from the Sadducees about the seven brothers and the one wife at the resurrection, as well as Jesus' answer, but he omits the charge that they do not know Scripture or God's power (20:27–33). The Sadducees drop out altogether and one of the scribes affirms Jesus' answer (20:39). Luke inserts a section on resurrection:

> The sons of this age marry and are given in marriage, but those who are accounted worthy to attain to that age and to the resurrection from the dead neither marry nor are given in marriage, for they cannot die any more, because they are equal to angels and are sons of God, being sons of the resurrection. But *that the dead are raised, even Moses showed*, in the passage about the bush, where he calls the Lord the God of Abraham and the God of Isaac and the God of Jacob. Now he is not God of the dead but of the living; for all live to him (20:34–8).

Although the Sadducees have disappeared from the story, Luke affirms the principle that a proper understanding of Scripture leads to belief in resurrection.

The same principle is underlined in Luke's story of the rich man and Lazarus (16:19–31), which is addressed to the Pharisees. The rich man in torment begs to warn his brothers, but Abraham answers, "If they do not hear Moses and the Prophets, neither will they be convinced if someone should rise from the dead" (v. 31). Understanding Scripture leads to recognition of reward and punishment in the afterlife and resurrection. One who truly understands the first will affirm the other. Here he is surely referring to Jesus as the "someone" who rose from the dead, since Luke shows elsewhere that the Pharisees affirm general resurrection. These two Lukan additions show resurrection as part of the classic theme of vindication of the righteous, especially the martyr, the earliest version of which appears in Isa 26:18–19; Dan 12:1–3, and 2 Maccabees 7. Both Lucan texts link resurrection of the dead to proof from Scripture.

*Summary*

In the Synoptic gospels, belief in resurrection of the dead appears as an issue connected to knowledge of Scripture and recognition of

God's power. In some cases it will be the exclusive experience of the righteous; in others it will be extended to righteous and wicked as reward and punishment. Its denial results in one group, the Sadducees, being dismissed as serious players in the drama. The Pharisees, criticized for a variety of things, are nevertheless portrayed as knowledgeable and legitimate leaders. They are never discounted for their theology of God's power nor belief in resurrection.

## Pharisees, Sadducees, and Resurrection in Acts

Of the New Testament authors, Luke is the most interested in the Pharisees and Sadducees and their differences. In all but two instances, material on these two groups appears in the speeches in Acts, material where Luke wields a strong hand.[22] In Acts, the Pharisees are most clearly defined by their belief in resurrection from the dead and Sadducees defined by their denial of it. Furthermore, Luke deliberately blurs the distinction between belief in general resurrection from the dead in the future and the belief that Jesus had already risen from the dead, thus aligning Peter and Paul with the Pharisees. For example, Peter and John are arrested because the Sadducees are irritated that by preaching Jesus, they were preaching the doctrine of resurrection: "And as they were speaking to the people, the priests and the captain of the Temple and the Sadducees came upon them, annoyed because they were teaching the people and proclaiming in Jesus the resurrection from the dead" (4:1–2). Oddly, it sounds as if preaching resurrection is the offense and Jesus is incidental. Luke makes the Sadducees responsible for their arrest and the ensuing ruckus (5:17), while the Pharisee Gamaliel defends the Christian preachers (5:34).

Paul, who is presented as a Pharisee in Acts (23:6; 26:5),[23] speaks to the Epicureans and Stoics at Athens, two groups the first of which

---

[22] Few doubt that the final compositional form of the speeches is Lucan. See Joseph Fitzmyer, *The Acts of the Apostles* (AB 31; New York: Doubleday, 1998) 103, 109. See also Marion Lloyd Soards, *The Speeches in Acts: Their Content, Context, and Concern* (Westminster: John Knox, 1994).

[23] Paul's status as a Pharisee is further implied in 22:3, where he is a student of Gamaliel, a leading Pharisee, and shows strictness (ἀκρίβεια) and zeal for the laws of the fathers, language associated with the Pharisees in Josephus. Paul's own statements about his Pharisaism do not mention resurrection, but underline his Jewish pedigree.

pointedly denies resurrection,[24] and the second of which finds it problematic.[25] He is called a "babbler" and "a preacher of foreign gods . . . because he preached Jesus and the resurrection" (17:18). Indeed, in his speech to the men of Athens, Paul preaches Jesus' resurrection as proof that God will one day judge the world (17:31). But the speech shades into the idea of general resurrection in v. 32, where it becomes the defining issue between Paul and those who join him or those who reject him: "Now when they heard of the resurrection of the dead, some mocked; but others said 'We will hear you again about this.' But some men joined him and believed . . ." (32–33).

In Paul's meeting before the Sanhedrin (23:6), he identifies himself as a Pharisee, seemingly to cause division and uproar. The divisive issue and defining feature of a Pharisee is belief in resurrection of the dead, "I am (present tense) a Pharisee, a son of Pharisees, with respect to the resurrection of the dead I am on trial." Luke again levels the difference between preaching Jesus' resurrection and preaching a general resurrection, as if Paul is simply a harmless Pharisee, preaching resurrection of the dead like everyone else. Luke underscores the crucial differences: "For the Sadducees say there is no resurrection, nor angel, nor spirit, but the Pharisees acknowledge them all." He is then defended by "one of the scribes of the Pharisees."[26]

Similarly, Paul before Felix professes puzzlement that some Jews oppose him, since he and they share a belief in resurrection from

---

[24] See discussion of the Epicureans in the Mishnah, pg. 39–43.

[25] Stoics held that only matter is real, so in certain periods they denied afterlife. But some teachers like Posidonius were influenced by Platonism and did espouse immortality. See Mason, *Josephus*, 164. Both Mason and Philipp Vielhauer note the Stoic ideas that actually appear in Paul's speech. See Vielhauer, "On the Paulinism of Acts," in Leander Keck and J. Louis Martyn, eds., *Studies in Luke-Acts* (Nashville: Abingdon, 1966) 33–50. One way to counter competing ideas is to coopt them.

[26] Mason sees this scene as a sort of burlesque, with the Pharisees as buffoons who believe in resurrection, but have missed an obvious example of it by not accepting Jesus' resurrection, "Chief Priests, Sadducees, Pharisees, and Sanhedrin in Acts," in Richard Bauckham, ed., *The Book of Acts in its Palestinian Setting*, v. 4 of *The Book of Acts in its First Century Setting* (Grand Rapids: Eerdmans, 1995) 153. Similarly, John Darr says the Pharisees emerge as "a paradigm of imperceptiveness." By the time readers get to the second half of Acts, they can only read a passage like this with distrust of the Pharisees (*On Character Building* [Louisville: Westminster/John Knox, 1992] 85–126). These interpretations do not affect my argument, except to reinforce my contention that resurrection is seen as a primary article of faith among the Pharisees.

the dead, thus deliberately ignoring the particularity of preaching Jesus' resurrection: "But this I admit to you, that according to the Way, which they call a sect, I worship the God of our fathers, believing everything laid down by the law or written in the prophets, having a hope in God that they themselves accept, that there will be a resurrection of both the just and the unjust" (24:14–15). Here too, resurrection of the dead is the defining element, and it is the result of knowledge of the Torah and the prophets and acceptance of God. Jesus is not mentioned. In v. 21, Paul claims the reason for his arrest: "With respect to the resurrection of the dead I am on trial before you this day."

When Paul stands before Agrippa and Festus, he emphasizes that he is a Pharisee: "According to the strictest party of our religion I have lived as a Pharisee" (26:5). Once again he claims to be accused on the basis of something shared by many Jews: "And now I stand here on trial for hope in the promise made by God to our fathers, to which our twelve tribes hope to attain, as they earnestly worship night and day. And for this hope I am accused by Jews, O king! Why is it thought incredible by any of you that God raises the dead?" (vv. 6–8). Which hope, whether God's raising Jesus from the dead or ultimate general resurrection, he leaves unexpressed. In this same speech, Paul claims his own teaching is "nothing but what the prophets and Moses said would come to pass, that Christ must suffer, and that, by being *the first to rise from the dead*, he would proclaim light to both the people and the Gentiles" (26:22–23). Festus reacts by calling Paul mad. Which offends Festus, the claim of Jesus' resurrection or the idea that it is only the first installment of general resurrection? We are left wondering. But again, Luke underscores the theme of resurrection as proven from Scripture and characteristic of a Pharisee.

When Paul meets with the Jewish leaders of Rome in 28:17, he claims to have done nothing against "the customs of our fathers," probably an allusion to the Pharisaic "tradition of the elders." He is in chains only because of "the hope of Israel." Unspecified here, that hope in 24:14 and 26:4–8 is in resurrection.

*Summary*

Luke tells us six times that to be a Pharisee is to believe in resurrection from the dead (Acts 23:6–9; 26:6–8; by implication 17:18, 31–32; 24:21), four times that resurrection is testified to by the law and the prophets (Luke 16:31; 20:37; Acts 24:14–15; 26:22–23), three times that Pharisees are characterized by "scrupulousness" (*akribeia*) and devotion to their traditions (Luke 18:12; Acts 15:5; 26:5), and twice that to be a Sadducee is to deny resurrection (Luke 20:27; Acts 4:1). He implies that the differences between Paul (or Peter) and the Pharisees are mere misunderstandings, since they all share a belief in resurrection.

The friendliness of the Pharisees to the church in Acts is matched by the friendliness of the Pharisees to Jesus in the gospel in the instances where they share table-fellowship (7:36; 11:38; 14:1). Scholars have generally understood that this alignment of the Pharisees with Christians serves Luke's apologetic, though they disagree on how.[27] Yet all of these interpretations share the idea that the Pharisees represent respectability and that Luke is trading on their legitimacy. Because Luke's agenda propels the narrative, we may wonder how accurate he is about the Pharisees and Judaism, but his apologetic will succeed only if his hearers recognize his description of the Pharisees. Furthermore, the characteristics of Luke's Pharisees cohere with the reports of Josephus about their popularity, knowledge of Scripture and authority, meticulousness in practice, and belief in the resurrection of the dead.

*Pharisees and Sadducees in Rabbinic Literature*[28]

The disputes between Pharisees and Sadducees in rabbinic literature echo the issues attributed to the Pharisees in the gospels: questions of practice, particularly ritual purity and tithing.[29] In one Tannaitic source, however, resurrection is at the heart of the formation of the Sadducees:

---

[27] Characteristic is Jack Sanders' assessment that the friendly Pharisees in Acts show that Christianty is the "true and authentic Judaism" (*The Jews in Luke-Acts* [Philadelphia: Fortress, 1987] 97). See also Fitzmyer, *Acts*, 333; and Robert Brawley, *Luke-Acts and the Jews* (SBLMS 33; Atlanta: Scholars, 1987) 105–6.

[28] Because the redaction of the earliest rabbinic material is not until the third century, we do not take them at face value in describing pre-70 groups. Shaye Cohen notes how few issues are actually linked to individuals of the early period (*Maccabees*, 158–59). Stemberger shows how infrequently they appear in the Mishnah (*Pharisees*, 50). In *m.Yad.* 4.6, Yochanan ben Zakkai initially opposes their position, then accepts it.

[29] Later rabbinic complaints about the *perushim* are curiously reminiscent of the gospels: that their stringencies are from wrong motives, arrogance, and a sense of superiority. See S. Weinstein, *Rabbinic Criticism of Self-Imposed Religious Stringency* (Ann

[Antigonus of Soko took over from Simeon the Righteous. He used
to say: Be not like slaves that serve their master for the sake of reward:
be rather like slaves who serve their master with no thought of reward.
And let the fear of heaven be upon you] and you will receive a reward,
both in this world and in the world to come, as if you had done it
yourself.

    He had two disciples, Saddok and Boethus, and when they heard
this saying, they taught it to their disciples. And their disciples quoted
the statement of their master but they did not offer its interpretation.
[The last mentioned disciples] said [to those who had quoted Antigonus'
statement]: If you had known that resurrection of the dead is the
reward of the just in the age to come, would you have spoken in this
manner? They went and withdrew and two sects developed from them:
The Sadducees and the Boethusians, the Sadducees named after Saddok
and the Boethusians named after Boethus[30] (*'Abot de Rabbi Nathan* B 10).

The original maxim of Antigonus (in brackets) would favor a Sadducean
argument that the Pharisees are only motivated by hope of reward
in the afterlife and it is more righteous to serve God for its own
sake. But the additional phrase mentioning the world to come, and
the succeeding discussion, turns it to the Pharisaic/rabbinic position.
In the later recension of this work, the discussion is expanded even
more and subjugated to the belief in resurrection of the dead, with
disciples exclaiming, "Why did our ancestors see fit to say this thing?
Is it possible that a laborer should do his work all day and not take
his reward in the evening? If our ancestors, indeed had known that
there is another world and that there will be a resurrection of the
dead, they would not have spoken in this manner ... So they arose
and withdrew from the Torah, and split into two sects, the Sadducees
and the Boethusians. . . ." Furthermore it attributes to the Sadducees
a jibe: "It is a tradition amongst the Pharisees to afflict themselves
in this world; yet in the world to come they will have nothing" (*'Abot
de Rabbi Nathan* A 5).[31] While the incident is historically doubtful, it
is noteworthy that this source recalls resurrection as the issue that
divided Pharisees and Sadducees, even causing the initial split between
them. Both versions A and B depict the Sadducees as the separatists,

---

Arbor: University Microfilms, 1995). In *m.Sot.* 3.4, the rabbis complain about the
ill effects of "the wounds of the *perushim*."

    [30] Translation by Anthony Saldarini, *The Fathers according to Rabbi Nathan (*'Abot de
Rabbi Nathan) version B* (Leiden: Brill, 1975) 85–86.

    [31] Translation by Judah Goldin, *The Fathers according to Rabbi Nathan* (Yale Judaica
Series 10; New Haven: Yale, 1955) 39.

saying they "withdrew" (*piršu*), using the same verb that elsewhere designates the Pharisees (*perushim*).

## Summary

While limited by the dating and tendentiousness of our sources, a striking agreement emerges in the attributes they associate with the Pharisees: (1) knowledge of Scripture; (2) ability in the interpretation of Scripture according to their own traditions, which they attribute to earlier teachers; (3) punctiliousness in observance; (4) authority with the people; (5) an understanding of God as powerful in human affairs, and a belief in the afterlife that includes resurrection from the dead. The sources do not the reveal the content of their resurrection belief, only that it was for reward and punishment. What happened to the body, how it came back to life, in what state or stage it was restored, we do not know.

The preaching of resurrection served in some way to shore up the influence and authority of the Pharisees. Saldarini argues that they represent a retainer class: a group that depended on the governing class, but also acted as patrons of those groups who depended on them. Furthermore, the governing class could not operate without the help of groups like the Pharisees. Josephus promotes them to his Roman audience as the authors of order and stability. Baumgarten calls them a "reformist" sect, attempting to change society while remaining part of it. Certainly the Pharisees' distinctive rules prevented them from being totally absorbed by society, and their stringent way of life represented an implicit criticism. Both Saldarini and Baumgarten agree, however, in representing the Pharisees as a group in a median position, neither withdrawn from society (like Qumran) nor utterly continuous with it. They were not identical with those in the highest eschelon of power, but in some way they needed to be in relationship with them.

I suggest that the concept of resurrection was part of a strategy that allowed the Pharisees to negotiate their position as mediators between the Romans and the people.[32] Resurrection carried with it a set of affirmations about God's power, ultimate justice, vindication

---

[32] Saldarini uses the general term "governing class," namely, Roman bureaucrats and their local sympathizers. For the Galilee, he speculates that the Pharisees are retainers of Herod Antipas, the Jerusalem priests, or wealthy landowners (*Pharisees*, 284–85; 295–96). The sources have not left us enough information to be definitive.

of the righteous and punishment of the wicked. Yet it could seem
innocent to an outsider, and as Josephus shows, it could be pack-
aged to sound like the Greco-Roman idea of the immortality of the
soul. For the people who looked to the Pharisees as their patrons
or representatives, it would be a shorthand that reassured them of
the continuing power of the God of Israel and Scripture's story, as
well as their own eventual vindication. For the local Roman bureau-
crat or his deputies, it would be an innocuous belief, perhaps not
recognizably different from Greco-Roman ideas of immortality. For
the Pharisees and their successors it serves as a useful tool in the
symbolic construction of community in a period of social change.

*Resurrection of the Dead in Jewish Liturgy: The* Gevurot *Benediction*

Sometime before the redaction of the earliest rabbinic literature at
the beginning of the third century, a blessing took shape that affirmed
God as the one whose power revived the dead. In its present arrangement, it appears as the second blessing of the central prayer of Jewish
daily liturgy, the *Shemoneh Esreh*, recited three times a day:

> You, O Lord, are mighty forever; you revive the dead; you are pow-
> erful in saving. You sustain the living with loving kindness. You give
> life to the dead in great mercy. You support the falling, and heal the
> sick, and free the captive, and keep faith with those who sleep in the
> dust. Who compares with you, Master of power, and who is like you?
> [You are] king over life and death, causing salvation to flower. You
> are faithful in bringing life to the dead. Blessed are you, O Lord, who
> revives the dead.[33]

Our present collection of prayers has come down to us only in much
later versions, from the twelfth century and later. Both the Babylonian
rite, from which our present-day versions derive, and the Palestinian
rite,[34] contain the *tehiyat hametim* blessing, though we cannot know
the exact wording of the earliest forms.[35] However, scattered remarks

---

[33] My translation, which is more literal than some prayerbooks.

[34] The version in the Cairo Geniza, for example, contains two examples of *mehayeh
hametim.* "who gives life to the dead," and one *mekayyem hametim*, "who raises up the
dead." But in spite of the claims of Ismar Elbogen and others, the Cairo Geniza
version has no claim to be earlier or more authentic. It demonstrates that resurrection of the dead is part of both Babylonian and Palestinian traditions.

[35] Perhaps because there was a ban on writing down blessings, as it says in *t.Sab.*
13.4. Yitzhak Heinemann counsels jettisoning the whole idea of "the original text"

in the rabbinic literature allow us to push the theme of God as *mehayeh hametim*, "he who gives life to the dead," back much earlier.

The Mishnah, pronouncing on the ordering of blessings, refers to a prayer called *tehiyat hametim*, "resurrection of the dead," in one place (*m.Ber.* 5.2) and *gevurot* in another (*m.Roš.Haš.* 4.5). The Tosefta also reports that *tehiyat hametim* is to be recited as part of the *birkat avelim*, the Blessing for Mourners said to the newly bereaved, and should end with the phrase *mehayeh hametim*, "who revives the dead" (*t.Ber.* 3.23–24).[36] So by the time of these works (around 200), there is an established benediction called "resurrection of the dead," which is part of the block of prayer called *Gevurot*, "might" referring to God's works of power.

A *beraita*, from the same period, places the ordering of the blessings at Yavneh in the post–70 period: "As it is taught, Shimeon haPakuli arranged in order the Eighteen Blessings before Rabban Gamliel at Yavneh" (*b.Meg.* 17b). The word *hisdir*, "arranged in order," implies further that the individual blessings were already common knowledge, but their order was not yet fixed.[37] In the same discussion (although not in a *beraita*) a statement is attributed to Rabbi Yochanan that moves the institution of the *Shemoneh Esreh* back to the men of the Great Assembly, a near-mythic group in the fifth-second century B.C.E. who are cited as part of the chain of tradition in *Avot* 1.1.[38] Hoffman harmonizes the two statements, suggesting the prayer was composed by the men of the Great Assembly, but put in order at Yavneh.[39] Both statements are likely attempts to legitimize the prayer by linking it to an early authoritative body.

---

in the face of so many versions and fluid custom (*Prayer in the Talmud* [trans. Richard Sarason; Berlin: de Gruyter, 1977] 37–38).

[36] See the discussion in Lawrence Hoffman, *The Canonization of the Synagogue Service* (Notre Dame: University of Notre Dame, 1979) 146–47. He cites Saul Lieberman, who suggests the blessing was part of the Grace after Meals said in the home of a mourner.

[37] Thanks to Debra Reed Blank for this insight.

[38] The same statement is attributed to R. Jeremiah in the Palestinian Talmud, *y.Ber.* 2.3, 5d.

[39] *Canonization*, 50. He argues that some institutionalization of the *Shemoneh Esreh* took place at Yavneh, but it built on earlier forms. The themes were fixed, but there was still latitude in wording. He notes that the Amoraim are still arguing about exactly how to address God in the prayers (*b.Ber.* 12a, 40b). Another view is expressed by Ezra Fleischer, who argues the prayer was composed at Yavneh, and that no obligatory prayers existed during the Second Temple period. Only sectarians, he maintains, competed with the Temple by requiring regular prayer ("On the Beginnings of Obligatory Jewish Prayer" [Heb.], *Tarbiz* 59 [1990] 397–44).

Whether instituted at Yavneh or earlier, by the time of the Mishnah and Tosefta at the beginning of the third century, the *tehiyat hametim* blessing is sufficiently well-known to be referred to in a kind of shorthand. Neither document needs to define or explain it, so it has been in use for some time.[40]

The prayer is a finished product, and leaves no hints as to what other groups might have said or not said in their prayers. We can only speculate about the controversies that contributed to its composition and usage and the extent to which it was part of the process of self-definition and drawing boundaries between groups.[41] But public prayer, by its nature, contributes to a sense of "us" and "them," and the implicit drawing of boundaries. The well-known *birkat haminim*, while not specifically anti-Christian by most estimates, is clearly anti-sectarian.[42] Hoffman uses the language of anthropology to work back from prayer to the community that produces it. He notes how prayer both "censors in" and "censors out." It "censors in" by presenting itself as possessing ideas close enough to the larger society's definition of religion to be taken seriously as religion, but also "censors out," by drawing boundaries that distinguish a group from the society at large. Prayer is a series of signs, he says, but also synecdoche, a part that stands for the whole.[43] Using Hoffman's insights, we may extrapolate that, for the early framers of the liturgy, *tehiyat hametim* stands for a whole set of assertions about God and the world. It also functions as a way of negotiating a median position in the larger society that draws boundaries to maintain the integrity of the group, but allows it to still function within society and reform it from within.

---

[40] An earlier generation of scholars assumed the insertion of this prayer goes back to the Pharisee/Sadducee split and represents a Pharisaic triumph, but no explicit evidence supports this conclusion. See Ismar Elbogen, *Jewish Liturgy* (trans. Raymond Scheindlin; Philadelphia: JPS, 1993) 26. Louis Finkelstein moved it back even earlier, to "proto-Pharisees": "The Development of the Amidah," *JQR* n.s. 16 (1925/26) 1–43.

[41] Heinemann and the form-critical school have argued against matching every prayer to historical circumstances, anti-sectarianism, foreign ideology and the like, just as they have argued against searching for the original text. See Lawrence Hoffman, *Beyond the Text* (Bloomington: Indiana University, 1987) 4–5.

[42] The influential article of Reuven Kimelman has changed the current of thought on this prayer in the last 20 years: "*Birkat ha Minim* and the Lack of Evidence for an Anti-Christian Jewish Prayer in Late Antiquity," in E. P. Sanders, Albert Baumgarten, and Alan Mendelson, eds., *Jewish and Christian Self-Definition* (3 vols.; Philadelphia: Fortress, 1981) 2:226–44.

[43] All of these insights are from Hoffman, *Beyond the Text*.

The early presence of the *tehiyat hametim* blessing is evidence that, for the Tannaim, and some generations before them, the belief that God would raise the dead is current, is a manifestation of God's *gevurah*, or power, and should be imposed upon everyone in the fold by including it in public prayer. This fits with earlier materials that describe the Pharisees and Sadducees that also connect resurrection to God's power. Whether or not a latter-day Sadducee or someone who rejected the belief in resurrection would be unwelcome in a congregation reciting the prayer, surely he would be forced to confront his dissent every time he participated in public prayer.[44] As with the Pharisees, for the early framers of liturgy, resurrection of the dead is explicitly linked to a certain theology of a powerful God, and by implication is part of an assertion of their own legitimacy and authority. The early rabbis and their predecessors who frame or arrange prayers for a group are claiming a measure of authority, and whatever the alternative prayers that may have been circulating at the same time, *tehiyat hametim* is successfully situated by those people in the liturgy.

### The Mishnah and Tosefta

In the earliest rabbinic literature, a peculiar mishnah provides evidence that the belief in resurrection of the dead continued to distinguish groups from one another and underscore legitimacy:

> All Israel has a share in the world to come, as it is said, *Thy people shall all be righteous, they shall inherit the land forever; the branch of my planting, the work of my hands that I may be glorified* (Isa 60:21). And these are the ones who have no portion in the world to come: he who says there is no resurrection of the dead [to be derived from the Torah], the Torah does not come from heaven, and an Epicurean. R. Akiva says, Also, he who reads heretical books, and he who whispers over a wound and says, *I will put none of the diseases on you that I put on the Egyptians, for I am the Lord who heals you* (Ex 15:26). Abba Saul says, Also he who pronounces the Divine name as it is spelled out (*m.Sanhedrin* 10.1).[45]

---

[44] The dispute over bodily resurrection was a major part of Reform Judaism's "censoring in" and "censoring out" process in the nineteenth century. See Gillman, *Death*, 193–204. Most influential was David Einhorn's reform, which substituted "who has planted in us eternal life" for the traditional "who raises the dead," opting for a sense of the soul's immortality as against physical resurrection.

[45] Translations of rabbinic works are my own unless otherwise noted.

This mishnah is peculiar in its inclusion of transgressions that are transgressions of belief and imposing a penalty that cannot be carried out in this world. With the exception of the mishnayot in 10:1–3 and the beginning of mishnah 4, *Sanhedrin* is about crimes of action like sexual relations with the wrong person, violation of the Sabbath, sorcery, murder, and manslaughter. The rabbinic response mentions capital cases, how many judges there should be, who may be a judge, what kind of evidence is admissible, treatment of witnesses, and kinds of penalties handed out, including forms of execution. Our mishnah, by contrast, legislates belief; it views as transgressions the denial of two articles of faith, resurrection of the dead and the divine origin of the Torah, and adhering to an alternative belief system, Epicureanism. The penalty is not one of the gruesome methods of execution discussed in Sanhedrin, nor even excommunication, but denial of life in the next world.

Let us consider the three groups the framers of the Mishnah consign to eternal loss. First there are those who say there is no resurrection from the dead or, according to some manuscripts, that there is no resurrection from the dead to be derived from the Torah.[46] Whether these people opted for immortality of the soul, denied the afterlife completely, or simply said it was not in the Torah, we do not know. But their denial reaps them the ultimate punishment; they do not receive it. Denying the next world to people who do not believe in it may not be as absurd as it seems. David Kraemer has shown that the rabbis' mourning and burial practices and their teaching indicate they believed the dead remained sentient beings for some period after death.[47] So, from the rabbinic perspective, a denier might confront his/her horrifying loss of the next world soon after death. The severity of the punishment shows denial of this principle is a threat to the rabbinic agenda. In later texts it is a sign of sectarianism.[48]

---

[46] "Min ha Torah" does not appear in the Palestinian Talmud's version (*y.San.* 10.1) nor the Tosefta's (*t.San.* 13.5). *Dikduke Soferim* views it as an interpolation. It may be added later, under the influence of the Gemara, where there are numerous proofs of resurrection from the Torah. See, for example, *b.San.* 90a–92a, where resurrection is proven from a variety of verses, Deut 31:16; Num 18:28; 2 Chron 31:4; Ps 72:16, as well as from the more predictable Isa 26:19 and Ezek 37.

[47] David Kraemer, *The Meanings of Death in Rabbinic Judaism* (New York: Routledge, 2000) 12–13, 39.

[48] In a much later text, *Ex Rab* 44.6, one who even asks "Do the dead live?" is accused of talking like a *min*, a sectarian.

The second group, those who say "the Torah is from Heaven," similarly undercut the authority of the rabbis as its interpreters. Another mishnaic statement links the Torah to life in the next world, in language that implies bodily resurrection: "Great is Torah, for it gives to those who fulfill it life in this world, and in the world to come, as it is said, *For they are life to those who find them, health to all their flesh . . . (m.Avot* 6.7).

The third one denounced is an Epicurean. Although a variety of competing philosophies and religious systems are current, the rabbis single out the Epicureans for censure. Study of the Torah is essential, and will provide one with the ability to answer the scoffers: "Rabbi Elazar said: Be eager to study the Torah; know what to answer an Epicurean" (*m.Avot* 2.19). Several scholars suggest the rabbis use it in a general, stereotypic way, as a catch-all for whatever they disapprove of, analogous to a modern-day rabbi who might rail against "the secularists." As Goldin notes, however, it only appears twice in the mishnah and does not seem to be an over-used epithet in the early literature, nor is the manuscript tradition on it in the Mishnah confused.[49]

The Epicureans, while never achieving the respectability of the Stoics, were an attractive group to many. They are one of the groups the Lukan Paul must convince at Athens (Acts 17:18). The digest of references to Epicureans by John Ferguson shows an upsurge in the popularity of Epicureanism as well as in anti-Epicurean rhetoric in the second and early third century.[50] Their visibility outside the academy is evident from the second century inscription of Diogenes of Oenoanda.[51] Fragment 18, as reconstructed by Smith, shows their attitudes towards the gods: "[Let us not think the gods are capable of examining people who are unjust] and base and [noble] and just. [Otherwise the] greatest disturbances [will be created in our souls]."[52] Similarly, the argument in fragment 19 appears, "[let not the imperishable beings be falsely accused at all] by us [in our vain fear that

---

[49] Judah Goldin, "A Philosophical Session in a Tannaitic Academy," *Essays in Greco-Roman and Related Talmudic Literature* (New York: Ktav, 1977) 369–71.

[50] John Ferguson, "Epicureanism under the Roman Empire," *ANRW* II 36.4:2257–327.

[51] Martin Ferguson Smith, ed., *Diogenes of Oinoanda: The Epicurean Inscription* (Naples: Bibliopolis, 1993).

[52] Smith, *Epicurean Inscription*, 376.

they are responsible for all misfortunes], bringing [sufferings to us] and [contriving burdensome obligations] for themselves."[53]

These references reveal what must have been the most troubling aspect of Epicureanism for the rabbis, their denial of Providence, the idea that if God or gods existed at all, they had no interest or involvement in human affairs. Accepting these ideas undercuts the foundation of the rabbinic system where God is creator and sustainer, who rewards and punishes humans for their deeds. The Epicureans, says Henry Fischel, "denied Providence and de-personalized the Universe." A common phrase associated with the opponents of the rabbis is *lyt din wlyt dayan*, "there is no judgment nor judge," which Fischel suggests is directed against Epicureans, since it also appears in Epicurean, anti-Epicurean, and patristic sources.[54] An early example is in *Targum Neofiti I* on Gen 4:8.[55] The phrase is often combined with a denial of the next world:

> There is no Judgment and no Judge;
> And there is no Other World;
> There is no bestowal of recompense for the just;
> And there is no reckoning for the wicked.

Such sentiments are attributed to Cain in four of the targums on this verse, and to Esau, Manasseh, and others in later literature.[56] Often these statements are a response to incidents of evil or injustice. In the Palestinian Talmud, a similar statement is linked to a denial of resurrection of the dead, *ayn matan skar wayn tehiyat hametim*, "there is no giving of reward and there is no resurrection from the dead" (*y.Hag.* 2:1, 77b).

In *t.San.* 13.3–5, an echo of our mishnah, the denial of resurrection and the denial of Torah are listed with Epicureanism as transgressions that earn the ultimate punishment. Three types of recompense

---

[53] Smith, *Epicurean Inscription*, 376.

[54] Henry A. Fischel, *Rabbinic Literature and Greco-Roman Literature* (Leiden: Brill, 1973). While some of Fischel's work has not been accepted on the level of formal parallelism, particularly his identification of the famous story of the four who entered *pardes* in *b.Hag.* 14b as an anti-Epicurean polemic, he has contributed to an appreciation of the parallelism between Talmudic and Greco-Roman literatures. Even his critics concede that he is right on this particular point. See A. Wasserstein's review, *JJS* 25 (1974) 459.

[55] This targum is a Palestinian work, dated to the third–fourth century, although it contains earlier material. The same statements attached to Gen 4:8 also appear in later targums. Fischel, *Rabbinic Literature*, 36–37, 129, n. 13.

[56] Fischel, *Rabbinic Literature*, 41–43.

are described: eternal life; eternal punishment; and limited, temporary punishment. I have here condensed the text and removed material that is not germane:

> The House of Shammai says, "There are three groups, one for eternal life, one *for shame and everlasting contempt* (Dan 12:2)—these are those who are completely evil. An intermediate group go down to Gehenna and scream and come up again and are healed . . . but heretics, apostates, traitors, Epicureans, those who deny the Torah, those who separate from the ways of the community, those who deny the resurrection of the dead, and whoever both sinned and caused the public to sin— for example Jereboam and Ahab, and those who sent their arrows against the land of the living and stretched out their hands against the lofty habitation (the Temple), Gehenna is locked behind them, and they are judged therein for all generations . . .

This matches our mishnah, where those who deny Providence and resurrection strike at the heart of rabbinic authority, whether by dangerous views or by actions that put them outside the community.

These Epicureans were likely Jews who were attracted to Epicureanism.[57] They were particularly threatening to the rabbis because they shared certain ideals with them. They promoted the ideal of the philosopher/sage, the moderate, disciplined life, the joy of study, the cultivation of a community of learners, the cult of friendship, and the unity of the body and soul. Rabbis probably experienced ambivalence towards Epicureanism as a popular, competing philosophy that outwardly shares their ethics and way of life, but dangerously removes Providence from the world of human affairs.

*Summary*

In both the Mishnah and Tosefta, "Epicurean" is likely a shorthand for the people who deny Providence, God's powerful work in the world. Thus both documents link resurrection, a correct understanding of Torah, and an affirmation of God's power in the world and ultimate justice. The denial of justice is the assumption behind "Epicurean" claims in rabbinic literature that "there is no justice and no judge." The rabbis promote their own legitimacy as the correct interpreters

---

[57] See my article, "Talking their Way into Empire: Pagans, Jews, and Christians Debate the Resurrection of the Body," in *Judaism in its Hellenistic Context*, ed. Carol Bakhus: *JSJSup*. (Leiden: Brill, forthcoming). Both in the Mishnah and Tosefta passages, the Epicureans are listed with other Jews who have a fractured relationship to the community. Were they non-Jews, they would be less likely to be of interest to the rabbis.

of Torah, and assume their right to pronounce on the fate of categories of people. In the Tosefta, a motley list of opponents are excluded, people whose only common trait is a non-acceptance of rabbinic principles and authority.

As with the Pharisees, in the rabbinic literature, resurrection functions as part of a constellation of values—God's power, a proper interpretation of Scripture, the legitimacy of a certain group as authorities for their community, and in light of the entire rabbinic enterprise, the promoting of a certain set of practices. Like the Pharisees, the rabbis stand in a median position, subject to the powerful Roman empire and its local deputies, but defining themselves and their followers as distinct and discontinuous with empire. Like the Pharisees, they are not withdrawn from the world, but see themselves as reformers within it.

## Resurrection as Symbol and Strategy in Early Jewish Groups

By now it should be clear that resurrection is a particularly hardy and visible symbol for several Jewish groups for more than two centuries. Furthermore, it never stands by itself but carries with it several deeper concepts. Using some of the categories proposed by sociologist Anthony Cohen in his work on the use of symbols in modern constructions of community, I will suggest some of the reasons resurrection worked so effectively as a symbol for these early Jewish groups. Cohen argues that symbols of community are held more intensely in periods of extreme social change and weakening of tangible group boundaries.

### Resurrection condenses a worldview[58]

Like other symbols, the cross, the swastika, or the queen, the symbol of resurrection condenses a worldview. Certain other beliefs adhere to it and are mentioned along with it: the belief in God's power and involvement in human affairs, the primacy of the Torah, the crucial role of those who interpret the Torah correctly, the legitimacy of groups that espouse resurrection, a particular set of practices associated with these groups, and a concern for ultimate justice.

---

[58] Cohen uses the term "condensation symbols" to refer to a mnemonic that evokes an emotional response, often draws on a mythic past, and sums up a whole set of values, in *The Symbolic Construction of Community* (London: Tavistock, 1985).

For the Pharisees, even through the filter of Josephus and the New Testament, resurrection is linked to belief in Providence, their own popularity and legitimacy, and the notion that they understand the scriptures correctly. For those who fixed the *tehiyat hametim* blessing, it is situated in a prayer about God's power to act in human affairs, and the issues of legitimacy and authority to interpret are implied by the process of fixing public prayer for a community. In the Mishnah, the rabbis place resurrection in a context that also asserts the primacy of the Torah and, by rejecting the Epicureans who assert the opposite, God's powerful role in the world. The assertion of their own authority is implied in the process of codification itself.

Why is resurrection of the body such an apt symbol? Most religionists now endorse Mary Douglas's essential insight that "body attitudes are condensed statements about the relation of society to the individual."[59] What about attitudes towards resurrected bodies and their implied statements about the social order? On this scholars do not agree. John Gager asserts that "denial of bodily resurrection signals an alienation from the body politic," while more radically spiritual systems typify sectarian movements.[60] Similarly, Rubin argues that the movement from the idea of the individual as a unity of body and soul in the early period to a sharper dualism reflects the rabbis' increasing alienation.[61] By contrast, Segal says "resurrection was the preserve of the disenfranchised classes of people who could not abide foreign domination, whereas notions of immortality of the soul were typical of people who benefited from Greco-Roman society and were more at home in the culture.[62] Like any symbol, resurrection of the body can be understood in multiple, opposing ways. These opposing theories are suggestive, however, that resurrection "worked" in some way to solve social problems.

---

[59] *Natural Symbols*, 195. The literature on embodiment and its implications for the study of Judaism and Christianity since then has been enormous and varied, including such scholars as Peter Brown, John Gager. Caroline Walker Bynum, Howard Eilberg-Schwartz, Daniel Boyarin, David Biale, Sarah Coakley, and Naomi Goldenberg. Much of it has focused on sexuality and gender, rather than death and resurrection. A helpful discussion is Caroline Walker Bynum's "Why All the Fuss about the Body?" *Critical Inquiry* 22 (1995) 1–33.

[60] John Gager, "Body-Symbols and Social Reality: Resurrection, Incarnation and Asceticism in Early Christianity," *Religion* 12 (1982) 353.

[61] Rubin, "Sages' Conception of Body and Soul."

[62] Segal, "Life After Death," 102.

*Resurrection is an imprecise and abstract symbol*
Cohen argues that the most effective symbols of community are
imprecise. They capture and contain the variety of subjective meanings and individual interpretations that any group of human beings
contains.[63] A symbol, he notes, presents a public face to outsiders
that is fairly simple, while the internal understandings of it within
communities is normally more complex. The Sadducees, for example, are simply labeled by the Synoptics, Acts, and Josephus as those
who deny resurrection. Similarly, "everyone knows" the Pharisees
believe in resurrection, but not when, how, and in what form.
Resurrection appears in proximity to a set of related ideas in the
*gevurot* section of the liturgy. In the Mishnah and Tosefta, those who
deny resurrection appear in lists of vague and overlapping types who
reject the rabbis' theology.

Bynum notes that body itself seems to mean two very different
things: limits, both biological and social; and a lack of limits, the
infinite potentiality of desire, fertility, and sexuality.[64] How much
more so is this true for the resurrected body? On the one hand it
is subject to death, the ultimate limit, the body shorn of all possibility. Yet resurrection and restoration of the body reveal its other
side, a complete lack of limits, a sense that it is all possibility. If the
body is socially constructed, how much more so the resurrected body,
where the limits are expanded? The resurrected body, in its malleability and possibility, is a symbol that carries with it certain central ideas, and is part of a strategy useful for groups who hold these
ideas.

*Belief in resurrection draws boundaries*
In sources describing the Pharisees and Sadducees, all coming from
outside the Pharisaic movement (Josephus being debatable), belief in
resurrection is a visible marker that distinguishes the Pharisees from
others. For Mark, denial of resurrection is the chief characteristic
that distinguishes the Sadducees. It is implicit in its inclusion in the
*gevurah* because public prayer by its nature sketches the horizon of
community. The rabbis in the Mishnah and Tosefta are most explicit
that belief in resurrection puts one within the bounds of community

---

[63] Cohen, *Symbolic Construction*, 21.
[64] Bynum, "Why All the Fuss," 5.

and rejection of it puts one outside. Rejection of resurrection forfeits the next world, a privilege extended to "all Israel."

Cohen notes that symbolic boundaries are increasingly important as structural bases of community weaken. In a period of rapid social change, like the period around the destruction of the temple in 70 and the reconstruction of a new form of Judaism by the rabbis, political, class, and even ethnic boundaries were no longer reliable. Being a priest carried no real advantages. Even non-Jews could be found in the synagogues. The lack of clear boundaries renders symbolic ones more crucial and the construction of community based on ideas more pressing.

*Belief in resurrection constructs community*
By constructing symbolic boundaries, people within groups strengthen their own sense of identity, who they are and are not, particularly as they encounter other Jews and non-Jews. People are most aware of their culture when they interact with those of a different culture. Boundaries created by belief in resurrection were perceived differently by different people and were probably imperceptible to others. Jewish belief in resurrection might seem quite harmless to a Roman, since it had no effect on how Jews behaved as subjects, but would be a serious matter to those same Jews who struggled with the question of God's justice.

*Resurrection confers legitimacy on those who preach it*
A symbol only works if others recognize it. Josephus says explicitly that the Pharisees were popular with urban Jews because they espoused resurrection. Acts implies the same with its presentation of the Pharisees as the most legitimate group (whose legitimacy Christians borrow) and its multiple references to their belief in resurrection. Furthermore, the early presence of *tehiyat hametim* in the liturgy shows those who asserted resurrection won any battles over liturgy. The rabbis attempt to assert their authority in the process of pronouncing on who will and will not merit the next world. Resurrection, I suggest, confers authority on those who promote it because it is recognizable to a significant number of Jews as a shorthand for their cultural values, and because it is part of an effective strategy to solve some problems created by their subjection to Rome.

*Resurrection is fabricated out of the "tool-kit" of Jewish culture*

Though abstract and indemonstrable, the concept of resurrection is part of a strategy used by the Pharisees and continued by the rabbis even as circumstances changed. People use ideas because they work, coinciding with the way they think, the way the world is, and the way they would like it to be. In a frequently-cited article, Ann Swidler proposes the idea of culture as a "tool-kit of symbols, stories, rituals, and worldviews" that allows groups to construct strategies to solve problems.[65] Swidler notes that people rarely invent strategies that are entirely new, but "construct chains of action beginning with at least some pre-fabricated links," provided by culture.[66]

Resurrection of the dead is a rhetorically powerful symbol because it trails in its wake a set of ideas about God's activity in the world, justice, reward and punishment. In Swidler's language, it is a pre-fabricated set of linking beliefs. What makes the image of the tool-kit useful is its combination of the idea of a certain fixed and limited set of resources with the idea of human volition. The components of a theology of resurrection are present as early as the Isaian apocalypse, Daniel, and 2 Maccabees, where resurrection is the reward of the righteous, especially the martyr. Not every Jewish group chose the same tools or used them effectively. The Sadducees, for example, were unable to fashion an effective strategy of survival when their Temple and its practice were taken away.

Swidler proposes two models of culture, one for "settled lives," where culture is less overt and tacitly reinforces already-existing strategies of action and worldview. In "unsettled lives"—periods of social transformation—when different forms of organization compete with one another, culture acts more directly to shape action. Symbols and rituals are highly charged. By any reckoning, our documents emerge from a period of "unsettled lives." In the Second Temple period, Pharisees are competing with several other groups for legitimacy and power. Sectarianism prevails and no single authoritative form of Judaism obtains. After 63 B.C.E., the Jews of Palestine are a colonized people, under the administration of the Herods, then Roman administrators. The people suffer from high taxes and economic deprivation. In the period after 70, in the wake of a disastrous Jewish

---

[65] Ann Swidler, "Culture in Action: Symbols and Strategies," *American Sociological Review* 51 (1986) 273–86.

[66] Swidler, "Culture in Action," 277.

revolt, former Pharisees (rabbis) are, with Christians, the only viable groups left. The Jews are not entirely in control of their land, economy, or destiny, subject to the relative competence and good will of others.

But nor are the Pharisees or rabbis slaves. They see themselves, and are seen by others, as possessing some authority and power. A successful Roman administrator, or a successful movement like Christianity, cannot afford to dismiss them. These groups—half-subject, half-authority—are societies within society, and are in a position to construct a strategy, a response to the upheaval and problems facing their communities.

*Resurrection solves a set of problems*

The problems to explain after the Romans incorporate Palestine are pressing: loss of Jewish sovereignty, the suffering of the Jews under Gentile domination, and the seeming withdrawal of God's favor towards Israel. Without direct documents, we can only speculate about the specifics of the Pharisees' response. They have at hand a rich culture from which to construct a response. They still possess their Scripture and its story of a powerful God who shows favor to his people, and its many laws and regulations whose ethos confers a distinctive identity on those who follow it. In a few places like Daniel and Isaiah, it offers the conviction that God will vindicate the righteous after death. It seems clear, particularly from Josephus's testimony and their image in Acts, that one way the Pharisees drew from these resources and fashioned a response that solved these problems for a recognizable number of people was by preaching the resurrection from the dead.

By the time the Mishnah is being fixed, the Temple is destroyed and a second Jewish revolt has been put down and Roman hegemony reasserted. Sects have dissipated. A mode of piety is being constructed that replaces Temple practice with a system of Torah-observance, Torah study, and prayer. Whether the rabbis are dominant or not,[67] they enjoy the circumstances to create a body of civil

---

[67] We cannot know what percentage of Jews actually followed rabbinic practice. Many scholars today assume that we have over-estimated their influence because their literature survives and because they are seen as the spiritual ancestors of today's Jews. See the discussion in Kraemer, *Meanings of Death*, 4–9. See also the comprehensive discussion by Seth Schwartz, *Imperialism and Jewish Society* (Princeton: Princeton University, 2001) 103–28.

and religious laws, and interpret and begin codifying them. The rabbis too, had to draw on a culture that was recognizable to their adherents. They possessed the same elements as the Pharisees: Scripture, the story of a powerful God, observance of a distinctive set of practices, and a claim of resurrection. They also claimed the antiquity and authority of the Pharisees themselves. Their use of culture is so seamless that one might not realize their mode of Torah-observant piety is a dramatic solution to Israel's problems.

Much of the Mishnah is theoretical and reads "as if" the rabbis hold the reins of civil power. *M.San.* 10.1–3 stands out because it moves everything to the next world. The concept of an afterlife is apparently so well-fused into the culture that the rabbis assume their right to pronounce on who merits the next world. The anomaly of this mishnah and the relatively small amount of space afforded it suggests that by now resurrection is either so universally accepted that it needs no defense, or is of minor importance. Its presence in the liturgy suggests the former.

*Resurrection allowed its adherents to live in the world as it is*
Symbolic forms, says Cohen, can reconcile the gap between beliefs and reality: "massage away the tension" created by the disparity between what is and what, according to a community's beliefs, ought to be.[68] It allows adherents to retain their commitment to a certain community and its history while managing the discordant reality of Roman triumph around them. By maintaining that the eclipse of God was temporary and only apparent, and that the righteous would ultimately prevail, it leaves God's power and the integrity of the scriptures intact. Those who suffered in body would be restored in body.[69] They could thereby continue to believe in a watchful God who acted in history, the election of Israel, and eventual reward for the righteous and punishment of evil-doers. The accompanying ethos of both the Pharisees and the rabbis supplied a way of life that matched and supported their beliefs.

---

[68] Cohen, *Symbolic Construction*, 92.
[69] The question of how bodies torn apart (sometimes literally) in martyrdom can be resurrected becomes crucial in Christianity. Some Christian writers conclude that the marks of martyrdom will remain but become badges of glory. See Bynum, *Resurrection*, 43–51.

The notion that these groups were engaged in a process we might call a strategy is supported by the work of Samuel Eisenstadt.[70] He describes a range of semi-autonomous religious groups operating within larger centralized empires. Like the Pharisees and the rabbis, they face the problem of carving out a place for themselves within these larger societies while maintaining a distinct identity. One of the ways these groups promoted themselves and competed for influence and resources was in the formalization and codification of religious traditions. "This formalization," says Eisenstadt, "was manifest in (a) the codification of sacred books; (b) the development of schools devoted to interpretation of the books; (c) the growth of special educational organizations for the spread of religious knowledge, and the elaboration of over-all worldviews and ideologies."[71]

These activities match the activities of the Pharisees and the rabbis. The codification of the Torah, while formalized at Yavneh, is a process that began earlier. The Pharisees' distinctive interpretation of the Torah is attributed to them by all our sources. They are actually presented as a philosophical school by Josephus. In this the Pharisees are competing with at least three other groups: Sadducees, Essenes, and Christians. For the post–70 period, the rabbis continue the process of codification and spread of their teachings, competing with a host of vaguely defined groups that populate the rabbinic literature: sectarians, scoffers, the deniers of the Root, Epicureans. These groups differed over issues such as who rightly understands and interprets the Torah, and what is the nature of God's role in the world when Israel is suffering. For both the Pharisees and the rabbis, the elaboration of a worldview in condensed form is, I suggest, part of the function of their teaching resurrection from the dead. Their belief helped mark the boundaries between them and these other groups.

*Summary*

The power of the resurrection of the dead is certainly as a solution to the human fear of death, what Bynum calls "the ultimate other," the one we carry within us. But in both the pre-70 period and later,

---

[70] Samuel N. Eisenstadt, "Religious Organizations and Political Process in Centralized Empires," *Journal of Asian Studies* 21 (1962) 271–94.
[71] Eisenstadt, "Religious Organizations," 279.

the rabbinic period, it serves as a useful symbol for the integrity of the community. It also becomes part of an effective strategy for solving the immediate problems of Israel's powerlessness and the metaphysical ones of the eclipse of God's favor and the suffering of the righteous. Constructed out of the cultural components of the Torah's primacy and God's power in history, it connects to a certain ethos that informs doctrine by supporting the claims of the Pharisees/rabbis of their own legitimacy. They are the ones with the right to interpret the Torah and the ones who correctly understand God's power in this world (and the next).

The belief in resurrection acts as an implicit protest against competing groups and the larger Greco-Roman society without, and as an instrument of self-definition and social control within the community. Dearly held ideas of God's power and favor to Israel are reconciled with the reality of her suffering and subjection to an alien power. Elegant in its amorphous, abstract nature—malleability and removal to another time (or place)—resurrection affirms the individual, physical body and the collective body of Israel in this world.

# CHAPTER THREE

# RESURRECTION AMONG BELIEVERS IN JESUS

## *The Historical Jesus*

Jesus' defense of resurrection in his encounter with the Sadducees in Mark 12:18–27 is an anomaly. It does not appear as a central theme in his preaching. Nevertheless, John Meier argues that this pericope goes back to an event in Jesus' Jerusalem ministry and is not, as some argue, an invention of the early church.[1] He notes that the passage does not serve Mark's apocalyptic theology. Nor does Mark otherwise show an interest in the Sadducees or the question of general resurrection. He does not multiply stories about the Sadducees as he does the Pharisees. Against the idea that this is invented by the early church, he argues that Exod 3:6 is nowhere else associated with the argument for resurrection. We have shown, however, that the argument for resurrection is strongly grounded in Scripture as a whole among early Jews and later Christians.

Meier suggests that general resurrection was a genuine, but relatively marginal part of Jesus' preaching because his apocalyptic message, like the message of John the Baptist, focused on the immediate arrival of the kingdom of God for the Israel all around them. The nature of Jesus' preaching, says Meier, was symbolic and enigmatic, not given to specifics. Furthermore, Jesus' prediction of the heavenly banquet, alluded to in his prophecy at the Last Supper, assumes resurrection: "Amen I say to you that I shall no longer drink of the fruit of the vine until that day when I drink it new in the kingdom of God" (Mark 14:25).

I would add another reason that resurrection was genuine but secondary to Jesus' preaching. It was already a given among the majority of Jews to whom Jesus preached. As an elite group, the Sadducees would hardly be representative of Jesus' audience. Furthermore,

---

[1] John Meier, "The Debate on the Resurrection of the Dead: An Incident from the Ministry of the Historical Jesus?" *JSNT* 77 (2000) 3–24.

Josephus's report on the Pharisees implies that a fixture of their popularity among the people was their preaching of resurrection.

Bruce Chilton does not dispute the historicity of this passage, but further explains the dearth of references to resurrection in the gospels' reports of Jesus' teaching.[2] He suggests that resurrection belongs to an intermediate level of instruction to catechumens, not appropriate for the elementary Synoptics or the advanced gospel of John. He points to a deliberate esotericism among early Christians, a policy of silence on teaching about Jesus' teaching on resurrection and Jesus' resurrection itself. He implies that Jesus' own teaching was more enigmatic than a literal resurrection of the body, and as Christians moved more towards a literal understanding of physical resurrection, Jesus' own teaching complicated catechesis.

If Jesus' dispute with the Sadducees is, as Meier effectively argues, a relic from the ministry of the historical Jesus, it reinforces the argument we have made, that a first century Jew would link the belief in resurrection of the dead to God's power and a correct understanding of Scripture. For Jesus, a Jew speaking in a Jewish context in the mid-first century, this may have seemed relatively unremarkable, a belief shared by most of his audience. For Paul, whose hearers were better versed in Greco-Roman ideas of immortality apart from the body, the idea was stranger. Because Paul is in a minority in preaching resurrection, accenting its importance becomes more crucial to his message.

## The Corinthian Church

Despite the centrality of the belief in Jesus' resurrection for the faith of many early communities, not all shared the expectation of resurrection of the dead for believers. Paul addresses some within the Corinthian church, "Now if Christ is preached as raised from the dead, how can some of you say that there is no resurrection of the dead? (1 Cor 15:12)." Since the resurrection of the dead is, in fact, *not* part of the earliest creed that Paul says he learned and then transmitted to the Corinthians (1 Cor 15:3–5), a believer could affirm all the essential elements of the earliest proclamation of Jesus, and not neces-

---

[2] Bruce Chilton, "Resurrection in the Gospels," Avery-Peck and Neusner, *Death, Life-after-Death*, 215–39.

sarily believe in a resurrection of the dead for all.[3] Paul utterly denounces such an interpretation, linking resurrection of the dead to
the crucial element in the proclamation, "Christ has been raised."
Belief in one, he claims, is embedded in the other: ". . . but if there
is no resurrection of the dead, then Christ has not been raised (1 Cor
15:13)."[4]

In a letter that deals with a series of disparate topics, Paul's discussion of resurrection in chapter 15 appears initially to be a misfit.[5]
It is an abstract and otherworldly aside in a letter about concrete
community matters—marriage, sexual behavior, lawsuits, divisions
between rich and poor, and patterns of worship. Paul's instructions
in 1 Corinthians normally prescribe behavior, not belief, yet the letter ends with Paul's ringing demand for belief in resurrection from
the dead.

Interpreters have answered the question of chapter 15's place in
the letter via historical and theological explanations. Many see Paul's
argument for resurrection as loosely fitting with the rest of the letter because it reins in an elitist, separatist group with alternative
views on resurrection and promotes the overall theme of church
unity.[6] Karl Barth argued that chapter 15 unifies the entire letter
around Paul's theme of the defeat of death.[7]

A second question revolves around Paul's unbending demand that
his hearers accept resurrection of the *body*. Could he not conceive
of pious Christians who lived decent lives, cared for each other and
the poor, but understood Christ's resurrection as conferring only spiritual immortality? Physical resurrection of believers is not part of the
earliest creed Paul heard and transmitted.[8] Nor is he himself with-

---

[3] Resurrection quickly becomes part of early catchesis, as shown by Heb 6:2.

[4] Joost Holleman discusses the various traditions used by Paul, in *Resurrection and
Parousia* (Leiden: Brill, 1996). The distinctive combination of Jesus' resurrection as
the vindicated martyr and the beginning of a general eschatological resurrection is,
Holleman argues, Paul's own distinctive response to misunderstandings in Thessalonica
and Corinth.

[5] This may not be the original arrangement of the letter. Conzelmann suggests
that it follows the order of the Corinthians letter to Paul, answering their queries
in turn. Some partition theories argue it is several fragments, but no theory has
won general agreement. In the absence of compelling evidence of separate fragments, we should interpret the letter as it presently exists.

[6] Margaret Mitchell, *Paul and the Rhetoric of Reconciliation* (Louisville: Westminster/John
Knox, 1992).

[7] Karl Barth, *The Resurrection of the Dead* (trans. H. J. Stenning; New York: Revell,
1933; German, 1924) 101–7.

[8] Resurrection quickly becomes part of early catechesis, as shown by Heb 6:2.

out ambivalence about the resurrected body.[9] Yet in this polemical
context he makes it the hinge upon which all else hangs. That he
means *bodies* is clear, since, as Wright points out, his seed metaphor
would have been unnecessary and unhelpful if he were reiterating
the standard view of the survival of the spirit.[10]

Richard Horsley and Neil Elliott provide insights into the letter
that take us further in solving the two questions of the continuity of
chapter 15 with the rest of the gospel and the importance Paul gives
to resurrection of the body. Both have understood 1 Corinthians as
an anti-imperial gospel, consciously designed to set up an alternative society in competition with the pyramid of patronage headed
by the emperor that was in place in first-century Corinth. Both build
on earlier historical and theological perspectives, but help us imagine the situation of human beings in Corinth struggling with specific
and tangible sources of suffering.

## 1 Corinthians as an Anti-Imperial Program

Elliott insists that Paul's focus on the cross of Christ is "unequivo-
cally political."[11] Paul holds up as the source of power and blessing
not the exalted emperor, but the symbol of resistance, the crucified
criminal. Interpretation, argues Elliott, has masked the political nature
of Paul's apocalyptic language, rendering the terms "sin," "death,"
"law," and especially "the powers" as they are used in the pseudo-
Paulines and Romans, as abstract elements. Yet the grisly death of
a lower-class trouble-maker, distasteful for the upper classes even to
discuss, is the ultimate concrete expression of Roman power and
suppression of dissent.[12] Paul's choice to emphasize the cross is an
open challenge to those forces, the rulers of this age, who in their

---

[9] Dale Martin points out that while Paul argues for resurrection of the body,
he cannot mean precisely *this* body, since "flesh and blood cannot inherit the kingdom." Martin suggests Paul is caught between accommodating lower-status Christians
and their apocalyptic hopes, and higher-status Christians influenced by philosophy
and currents of popular Greco-Roman thought (*The Corinthian Body* [New Haven:
Yale, 1995] 130).

[10] Wright, *Resurrection of the Son of God*, 343.

[11] "The Anti-Imperial Message of the Cross," in Richard Horsley, ed., *Paul and
Empire* (Harrisburg: Trinity, 1997) 167–83; an earlier version appears as chapter 4
in *Liberating Paul* (Maryknoll, N.Y.: Orbis, 1994).

[12] See Elliott, "Anti-Imperial Message," 167–71, and Martin Hengel, *Crucifixion*
(trans. J. Bowden; London: SCM, 1977).

ignorance crucified the Lord of glory (2:8). "The cross was for Paul the signature in history of the forces that killed Jesus."[13]

Another expression of Paul's challenge to the power politics of his day is his method of arguing by contraries, turning normal notions of what is valuable inside out, distinguishing between the apparent and the real. He holds up not strength, but weakness (1:27); not wisdom of the world, but the folly of the cross (1:21); not the worldly wisdom of those who govern, but the secret wisdom of those who know God's power (2:5–8).[14] In place of the exalted emperor—whose image as the "patron of the empire" dominated the colony, appearing on coins, statues, at games, and at official celebrations—Paul raises up the image of the crucified criminal.[15] The power of these forces that killed Jesus, however, is already beginning to wane (2:6).

Horsley argues that Paul's choice of terminology points to a conscious construction of an alternative society.[16] While Paul likely borrowed *ekklesia* from the Septuagint, he cannot have been naïve about its meaning in the eastern empire as "citizen assembly," a political-religious body.[17] Paul's talk of the community as "the body of Christ" adapts a primary symbol of the Republic, a unified organism whose head is the emperor.[18] Furthermore, as Mitchell has illustrated, his rhetorical forms echo Greco-Roman rhetoric, appealing to the actions that focus on the future. They appeal to advantage and support of the greater good;[19] however, Paul directs them not to the πόλις, but to the internal order of the ἐκκλησία.

Paul not only co-opts terminology from the dominant society, he undermines the imperial patronage arrangements of that society by encouraging alternatives. Horsley delineates these alternatives: (1) Paul

---

[13] *Liberating Paul,* 110.

[14] In 2 Corinthians Paul similarly wields Jesus' death and resurrection against his detractors, the Super-Apostles, inverting their categories of glory and success. See Calvin Roetzel, "'As Dying, and Behold We Live': Death and Resurrection in Paul's Theology," *Int* 46 (1992) 5–18.

[15] See John K. Chow, "Patronage in Roman Corinth," in Horsley, *Paul and Empire,* 104–25.

[16] Horsley, "1 Corinthians: A Case Study of Paul's Assembly as an Alternative Society," in Horsley, *Paul and Empire,* 242–52.

[17] Horsley, "Assembly," 208.

[18] Richard Gordon, "The Veil of Power," *Paul and Empire,* 129; and Horsley, "1 Corinthians," 248.

[19] Margaret Mitchell (τό συμφέρον), calls this a deliberative letter, combining epistolary and rhetorical forms. Paul particularly appeals to the greater advantage, *Paul and the Rhetoric of Reconciliation.*

encourages a network of small assemblies to consider themselves as responsible to each other, part of the larger community of believers, thus encouraging a social movement that crosses boundaries of city and province. (2) Paul recommends the community handle its affairs internally as much as possible, settling problems of group discipline themselves and avoiding the civil courts (6:1–8). (3) In Horsley's reading of 1 Corinthians 8–10 Paul prohibits the eating of idol meat, a move that effectively cuts church members off from the social and religious life of the empire. Horsley's reading departs here from much of the history of interpretation in giving primacy to 10:14–22, which forbids "sharing community with demons," and seeing 10:23–11:1 as an parenthetical afterthought.[20] Even if one disagrees with Horsley on this point, the bulk of his other evidence stands. (4) Paul promotes an economic system that differs from the imperial patronage system. In refusing to accept support from the community and "paying his own way" by continuing to work at his own trade, Paul rejects the patronage system in place in the empire. While Horsley recognizes Paul's desire to avoid becoming some wealthy patron's "house apostle," he also notes that Paul deliberately steps out of the pyramid of patronage and power in favor of a more horizontal, egalitarian system. (5) In taking up collections for the poor in other churches (16:1–4; Gal 2:9–10; Rom 15:25–27) Paul also encourages an economic support system that is international in scope and requires a horizontal sharing of wealth: a rejection of the tributary, top-down system of the larger society.

## The Place of Resurrection in an Anti-Imperial Program

If we look at 1 Corinthians through the lens suggested by Elliott, Horsley, and others, which reveals an open challenge to the power politics of Paul's day and a prescription for an alternative society, Paul's discussion of resurrection comes into focus as an integral part of the letter. It is no misfit, but will be the final proof that the pyramid of power has been overturned and an alternative society has emerged.

In chapter 1 of the letter, Paul studiously dismantles publicly-accepted categories of what is valuable. Salvation comes not through

---

[20] See discussion in "Assembly," 247–49.

wisdom and learning, but accepting the folly of the cross, which projects God's power (1:18–24). Not human wisdom or strength brings salvation, but the folly and weakness of God (v. 25, repeated in 3:18–20). Neither human power nor status will prevail, but God has chosen people of apparent weakness and low status to overthrow the existing order (lit., "those that are not, to destroy those that are" [1:28]). Horsley's suggestion that Paul is constructing an alternative community fits with his rejection of all that that community deems valuable.

Chapter 2 matches chapter 15 in language and form, as Judith Kovacs has observed, forming a frame to the letter.[21] In the second chapter, the decline of both the present Greco-Roman culture, as exemplified by philosophy (vv. 4–6) and the political rulers of the current age (v. 8), has already begun. It is being replaced by a process that leads to glory, secret and unimaginable things (vv. 4–5) for those who love God and understand his power (v. 5).

Paul continues the reversion of categories in 4:10–13, again lauding folly, weakness, and low status. He tellingly links it again to the beginning of the end, calling himself and other apostles "the last act," the ones who fight to the death in the arena (echoed in 15:30–33, fighting the wild beasts at Ephesus). The end here is not that of a gladiatorial contest, but the social and political hegemony of the society that enjoyed such contests.

In chapter 15, Paul brings his final "proof-text" for his own program to replace the existing order, namely the death and resurrection of Jesus. He states the essence of the kerygma in vv. 3–7, and underlines his pedigree as an apostle in vv. 8–11. Curiously, he then chains this kerygma and his apostleship to the belief in resurrection of the dead for believers, an element not explicit in the proclamation itself. It is the whole underpinning of their faith and understanding of God, and the nature of the lives they are living. In a series of "if-then" clauses (vv. 13–19), he says that the belief in resurrection is the necessary element in a whole set of realities: (1) the resurrection of Christ himself. Three times, he says that if there is no general resurrection, then Christ has not been raised (vv. 13, 15,

---

[21] Judith Kovacs, "The Archons, the Spirit, and the Death of Christ: Do We Need the Hypothesis of Gnostic Opponents to Explain 1 Corinthians 2:6–16?" *Apocalyptic in the New Testament: Essays in Honor of J. Louis Martyn* (*JSNTSup* 24; ed. Joel Marcus and Marion Lloyd Soards; Sheffield: JSOT, 1989) 217–36.

16); (2) the worth of his own and others' preaching (vv. 14–15); (3) the worth of the Corinthians' own faith, emphasized twice (vv. 14–17); (4) their freedom from their sins (v. 17); (5) the fate of believers who have already died (v. 18); (6) the value of their lives and their disciplined way of living (vv. 19, 32b); (7) the efficacy of their practice of baptism for the dead (v. 29); (8) Paul's living in danger (vv. 30, 32); (9) the meaning of their potential martyrdom (v. 32); and (10) a proper knowledge of God (v. 34).

In other arguments Paul can be hard to fathom, but here he is crystal-clear about which ideas are corollaries of resurrection of the dead, and what is at stake in accepting or rejecting it. Paul is still an apocalyptic Jew (and former Pharisee), who sees God's power and ultimate justice as wrapped up in his willingness and ability to give life to the dead. Wright observes a whole "creation theology" at work here, seeing chapter 15 as a meditation on Genesis 1 and 2, not a mere piling up of proof-texts.[22] Paul often points to God's power as proven by Jesus' resurrection and the resurrection of all believers, calling him "the God who raised Jesus" (1 Cor 6:14; 2 Cor 1:9–10; 4:7–12; Rom 8:11).

To disbelieve resurrection is to short-circuit the apocalyptic drama—to disrupt the process of liberation that began at Jesus' death and is still unfolding. In vv. 20–23, Paul brings several metaphors to communicate the idea of an unfolding process that begins with Christ's death, the first-fruits of the harvest, the first man at creation, and the τάγμα, a brigade or order of soldiers in a processional. The intensifying military imagery and processional language liken God's coming triumph to an imperial victory march. Paul Duff describes the Roman triumphal procession that celebrated victory over enemies.[23] A display of the structure and hierarchy of Empire, it included the magistrates, Senate, people carrying the goods taken in war, enemy captives, the conquering general, and his army. The enemy captives were executed at the end of the ceremony. Paul's metaphor reverses the process: he begins with the execution of the crucified criminal,

---

[22] Wright, *Resurrection of the Son of God*, 334.

[23] See Paul Duff, "Processions" *ABD* 5.469–73; idem, *Honor or Shame: The Language of Processions and Perception in 2 Cor 2:14–6:13; 7:2–4* (Ph.D. diss., University of Chicago, 1988); Scott Hafemann, *Suffering and Spirit. An Exegetical Study of II Cor 2:14–3:3 Within the Context of the Corinthian Correspondence* (Tübingen: Mohr Siebeck, 1986); Peter Marshall, "A Metaphor of Social Shame: *Thriambeuein* in 2 Cor 2:14," *NovT* 25 (1983) 302–17.

through the order (τάγμα), an allusion to the armies; he then continues to the ultimate defeat of every sovereignty, authority, and power, which cannot fail to include the reigning emperor. Since, as Duff has shown, Paul uses processional language explicitly elsewhere in the Corinthian correspondence (2 Cor 2:14–6:13 and 7:2–4), the metaphor is close at hand and seems to be implicit in 1 Corinthians 15. The use of the military metaphor τάγμα, a unit of soldiers, supports the image of a procession displaying the different parts of the Empire's might.

First Corinthians 15:22–28 provides the clearest proof that Paul has not merely translated Jesus' death to an apocalyptic plane and ignored its brutal political quality in real time. The powers are not, in this letter, elemental invisible forces, but real tyrants and their deputies. Had Paul moved entirely to the apocalyptic world, the hidden reality behind the apparent, says Elliott, the drama would already be complete with Christ's death. The other-worldly powers would already be overthrown. But in 1 Corinthians, Paul sees the "powers" as not yet conquered. Jesus' death was the beginning of "God's war of liberation,"[24] but it will not be final until the powers are overthrown at resurrection.[25] While the terms "sovereignty" (ἀρχή), "authority" (ἔξουσια), and "power" (δύναμις) would include the elemental invisible forces of the universe (Rom 8:38, cf. στοιχεῖα τοῦ κόσμου; Gal 4:3,9) that oppose God, they also point to political powers that have not yet been fully vanquished.[26]

Helmut Koester has also shown that the word for Jesus' return, παρουσία, in 15:23, appears elsewhere in Paul only in 1 Thessalonians (2:19; 3:13; 4:15; 5:23; it also appears in the deutero-Pauline 2 Thess 2:1, 8) and its common meaning is a political term used for the coming of a king or emperor.[27] Paul adapts the word to adjure the community to prepare for the coming of Christ, who "is destined to reign (βασιλεύειν) until God has put all enemies under his feet (v. 25)."

---

[24] J. Louis Martyn uses this term to describe Paul's apocalyptic eschatology, *Galatians* (AB; Garden City: Doubleday, 1997) 101, 105.

[25] Elliott, "Anti-Imperial Message," 180–81.

[26] Commentators who embrace quite different understandings of Paul agree on this point. In addition to Horsley and Elliott, see also Richard Hays, *First Corinthians* (Louisville: John Knox, 1997) 265; and Ben Witherington, *Conflict and Community in Corinth* (Grand Rapids: Eerdmans, 1995) 295–98.

[27] Helmut Koester, "Imperial Ideology and Paul's Eschatology in 1 Thessalonians," in Horsley, ed., *Paul and Empire*, 158–59.

In this last act of the apocalyptic drama, all enemies, both human rulers and cosmic elements, will be destroyed. The final enemy, death, will be defeated through resurrection of all believers. This defeat of death in v. 26 cannot refer to Christ's resurrection, which has already taken place, but is a yet-to-be accomplished feat. Furthermore, the many allusions to empire imply that Paul sees death not only as an abstract cosmic force,[28] but also expressed in local and political terms.

Paul continues to marshal his arguments by reminding the Corinthians in v. 29 of their practice of "baptism on behalf of the dead" (v. 29). No one knows exactly what this practice was, but Richard De Maris's examination of archaeological evidence reveals first-century Corinth as intensely pre-occupied with death and the underworld.[29]

Paul's reference to "fighting those wild beasts at Ephesus," (v. 32) whether literal or metaphorical (as in 4:9) is another indication that the Empire and its brutal methods of retaining its power are ever before Paul in this chapter. His "constant danger" and "dying daily" could be from many sources, but the many references to empire suggest at least some of them are from secular authorities. Facing these dangers would be an absurd risk, were it not for the hope of resurrection (vv. 30–32).

### Resurrection of the Body in an Anti-Imperial Program

Against some people in the church who deny it, Paul's passionate defense of resurrection makes clear it is *bodies* that will be raised. Mere survival of the soul or spirit is not sufficient to prove God's victory over the political and cosmic powers of the age. Paul's exasperation in vv. 35–36 seems to be towards those who question the physical body being raised (35), or suggest that some part of the self does not actually die (36).

Who are these people who say there is no resurrection from the dead, and what do they believe? Because they practice a baptism on behalf of the dead (15:29), they probably believe in some form

---

[28] Martin De Boer argues that death is the primary enemy in 1 Corinthians, conceived as a quasi-angelic force.

[29] Richard De Maris, "Corinthian Religion and Baptism for the Dead (1 Cor 15:29): Insights from Archaeology and Anthropology," *JBL* 114 (1995) 661–82.

of afterlife. Scholars have gone two directions, depending on whether they see the key to the deniers in later Gnostic texts or in Jewish wisdom speculation. The former group sees the deniers as triumphalist pneumatics, who believe that they *already* live a pneumatic existence by virtue of their dying and rising with Christ in baptism.[30] Others note Paul's unusual oppositional language of ψυχή and πνεῦμα and the unexpectedly negative evaluation of ψυχή. Normally, ψυχή simply means "soul" or the immortal part of the self.[31] This group sees the key in Jewish wisdom literature, arguing that the deniers reject the resurrection of the body in particular. Many now favor some form of this second view, that Paul is facing believers who tout an afterlife that does not involve the body.[32] These two positions are not far apart: both draw Paul's fire because they diverge from him on the nature of the resurrection.[33] In either case, the issue is different from other problems in the letter, calling for belief rather than behavior.[34]

Paul's extensive argument for bodily resurrection and his statement in v. 50, "flesh and blood can never possess the kingdom of God," would then seem to be at odds with each other. Whatever body is raised, it is not exactly the body that was buried. Martin cautions us against a starkly dualistic perspective that leaves Paul with the choice of either bodily resurrection or spiritual immortality. Cartesian dualism that organizes a human being by antinomies,

---

[30] De Boer, *The Defeat of Death* ( *JSNTSup* 22; Sheffield: JSNT, 1988); Christopher M. Tuckett, "The Corinthians who say 'There is No Resurrection of the Dead,'" *The Corinthian Correspondence* (ed. R. Bieringer; Leuven: Peeters, 1996) 247–75.

[31] De Boer, *Defeat*, 98–99. Birger Pearson, Horsley, and Gerhard Sellin posit the influence of Jewish wisdom literature similar to Philo, and its exegesis of Gen 2:7. See Pearson, *The Pneumatikos/Psychikos Terminology of 1 Corinthians: A Study in the Theology of the Corinthian Opponents of Paul and its Relation to Gnosticism* (Missoula: Scholars, 1973); Richard Horsley, "How Can Some of You Say 'There is No Resurrection of the Dead?' Spiritual Elitism at Corinth," *NovT* 20 (1978) 203–31; idem, "*Pneumatikos* vs. *Psychikos*: Distinctions of Status Among the Corinthians," *HTR* 69 (1976) 269–88.

[32] See Martin, Soards, Horsley, Hays, and Conzelmann.

[33] De Boer summarizes the many theories about the position of the Corinthian deniers in *The Defeat of Death* ( *JSNTSup* 22; Sheffield: JSNT, 1998) 96–97. For recent summaries of the discussion see also Gerhard Barth, "Zur Frage nach der in 1 Korinther bekämpften Auferstehungsleugnung," *ZNW* 83 (1992) 187–201; A. J. M. Wedderburn, *Baptism and Resurrection* (WUNT 44; Tübingen: Mohr Siebeck, 1987) 6–37; G. Sellin, *Der Streit um die Auferstehung der Toten* (FRLANT 138; Göttingen: Vandenhoeck & Ruprecht, 1986) 17–37.

[34] A fresh and interesting recent attempt to reconstruct their position is Tuckett, "Corinthians Who Say," 264–75, who includes a discussion of earlier attempts.

he points out, is not typical of the ancients. Things like ὕλη ("matter"), σῶμα ("body"), ψυχή ("soul"), and πνεῦμα ("spirit") were on a
continuum, and were thought of in terms of more or less, not
either/or. The body is a mixture of these substances that interact
with each other and constitute a "hierachy of essence."[35] The body
is continuous with its environment, and the self is a fluid, permeable, temporary entity.[36]

Like Martin, Wright rejects a sense of body-soul dichotomy for
Paul. He renders ψυχή ("soul") as similar to the Hebrew נפש, the
whole person. In Paul's use here, it stands for ordinary human life
versus the pneumatic life infused by God's spirit. But both encompass some form of bodily life.[37] While rather different in their
approaches, both scholars steer us away from a simple dualism and
reject a "spiritual resurrection" without a body. "Flesh and blood"
then stands for a certain kind of bodily life that will not inherit the
kingdom, but not a rejection of bodily resurrection. A wholly spiritual afterlife would be unremarkable in an ancient context and not
require Paul's extensive explanations.

The deniers in Corinth, whom Martin and others call the Strong
(because they claimed to eat idol meat, engage in sex with prostitutes, and attend pagan temples with no spiritual ill effects) differed
from Paul, argues Martin, in their constructions of the body. These
differing constructions, says Martin, matched different social and economic statuses. The deniers, or the Strong, were of higher social status and partook more freely of some currents of Stoic, Cynic, and
Epicurean philosophical and popular thought. Many may have thought,
like the pagan Celsus, "What sort of human soul would have any
further use for a body that has rotted?" (*Against Celsus* 5.14). The
deniers shared with others the idea that as long as the essences are
in their proper place in the hierarchy, with *pneuma* as the highest
element, harmony and balance prevail. Their ideology of society mirrors their ideology of the body. As long as the appropriate strata of
society remain in charge and inferior groups willingly submit to them,

---

[35] Dale Martin, *The Corinthian Body* (New Haven: Yale, 1995) 15.
[36] Martin shows that Platonic dualism is not strict Cartesian body/soul dualism,
and that Platonism is a minority position amidst a multiplicity of views held by
Aristotle, Stoics, and Epicureans (*Corinthian Body*, 3–37). For another discussion of
Paul's anthropology and Greek science, see Scott Brodeur, *The Holy Spirit's Agency
in the Resurrection of the Dead* (Rome: Gregorian University, 1996) 34–80.
[37] Wright, *Resurrection of the Son of God*, 282, 350–51.

society will function harmoniously.[38] As part of the upper echelons of society, they see themselves as possessing larger quantities of the higher "stuff" of a person, πνεῦμα. Therefore, any notion of after-life focuses on the predominance of πνεῦμα at the expense of σῶμα.

Martin shows that Paul constructs the body differently. He also sees the person as a combination of elements, but he emphasizes the body's continuity with its environment and vulnerability to the elements around it. Like the lower-status people he identifies with, says Martin, Paul thinks of the body more in terms of boundaries, and is more anxious about invasion and pollution. On a social level, their unsteady position translates this anxiety to fears of being subdued and controlled by more powerful outsiders. Similarly, Paul and the deniers differ on their views of community, the deniers being rela-tively comfortable Christians who think they possess more πνεῦμα and accept their higher status as their due, maintaining ideas of spir-itual immortality more in tune with their environment. Paul and his lower-status fellow Christians experience the surrounding culture as more hostile, see the body as threatened, and put forth resurrection in defiance of its standards.

In asserting resurrection of the body in particular, then, Paul again turns an accepted hierarchy of values on its head. In recommend-ing that the strong submit to the weak, the spirit to the body in res-urrection, the higher-status Christians to the lower-status Christians, he argues for a reversal of status that disrupts the pyramid of value.[39] To maintain spiritual immortality alone would leave the pyramid of value in place by discounting the physical reality. For Paul, bodies that suffer, face danger, and go through death are not dismissed as unimportant, but are transformed through God's power. They go from being "mere," ordinary, matter-laden bodies to transformed pneumatic bodies. Paul maintains the traditional categories of mat-ter, soul, spirit for the sake of argument, but in claiming bodies will be raised and transformed he reverses the continuum. The hierar-chy will eventually be overturned.

Paul does not literally read the deniers out of the community, per-haps because as the higher-status group, they are well-regarded, dis-proportionately powerful, and financially supportive of the church. But he makes perfectly clear that their rejection of bodily resurrection

[38] Martin, *The Corinthian Body*, 38–47.
[39] Martin, *The Corinthian Body*, 55–68.

is unacceptable, a litmus test for the value of their very existence as
a church. He draws a boundary that attempts to rein in, rather than
exclude.

Looking at 1 Corinthians as an anti-imperial gospel answers two
questions: the question of the seeming discontinuity of chapter 15
with the rest of the letter, and the question of why resurrection of
the body in particular is so crucial for Paul. The discussion of resurrection *is* continuous with the rest of the letter, because the resurrection of believers is the final proof of God's power to bring about
a new order, the culmination of the apocalyptic drama that began
with Jesus' death. Furthermore, belief that bodies are raised is crucial, because belief in spiritual immortality alone would leave the old
assumptions about value and privilege in place. Paul replaces the
old pyramid of patronage, and its sense of trickle-down benefits from
the emperor to his subjects, with the crucified Jesus whom God raises
in power. If he has been raised, so too must his subjects receive the
same benefit. Resurrection of bodies from the dead becomes a powerful idea wielded by Paul against prevailing political and cultural
assumptions.

*Resurrection as Symbol and Strategy*

In considering the essential question of this book, how did belief in
resurrection function, our findings in 1 Corinthians echo our findings
in the Jewish materials. Resurrection acts as a potent symbol in
Paul's construction of community. The same elements are embedded in it as in the Jewish literature, an affirmation of God's power,
a correct understanding of Scripture, and the legitimacy of those
who preach resurrection. God's powerful victory over every other
power, cosmic and political, is trumpeted in 1 Cor 15:24–28. Paul
proclaims Jesus' death and resurrection happen "according to the
Scriptures" in 15:3–7, and these events are inextricably linked to the
resurrection of believers. Last, the legitimacy of the preachers and
teachers flows from resurrection, for without it "our preaching is
empty and we are found to be false witnesses" (15:14–15).

*Resurrection condenses a worldview*
Resurrection acts as a shorthand for all that Paul and his hearers
hold dear. Three times he says that if there is no resurrection from
the dead, then Christ's resurrection also did not happen. Neither is

his preaching legitimate, nor their faith, way of life, or individual practices worthwhile. The work of Horsley, Elliott, Martin, and Wright helps us understand Paul's use of resurrection, his claim that it is not the immortal *pneuma* that is the site of God's power, but the fragile *soma*. Cohen's essential insight that condensation symbols often sum up a way of life and embody a sense of self [40] is amplified and nuanced by their work. These scholars have demonstrated how Paul co-opts the imperial and military language and substitutes an entirely different set of symbols: not the emperor, but the crucified criminal; not the strong, but the weak; not worldly wisdom, but foolishness; not the citizen assembly of the *polis*, but the *ekklesia* of believers; not the immortal *pneuma*, but the earthy *soma*. Paul's apocalyptic language paints a broad picture into which his hearers can plug the particulars of Rome: the emperor, the local aristocracy, and the system of patronage as well as the program of an emerging alternative community.

### Resurrection is imprecise and abstract

That its meaning is not agreed upon by all Christian believers is obvious from the fact that the Corinthian deniers went one way with the idea of resurrection, and Paul and those like him went another. Most scholars think the deniers agreed on survival after death, but denied the body would be raised. Cohen shows that symbols encompass both commonality and individuality. They put a simple public face on varying complex views.[41] Some of these individual interpretations deviated too much for Paul. He is annoyed when he must answer questions like "How are the dead raised?" or "With what kind of body do they come?" branding them ἄφρων, "foolish." The seed metaphor, de Boer points out, allows Paul to argue both the dissimilarity of the body that dies and the body that is raised, as well as the continuity of the two bodies.

### Belief in resurrection draws boundaries

Paul could not be clearer that only those who believe in resurrection of the body have truly understood Jesus' resurrection. Those who say otherwise are foolish and undermine the basis of community. But he does not use it as a boundary to keep the deniers out,

---

[40] A. Cohen, *Symbolic Construction*, 109.
[41] A. Cohen, *Symbolic Construction*, 74.

nor suggest they be ejected from the community. Rather, he draws
a line to keep the insiders in and maintain the purity and integrity
of the community, keeping the world and its hostile forces at bay.
As Martin understands it, Paul sees the body as permeable and in
danger of pollution and invasion. Similarly, he sees the community
in danger from weakening of boundaries. Mating with prostitutes,
bringing lawsuits between believers to the local courts, eating idol
meat, and eating in pagan temples all represent intrusions from outside and threaten to breach the boundaries of the group. Resurrection
is a useful in contructing symbolic boundaries, which Cohen shows
are increasingly important when structural boundaries are weak.

*Belief in resurrection constructs community*
Paul says this outright, in that the entire enterprise of their faith and
his preaching falls flat without belief in resurrection. The character
of their life and faith, the peril in which they live, their suffering,
and the fate of those who have died is rendered meaningless. Their
way of life, which includes a practice of baptism on behalf of the
dead, is particularly meaningless. The points of faith on which the
community turns, evaporate. Resurrection is the final scene of the unfolding apocalyptic drama, which is replacing the current society with
an alternative one. Paul not only thinks about the world differently
because he believes in resurrection, but as Horsley has shown, he
acts differently. Resisting the economic patronage system in place,
he works for himself and takes up collections for other churches. He
promotes different customs in prayer, banquets, legal disputes, and
personal conduct, all at odds with the surrounding society.

*Belief in resurrection confers legitimacy on those who preach it*
Paul refers to his own preaching, suffering, and peril as meaningful
only in light of resurrection of the dead. The discussion of resurrection in chapter 15 is preceded by a plea for his own status as an
apostle, in spite of his early persecution of the church. He claims
he worked harder than any of the apostles; yet without belief in resurrection, his preaching is κενὸς, "empty" (v. 14). just as God's grace
that conferred apostleship on him would be empty (v. 10). He and
his co-workers could be accused of misrepresenting God, since they
preached Christ's resurrection, which follows only (in Paul's mind)
if the dead are raised (v. 15). He and his hearers would be pathetic
without resurrection (v. 19). Certainly the danger he faces daily is

absurd without it (vv. 30–32). Since there is resurrection of the dead, all these subjunctive clauses change to indicative statements that underline Paul's legitimacy. He faces danger for good reason; he is not pitiable; *he represents God truly*; his preaching will bear fruit; and, not incidentally, he is a valid apostle. The point of representing God truly echoes Jesus' jibe against the Sadducees that they do not understand God's power because they deny resurrection, or the image of the Pharisees in Josephus as the ones who understand God's power because they preach it.

*Resurrection solves a set of problems*
Cohen reminds us that groups worry most about boundaries when they encounter other cultures. Many of the problems at Corinth stemmed from the encounter with the surrounding culture, causing Paul to worry about invasion, pollution, and the breaching of boundaries. As well, the gap between the group's belief in the expectation of God's reign and the reality of their shaky status and anticipated suffering required some explanation. This gap is bridged by the vision of God's not yet complete "war of liberation," the vision of an awakening new society to replace the old, the triumph of the righteous and the ultimate subjection of all nations to God. Resurrection will be the last act in the drama, the defeat of death itself along with the cosmic and the political power; "the last enemy to be destroyed is death" (v. 26); "we shall not all sleep, but we shall all be changed" (v. 51); "the dead will be raised imperishable" (v. 52); and "death is swallowed up in victory" (v. 54). Resurrection allowed the Corinthians to retain the idea of God's power and plan for history, manifested in Jesus' resurrection, and reconcile it with their experience of suffering and insecurity under Roman domination, while beginning to put another society in place.

*Belief in resurrection allowed its adherents to live in the world as it is*
Jesus' death and resurrection, essential elements in the earliest catechesis (15:3–5), carried with them the promise of bodily resurrection for all believers and the inauguration of a new reign. The power of Rome, the local authorities, cosmic elements, and even death itself, was only apparent and was already being dismantled. Paul is like the Pharisees and the rabbis in his expectation of bodily resurrection, but he differs in the immediacy of his expectation. For the Pharisees, we do not know when they expected resurrection. For the

rabbis, it becomes a generalized article of faith. Paul expects the end to come while some in the church are still alive. His apocalyptic vision places him and his community in the last act of the unfolding drama of God's liberation.

Paul attempts to exert some social control in Corinth. He utterly delegitimizes those who do not accept it, while legitimating himself. His largesse in accepting different preachers and baptizers in chapter 3 does not operate in the discussion of resurrection in chapter 15. How successful he was at Corinth, we do not know. Second Corinthians shows evidence of considerable reaction against Paul.[42] Whether Paul fails or triumphs in promoting bodily resurrection at Corinth, it becomes part of catechesis by the time of Hebrews and 2 Timothy, although alternative constructions continue to surface in the second and third century.

---

[42] See Dieter Georgi's classic study, *The Opponents of Paul in Second Corinthians* (Philadelphia: Fortress, 1986).

# CHAPTER FOUR

# RESURRECTION IN EARLY CHRISTIANITY

## *The Apostolic Fathers*

A smattering of references to resurrection appears in the apostolic fathers. It occurs as a standard idea in homily (*1 Clem.* 25–27; *Barn.* 21.1), doctrine (*Did.* 16.6; *Barn.* 5.6; *Mart. Pol.* 14.2; *Smyrn.* 3.1), and instruction (*Barn.* 5.6; *Did.* 16.6). The author of *1 Clement* argues for resurrection at some length, proving it from the cycle of day and night (24), the growth cycle of plants (24), the phoenix (25), the scriptures (26), and God's integrity and power (27). Later in the work he points to schisms, divisions, and strife (46.5; 54.2) but never says whether they are caused by differences over resurrection. Several references to "flesh" appear, but never the term "resurrection of the flesh."

Similarly, Ignatius voices complaints about heterodoxy, speaking of "evil teachings" and "division" (*Phil.* 2.1) and "evil plants" (*Phil.* 3.1). We know that he attacks the docetists on one hand, "unbelievers" who "say that he suffered only in appearance" (*Smyrn.* 2.1; cf. *Trall.* 9.1) and deny Jesus came in the flesh (*Smyrn.* 2–5; 12.2), and Judaizers on the other (*Phil.* 6.1; *Magn.* 8.1; 9.1; 10.3). While he makes multiple references to false teaching and division (*Trall.* 9–11; *Phil.* 2–4), Ignatius does not cite the bodily resurrection of believers as a point of conflict, though we are safe in assuming the docetists rejected it. If they argue that Jesus did not experience bodily resurrection, they would hardly claim it for his followers.

Resurrection of the body is assumed and is simply part of the hortatory, catechetical language throughout this literature. No sustained defense of resurrection appears that allows us to reconstruct a set of opponents. Perkins suggests the lack of outright controversy is the result of these authors inheriting Jewish-Christian traditions of resurrection where it is linked to ultimate justice, but not yet facing any thoroughgoing and organized opposition.[1]

---

[1] Perkins, *Resurrection*, 334.

While we cannot reconstruct any clearly-defined groups of opponents, two references in *2 Clement* and Polycarp's *Letter to the Philippians* allude to some opposition to the belief in resurrection of the body:

> And none of you should say that this flesh is neither judged nor raised. Think about it! In what state were you saved? In what state did you regain your sight? Was it not while you were in this flesh? And so we must guard the flesh like the temple of God. For just as you were called in the flesh, so also you will come in the flesh. Since Jesus Christ-the Lord who saved us- was first a spirit and then became flesh, and in this way called us, so also we will receive the reward in this flesh (*2 Clem.* 9.1–5).[2]

Most scholars assign *2 Clement* to the early to mid-second century, though authorship and provenance are unknown. Along with 2 Tim 2:18, Justin, and Athenagoras, it is another piece of evidence that resurrection of the body (or flesh) was an idea not shared by all Christians. His emphasis on "flesh" (σάρξ), repeated seven times in five verses, implies someone is denying the role of the flesh in resurrection. He links the resurrection of believers not to Jesus' resurrection, but to his incarnation, reflecting, says Perkins, "a general shift to the incarnation as the central image of salvation."[3]

In Polycarp's letter to the Philippians, he is more pointed:

> For anyone who does not confess that Jesus Christ has come in the flesh is an anti-Christ; and whoever does not confess the witness of the cross is from the devil: and whoever distorts the words of the Lord for his own passions, saying that there is neither resurrection nor judgment—this one is the first-born of Satan (7.1).

Polycarp paraphrases 1 John 4:2–3 and 2 John 7 here, and uses the term he employs elsewhere for Marcion (according to Irenaeus, *Adv. Haer.* 3.3,4; *H.E.* 4.14.7). He seems to be reacting to more than a nebulous threat. Not only is someone promoting this "false teaching," but it may even be the majority view at Philippi, since he calls it "that which deceives many" (2.1). Van Eijk suggests that Polycarp's blast is brought on not so much by Marcion, whose theology is not

---

[2] All references from *The Apostolic Fathers*, translated by Bart Ehrman (LCL; Cambridge: Harvard University, 2003).
[3] Perkins, *Resurrection*, 337.

mentioned again, but a more general crisis of faith brought on by the delay of the Parousia.[4]

Like *2 Clement*, Polycarp links resurrection to the incarnation, but further links it to the death of Jesus and correct interpretation of Jesus' teaching. In 2.2, Polycarp links resurrection of believers to Jesus' resurrection, using traditional formulae: "But the one who raised him from the dead will raise us as well" (2.2). He further employs the classic themes of resurrection as flowing from God's power, and as the reward for the righteous (2.1–3).

The shadowy references in these two works do not permit a full-scale investigation of controversies and community reconstruction. They do indicate a climate where bodily resurrection is not universally believed, a climate richly attested to by the Nag Hammadi documents. Language is becoming more explicit, with more references to "flesh." Paul's statement that "flesh and blood cannot inherit," as well as his talk of a "spiritual body," has led some to deny all but a spiritual resurrection. The fathers provide evidence of a growing orthodoxy that linked bodily resurrection of believers to the incarnation, the passion, and the bodily resurrection of Jesus. Elaine Pagels has argued that the physical resurrection of Jesus is essential to the establishment of apostolic authority in the early church.[5] Only those closest to this one-time event and their successors could rightly claim legitimacy. It follows that resurrection of believers is similarly linked to questions of authority and legitimacy. Bodily resurrection of believers is a corollary of Jesus' bodily resurrection. If believers looked for spiritual resurrection, or realized their own resurrection in this world, then their resurrection would be different in kind than that of Jesus. Inevitably one might be considered superior to the other, or independent of the other.

Though vague and fragmentary, these references show that the belief in resurrection of the body is linked to questions of authority, and on its way to becoming a litmus test for who belonged in the community. It is joined to issues of God's power as creator and who rightly interprets Jesus' teaching. For fuller evidence of these trends we turn to evidence in Justin and Athenagoras.

---

[4] Ton H. C. van Eijk, *La Resurrection des Morts chez les Pères Apostoliques* (Paris: Beauchesne, 1974) 131–33.

[5] Elaine Pagels, *The Gnostic Gospels* (New York: Random House, 1979) 3–27.

## *Justin Martyr*

A hundred years after Paul, Justin cites the belief in resurrection of believers as the mark of a genuine Christian. His stylized apologetic draws on pagan and Christian arguments and addresses multiple audiences.[6] By this time, an idea merely alluded to in the Apostolic Fathers[7] has assumed definite form: that belief in resurrection of the body is a mark of orthodoxy. Equally clear is the reality that not all believers in Jesus agree that his followers will attain bodily resurrection. In arguing with the Jew Trypho and defending the belief in a thousand-year reign of Christ in a rebuilt Jerusalem, Justin mentions some who do not deserve to be called Christians:

> For if you have been thrown together with some who are called Christians, but who do not confess this, but dare to blaspheme the God of Abraham, and the God of Isaac, and the God of Jacob; who say there is no resurrection of the dead, and that their souls, when they die, are taken up to heaven; do not assume that they are Christians, just as one would not consider those claiming to be Sadducees, or similar sects of Genistae, Meristae, Galileans, Hellenists, Pharisees,[8] Baptists, are Jews (do not hear me disagreeably when I tell you everything that I think), but are [merely] called Jews and children of Abraham, worshipping God with the lips, as God himself declared, but the heart was far from him. But I and others who are straight-thinking (ὀρθογνώμονες) Christians on all things, understand that there will be a resurrection of the flesh (σαρκὸς ἀνάστασιν), and a thousand years in Jerusalem, which will then be built, beautified, and enlarged, [as] the prophets Ezekiel and Isaiah and others declare (*Dial.* 80.4–5).[9]

---

[6] See M. J. Edwards, M. A. Goodman, and S. R. F. Price, who situate Justin and others within a general wave of Jewish, pagan, and Christian apologetic in the late first and early second century: *Apologetics in the Roman Empire* (Oxford: Oxford University Press, 1999). On questions of a possible *Grundschrift* for the *Dialogue* and its editing, see Oskar Skarsaune, *The Proof from Prophecy* (*NovTSup* 56; Leiden: Brill, 1987) and Timothy Horner, *Listening to Trypho* (Leuven: Peeters, 2001).

[7] *1 Clem.* 24.1, 26.1; *2 Clem.* 9.1, 19.3; Ignatius, *Tral.* 9.1–2; *Smyrn.* 1.1–2; Polycarp, *Phil.* 1.2–3, 2.1–2, 7.1; *Barn.* 5.6, 21.2; Shepherd of Hermas, *Sim.* 5.6.5–7; *Mart. Pol.* 14.2.

[8] Most scholars have assumed Justin is simply mistaken here. He may, however, know Jews who do not admire the Pharisees, or those perceived to be their successors, the Rabbis.

[9] All references are from Edgar Goodspeed, *Die ältesten Apologeten* (Göttingen: Vandenhoeck & Ruprecht, 1984). Two recent critical editions of *Apologies* by André Wartelle and Miroslav Marcovich do not differ on our passages. The translation is my own.

Although chapter 80 begins in a tone of liberal acceptance of differing Christian views, Justin is unbending towards those who deny resurrection of the body. As Justin explains it, first the resurrection will take place, then will be followed by the thousand-year reign of Jesus in Jerusalem. He is incensed toward those who deny the first proposition, but accepts that some perfectly good Christians do not accept the second (80.2). He turns angry, reading these resurrection deniers out of the community. Three times, he says they do not even deserve to be called Christians (vv. 3–4).

This is the first appearance of the term "resurrection of the flesh." While the apostolic fathers talk about "flesh" and "resurrection," they never put the two terms together (2 Clem 9.1 comes closest). Justin himself does not use it consistently.[10] It never appears in his *Apologies*, which address pagan arguments. His use of "resurrection of the flesh" may be a response to those who have taken Paul's statements "we will be raised a spiritual body" (1 Cor 15:44) and "flesh and blood cannot inherit the kingdom of God" (1 Cor 15:50) to argue for a spiritual resurrection and deny a resurrection of the physical body.[11]

Although Justin discusses resurrection ostensibly in argument with Trypho (80; 81; 105; 117; 130), Trypho himself never objects to the belief in resurrection, nor does Justin ever accuse Jews of disagreeing with Christians over the issue. While the audience for *Dialogue* is not articulated by Justin, Tessa Rajak and others are probably correct that it is primarily other Christians, meant to provide them with arguments to discourage dabbling in Judaism or joining the many heretics named in Chapter 35, Marcionites, Basilidians, Valentinians, Saturnilians, and others.[12] Whether this chapter is specifically Marcion,[13] or responding to a larger climate of heterodoxy, the internal quality seems particularly evident in the discussion of resurrection,

---

[10] See M. O. Young, "Justin Martyr and the Death of Souls," *StPatr* 16 (1985) 209–15.

[11] Canon specialists note that Justin never cites Paul, though he does know some of the gospels. Arguments from silence are risky, but Justin's failure to cite Paul's statements about resurrection may mean they are being used by the resurrection deniers.

[12] Tessa Rajak, "Talking at Trypho: Christian Apologetic as Anti-Judaism in Justin's *Dialogue with Trypho the Jew*," in *Apologetics in the Roman Empire*, ed. Edwards, Goodman et al., 59–80.

[13] As argued by Paul J. Donahue, *Jewish-Christian Controversy in the Second Century* (Ann Arbor: UMI, 1990).

where Justin calls the deniers heretics, atheists, and sectarians, unworthy of the name "Christians." Justin officially addresses the *Apologies* to the emperor and senate, but surely they too are meant to provide material for Christians in their debate with paganism.

For Justin, as for earlier Jews and Christians, resurrection of the dead (now flesh) is a conviction that carries within it other ideas:

(1) Resurrection demonstrates God's power. In 1 Apol. 19, Justin makes what will become a familiar argument, the argument from creation. If a human being can come forth from a drop of semen, bodies dissolved in the earth can come forth again. He argues a material continuity that Bynum notes is characteristic of second-century arguments. Twice, he brings a verse that Celsus claims is used all the time by Christians promoting resurrection (*Cels.* 5.14), a paraphrase of Matt 19:26: "what is impossible with men is possible with God."

(2) Belief in resurrection demonstrates fidelity to God and his teaching, as opposed to humans and their doctrines: "For I choose to follow not human beings nor the instructions of humans, but rather God and the lessons [taught] by him" (*Dial.* 80.3). Justin parallels the anti-Pharisaic polemic of the gospels (Mark 7:6–8; Matt 15:3–9), where the Pharisees' teaching is exposed as mere human invention. Similarly, Justin applies the same charge to those who deny resurrection of the body.

(3) Resurrection is connected to loyalty to the God of Abraham, Isaac, and Jacob. This phrase is attached to proof of resurrection in Jesus' dispute with the Sadducees (Mark 12:26; Matt 22:31–32). Justin lifts the ideas, still connected, and applies them to the opponents of his own day. In the next lines, he says outright that his opponents are no better than Sadducees. Implicit is the notion that the deniers misunderstand biblical history. Both the anti-Saducean jibe here and the anti-Pharisaic jibe above, in their gospel contexts, refer to disputes over who rightly understands the promises of the Hebrew Bible. Justin borrows both and turns them against the resurrection deniers of his own day: they do not understand Scripture.

(4) Belief in resurrection is the sign of an authentic Christian. Some people claim the name "Christian" but do not deserve it. Belief in resurrection of the flesh is a sign of a "right-minded" or "straight-thinking" Christian (*Dial.* 80.5). The so-called Christians argue for a resurrection of the soul (*Dial.* 80.4). So while Justin speaks in *Dial.* 1.4 of the resurrection of the dead (νεκρων ἀνάστασιν), and in sev-

eral places of immortality (*Dial.* 45.4; 46.7; 69.7; 117.3), language that might allow a spiritual interpretation, here he leaves no doubt that he means fleshly resurrection. Similarly, in *1 Apol.* 9.4 he speaks of bodies, dissolved in the earth, rising again. Furthermore, denial of resurrection signals a sectarian. An emerging sense of orthodoxy colors Justin's remarks, as when he compares deniers to a list of sectarian Jews, branding them blasphemers, atheists, and heretics.

(5) Resurrection is part of a system of justice, recompense for the righteous, and punishment for the wicked. Insensibility, says Justin, would be a godsend for the wicked (*1 Apol.* 18.1). In *Dial.* 117.3, he implies that the final resurrection will be the time to settle accounts with Jews. The "filthy garments" put on Christians by Jews will be taken away and all will be raised. Some will live free from sorrow in the eternal kingdom, but others will be sent to eternal punishment. In a passage strangely reminiscent of *t.San.* 13.3–5, which speaks of everlasting punishment, Justin says transgressors will be rendered immortal, so that in their suffering they will be a spectacle to all humanity (*Dial.* 130.2).

(6) Resurrection will finally establish who correctly interprets Scripture. In settling accounts with Jews, final resurrection will not only rectify sufferings Justin claims are visited on Christians,[14] but will also establish who rightly possesses Scripture. *Dialogue* 80 begins with a dispute over who really understands the Scriptures, Trypho or Justin, and returns to the question at the end of the chapter, framing the resurrection discussion. In the next chapter, Justin continues with the prediction of a thousand years in a restored Jerusalem, cited as an argument between Jews and Christians in connection with interpretation of Mal 1:10–12 in *Dial.* 117. So while the belief in resurrection is something on which Christians and Jews do not disagree (and here he would surely mention it if they did), final resurrection will be instrumental in settling grievances between them.

## On the Resurrection

A fuller treatment of resurrection appears in *On the Resurrection*, a work attributed to Justin by Procopius and the fifth-century *Sacra*

---

[14] See my summary of Justin's anti-Jewish charges, where Justin claims that Jews persecute and hate Christians, but never brings a single example of their doing so directly (*Jewish Responses to Early Christians* [Minneapolis: Fortress, 1994] 128–46).

*Parallela.* While the attribution to Justin is disputed,[15] Pierre Prigent
has argued persuasively on linguistic grounds that it is authentic.[16]
He has been seconded by recent scholars such as A. van Eijk[17] and
Wartelle,[18] as well as Bynum,[19] who notes the stress on material continuity is in line with second-century attitudes. For my purposes, I
will refer to the author here as Justin. But whether this work is
authentically Justin or an anonymous second or early third century
work does not substantially alter my argument that resurrection of the
body is a conspicuous part of the early construction of community.

Although the audience is not indicated explicitly, Bernard Pouderon
argues that the work is meant for oral discourse, possibly a public
debate.[20] He suggests it is directed at three sets of hearers: pagans
who are potential converts, Christians of shaky faith who are vulnerable to heretical doctrines, and convinced Christians who will use
its arguments in debate. The systematic, question-and-response for-
mat supports the idea that it meant to demonstrate its position to
the not-yet-convinced.

In this work, the position of the opponents comes into clearer
focus, although their identity remains unclear.[21] This work articulates the contrary position first, allowing us to glimpse the nature of
the anti-resurrection arguments, and then gives Justin's refutation.
Here I summarize the opponent's claim and Justin's response. The
opponents maintain:

(1) There is no resurrection of the flesh, because something already
dissolved could not be restored. A similar objection appears in *1 Apol.*
19. Nor would restoration of the flesh even be desirable, since the
flesh is a source of sin and prone to infirmity. If the body were to
be restored, it would be complete, as in this life, or incomplete,

---

[15] Eusebius does not mention the work in connection with Justin. Irenaeus,
Tertullian, and Methodius know the work, but do not attribute it to Justin.

[16] Pierre Prigent, *Justin et l'Ancien Testament* (Paris: Gabalda, 1964) 50–61.

[17] A. van Eijk, "'Only that can rise which has previously fallen': The History of
a Formula," *NTS* n.s. 22 (1971) 517–29.

[18] André Wartelle, "Le Traité *De la résurrection* de Saint Justin ou Le destin d'une
œuvre," Yves Ledure, ed., *Histoire et culture chrétienne* (Paris: Beauchesne, 1992) 3–10.

[19] *Resurrection of the Body*, 28–29.

[20] Bernard Pouderon, "Le contexte polémique du *De Resurrectione* attribué à Justin:
destinataires et adversaires," *StPatr* 31 (1997) 143–66.

[21] Pouderon reviews the many proposals for the identity of the opponents, "Contexte
polémique" (144–45). He argues that the opponents are disciples of Simon Magus
(163–66).

therefore imperfect. If God raised it incomplete, without all its parts, it would show his lack of power. If he raised it complete, with its sexual and digestive organs, it would be absurd, since Mark 12:25 indicates that after the believers rise from the dead, "they neither marry, nor are given in marriage, but shall be as the angels in heaven." Moreover, Jesus himself, the opponents say, only rose spiritually.

Justin responds that bodies may be raised complete, but not all organs need be used. Even in this world, virgins of both sexes do not procreate. The claim that Jesus did not rise in the flesh, he simply dismisses as an attempt "to rob the flesh of its promise" (2.14).[22] These arguments are ploys to distract others from the faith.

(2) If the flesh rises, the deniers say, it must be with the same defects it had in this world, so God would be raising deformed bodies, which provokes the charge that God lacks power. Justin counters that just as Jesus healed sickness and deformity on this earth, how much more so will he heal at the resurrection.

(3) Flesh, by its nature, cannot be recreated once it has disintegrated. Using the same metaphor as he did in *1 Apol.* 19, Justin argues from creation, first of Adam, and of all humanity. If, by God's power, a human can come forth from a drop of semen, a human being can certainly be recreated: "We have proofs (of his power), first in the making of the first form, for he was made from the earth by God, and this itself is a sample of God's power; and along with that one can see how people are generated from each other, and then can marvel even more that from a tiny drop of moisture so great a living creature is made" (5.7). Furthermore, resurrection of the flesh is desirable, because the body is God's handiwork: "To God nothing is foreign, not even the world itself, for it is his workmanship" (5.12). Even to nonbelievers, says Justin, he can make his case. He claims that the philosophers, Plato, the Stoics, and the Epicureans agree on the permanence of elements of matter. God, like a metal-worker or jeweler, can refashion what he made in the first place from the same elements.

(4) The flesh is contemptible and not worthy of resurrection. Justin answers that the body is valuable to God. Gen 1:26 and 2:7 mean

---

[22] All references from the recent critical edition by Martin Heimgartner, *Pseudo Justin: Über die Auferstehung* (*PTS* 54; Berlin: de Gruyter, 2001). It does not differ significantly on our passages from J. Otto, *Corpus Apologeticarum Christianorum: Justini Philosophi et Martyris* vol. 3 (Oxford: Blackwell, 1968). The translations are my own.

that the human created in God's image was one of flesh: "But that
the flesh is a valuable possession to God is apparent, first because
it is formed by him, the image is at least valuable to the one who
forms it and the artist; and besides, its value can be gathered from
the creation of the rest of the world. For that on account of which
the rest is made, is the most valuable of all to the maker" (7.13).

(5) The flesh sins, say the deniers, and drags down the soul along
with it. Justin retorts that the body cannot sin alone. Body and soul
are like oxen yoked together. Neither can do anything alone. Even
more cleverly, Justin says that if flesh could sin by itself, then on its
account the savior came, because "I come not to call the righteous,
but sinners to repentance" (7.12).

(6) Even admitting the flesh is valuable as God's work does not
guarantee the promise of resurrection. Justin counters that God could
not neglect his own handiwork and possession. He promised to save
humans. By definition, a human being is neither body nor soul alone,
but both.

(7) The soul is incorruptible and part of God's nature. God will
only save that which is part of himself. Justin replies that God is
not grudging. If God is good, he will save both that which is part
of him and that which is not. How good would he be if he only
saved himself? Jesus preached "Love your enemies"; therefore, God
is benevolent both to that which is part of himself and that which
is not.

(8) Jesus had no need of the flesh, the opponents maintain, and
experienced only spiritual resurrection. Justin responds that he healed
the flesh and raised the flesh in his miracles. When he raised the
dead, for example, he clearly raised the body too, since the miracles do not mention the body lying dead and apart from the soul.
Furthermore, he himself rose in his body, because he encouraged
his disciples to touch him, showed them the nail-prints in his hands,
and ate with them. He ascended into heaven in the flesh. Given all
this evidence, anyone demanding further proof of resurrection of the
flesh is no better than a Sadducee, since the resurrection of the flesh
is the power of God.

(9) The spirit is immortal, say the deniers, but the body is mortal and incapable of being revived. Jesus proclaimed salvation to the
soul alone. Justin answers, the spirit *is* immortal, but the soul is the
house of the spirit. The soul cannot exist without the body, and vice

versa. Therefore, all three will be saved. If philosophers like Plato and Pythagoras proclaimed salvation of the soul, what would be unique in Jesus' proclamation of the same thing? Rather, he announced "the good news of a new and strange hope coming for men . . . to turn that which is not immortal to immortality" (10.9–10). If the flesh does not rise, says Justin, why do we not indulge it completely, as physicians do someone who is terminally ill? We guard against sins of the flesh because flesh has the hope of salvation, just as physicians prescribe a strict regimen to guard the health of someone they expect to save.

In these often ingenious arguments, the author of *On the Resurrection* argues that certain convictions are embedded in the belief in resurrection of the body. God's power and goodness are at the heart of the conviction that the flesh of the dead will be raised. He can raise the body in a perfect form, just as he could create it in the first place. Resurrection is the other side of creation. If God can cause a person to come forth from a drop of semen, he can certainly re-create a body that has already existed. Nor would God create the body only to destroy it. A good God would not destroy his own creation, nor save only the soul, which is part of himself.

The author further asserts the nature of the body as essential to personhood, and of supreme value. It is in the nature of the body that it can be raised. Human beings are body, soul, and spirit. The three are intertwined and cannot act alone, so will not be saved alone (10). Material continuity, which even the pagan philosophers teach, proves that the elements that make up the bodies still exist, and under God's power may be reassembled.

Furthermore, Justin refutes the same claim that others made in *First Apology*: that recreating the body is not even desirable. Justin articulates a view of the body that appeals to our modern sensibilities: that the body is God's workmanship. The body made in God's image at creation is a fleshly one. The whole world was created for humans' sake in Genesis 1, therefore for the sake of a fleshly being. Those who argue against resurrection of the body "try to rob the flesh of its promise" (2.14).

Last, resurrection of the body is proof of Jesus' uniqueness. If he only came to preach spiritual resurrection, he would bring nothing new. Yet his miracles were performed on bodies, he raised bodies from the dead, and his own resurrection was in his body.

*Summary*

The works of Justin and *On the Resurrection* represent the flowering of an articulate resurrection apologetic. He adds quantity and specificity to the arguments from nature that appear in the apostolic fathers a few decades before. Furthermore, he adds precision in language, using for the first time the expression "resurrection of the flesh." He links general resurrection to a millennium-long reign of Christ in a re-built Jerusalem. Further, although both Jewish and Christian sources have generally associated belief in resurrection with a correct inter-pretation of Scripture, he painstakingly proves resurrection from Isaiah, Ezekiel, and Psalms (*Dial.* 81).

The leap of intensity in the defense of resurrection of flesh and material continuity accompanied second-century developments: in particular, the emergence of alternative understandings of the res-urrection of Jesus and the believers among other groups, the pagan intellectual challenge, and the increasing possibility of martyrdom. Justin's pseudo-Christians, who deny resurrection of the body, and the opponents in *On the Resurrection*, who denigrate the flesh, provide more evidence for a strain of Christianity that opts for immortality of the soul or some form of realized resurrection in this life (see appendix). Probably as a response to these currents, Justin coins the phrase, "resurrection of the flesh" and emphasizes flesh as God's creation.

Frances Young describes the task of the second-century apologist as a "justification of an anomalous social position,"[23] the puzzling rejection of the classical values and traditions held up as superior in the surrounding culture. Justin argues in two directions: that Christian faith is congruent with the best in Greco-Roman philosophy, but also more ancient and superior to it. In resurrection of the flesh, he must confront outright evaluations of the body in Greco-Roman thought, as well as the predominance of the belief in immortality of the soul.

Although widespread persecution of Christians did not character-ize the Antonine age, martyrdom on a local scale is a threat in some of the Greek-speaking provinces of Asia. Justin refers to the mar-tyrdom of Ptolemaeus and Lucius in *2 Apol.* 2. Polycarp and other Christians in Smyrna are martyred in the mid-second century, and

---

[23] Frances Young, "Greek Apologists of the Second Century," in *Apologetics in the Roman Empire*, ed. Edwards, Goodman, et al., 104.

Justin himself is caught in some of the persecutions coming slightly later, in the reign of Marcus Aurelius and Verus, around 165. We have observed the marked association of martyrdom and belief in resurrection as early as 2 Maccabees. Similarly, in the second century the increasing possibility of the annihilation and scattering of the martyr's body made the assertion of fleshly resurrection more pressing.

Other proposed factors,[24] such as the growth of millenarianism and the assimilation of Jesus' resurrection into the resurrection of believers, beg the question: which came first? If the belief in a Messiah ruling from Jerusalem for a millennium on earth requires bodily restoration, which is brought to prove the other? Similarly, thinkers who argue from the material elements of Jesus' resurrection appearances—such as the eating of a broiled fish or showing his wounds—to the bodily resurrection of believers are choosing a particular understanding of Jesus' resurrection that is not shared by all believers.

## Resurrection as Symbol and Strategy in Justin

The categories I have proposed to understand how resurrection functioned come into clearer focus in the apologetic material. Belief in resurrection continues to function in ways that characterize earlier communities.

### Resurrection condenses a worldview

In spite of the new challenges the apologist faces and the more elaborate arguments he mounts, the second-century apologetic does not really depart from the fundamental associations with resurrection that appear in earlier descriptions of the Pharisees, Paul's argument in 1 Corinthians 15, and Jesus' encounters with the Sadducees in the gospels. Justin links belief in resurrection to God's power as creator, the correct interpretation of Scripture, the accomplishment of ultimate justice, and the legitimacy of those who preach it. These concepts are so deeply embedded in the concept of bodily resurrection that the opponents do not seem to be able to employ them for their arguments, relying instead on negative evaluations of the flesh and an extreme dualism of body and soul.

---

[24] See J. Davis, who argues for four factors in the growth of belief in resurrection of the flesh, including an anti-docetic interpretation of the resurrection appearances and millenarianism, in "Factors Leading to the Emergence of Belief in Resurrection of the Flesh," *NTS* 23 (1972) 448–55.

Like Paul, Justin links belief in resurrection to these fundamental parts of the faith, as well as the nature of Jesus' own resurrection and the uniqueness of Jesus and his miracles. What is new here is the emphasis on the essential value of the fleshly body, as well as an elaboration of the body's relation to the soul and the spirit.

*Resurrection draws boundaries*
Justin reserves the name "Christian" only for those who share the belief in resurrection of the physical body (*Dial.* 80.3–4). Justin can tolerate divergence over other issues, such as Christians who continue to observe the commandments of the Hebrew Bible (*Dial.* 47.1) or those who are not millenarians (*Dial.* 80.2), but shows no such largess on the issue of resurrection. He calls the deniers impious, atheistic, foolish, sectarian—no better than Sadducees. *On the Resurrection*, which is not generally given to name-calling, nevertheless calls the resurrection deniers latter-day Sadducees (9.9) and apostles of the devil (10.11).

*Resurrection constructs community*
The resurrection deniers threaten the very life of the community, carrying out the devil's work: "The adversary on one hand leads astray the faithful, and on the other hand prevents the unbelievers from coming to faith" (*On Res.* 1.12). Justin even implies some action against them is called for: "Why do we any longer entertain those unbelieving and scandalous arguments?" Attributing competing ideas to the devil is a standard dismissal of opponents, which Justin employs against Marcion, Simon, Menander, and other heretics (*1 Apol.* 26, 56–58, 62).

Like Paul, Justin makes a number of symbolic reversals, subordinating revered public values to internal Christian ones. James Scott suggests that upside-down imagery is a form of "resistance below the line" that typifies subordinate groups. Off-stage discourse is a counterpart and precursor of an open break with a more powerful society. In negating public symbols and proposing an alternate set of symbols, the subordinate group develops a sense of its own dignity and separateness from the larger culture.[25] Justin, for his part, argues that Moses is superior to Homer; the fleshly body is God's own

---

[25] James Scott, *Domination and the Arts of Resistance* (New Haven: Yale, 1990) 198–200.

handiwork, and not the despised partner to the soul; and death brings not blessed insensibility and liberation from the body, but the initiation of reward and punishment.

*Resurrection confers legitimacy on those who profess it*
Only those who believe in resurrection, Justin calls the "right-minded ones" who understand the promise of Scripture and the implications of creation in Genesis 1 and 2. Only those inspired by Satan deny it.

*Resurrection solves a set of problems*
Early Christians faced the discrepancy between their seemingly upstart faith and ancient and revered philosophies, as well as the logical problem of the obvious decomposition of the body after death. Justin treads a delicate path. He shows resurrection (and Christian faith as a whole) is as good as, and compatible with, other philosophical systems, but also superior to them. Resurrection helps underscore the differences from the broader culture in its evaluation of the body, and its schema of reward and punishment. Of the survival of the spirit, he says, "This we used to hear from Pythagoras and Plato, even before we learned the truth" (*On Res.* 10.7). Belief in bodily resurrection shows the uniqueness of the Christian faith.

Resurrection solves a set of logical, philosophical problems raised by the apparent decomposition of bodies after death, and the negative evaluation of the body in some philosophical systems. To the problem of decomposition, Justin answers with God's power as creator. Extolling God's workmanship in creating a human being from a drop of semen, Justin renders re-creating a human being from decomposed elements a relatively easier feat. In chapter 2 of *On Res.*, the author reacts to ideas of the body as subject to infirmity, and in chapter 5 refutes the notion of the body as despicable. Absence of sexuality, eating, and drinking in the next world indicated to some that they would not possess their bodies. He argues from the threefold nature of the human being as God's workmanship that all three aspects will be saved. God's power means that he can save his creation, and his goodness means that he will.

*Resurrection allows people to live in the world as it is*
Justin provides early Christians with a rationale for claiming Christian faith above other philosophies. He shows the resurrection is compatible with principles of material continuity in some philosophical

systems, but ultimately is superior to them. He provides an alternate set of symbols: Moses over Homer, the body as God's workmanship over the body as the inferior partner to the soul, and resurrection to reward and punishment over liberation of the soul.

Justin's context is not mere dispassionate debate among competing philosophies. As we have noted, while nothing comparable to later, state-sponsored persecutions takes place, clearly Christians are not at ease either. Justin mentions in both the *Apologies* and the *Dialogue* traditional charges against Christians from the reign of Antoninus Pius—atheism, sexual excess, and Thyestean feasts—as well as the recent martyrdom of certain Christians. Grant thinks that the *Apology* is occasioned by Polycarp's martyrdom in Smyrna.[26] A stream of disfavor is running against Christians in some provinces, even if it is not yet a flood.

Resurrection here offers the same answer to injustice and suffering as it does in earlier works. Justin says, "For if we looked for a human kingdom, we would also deny [Christ], that we might not be killed . . . since our hope is not in the present, we do not care when men kill us, since in all cases one must die" (*1 Apol.* 11.2).

### Athenagoras

Two decades after Justin, Athenagoras promotes the Christian belief in bodily resurrection in two ways: using it as a weapon of defense against widespread charges against Christians in one work, while defending the doctrine itself in the other. Like Justin, he recommends Christianity to the emperor as compatible with the philosopher's search for truth. His *Plea on Behalf of the Christians*, addressed to the emperor Marcus Aurelius and his heir apparent Commodus, is dated around 176, and his *On the Resurrection*, promised at the end of *Plea*, is dated sometime later. Athenagoras is identified as "an Athenian Christian philosopher" in the tenth-century codex that preserves the two works,[27] but we know nothing of him apart from these works, and no other early writer mentions him except Methodius.

---

[26] *Greek Apologists of the Second Century*, 53. The dates of the emperor Antoninus Pius fit with the martyrdom, and he argues that Justin's emphasis on punishment by fire for the wicked is a response to the elderly bishop's death by fire.

[27] Louis Ruprecht argues that he is a Corinthian, since he seems to know Corinthian stories and use Corinthian traditions comfortably ("Athenagoras the Christian,

No one questions the authenticity of *Plea*, but *On the Resurrection* is seriously disputed. Responsible people are on both sides of the question,[28] but I am persuaded by L. Barnard's arguments for authenticity.[29] Bynum notes that, as with the disputed work of Justin, the materialist view of humans fits with other second-century texts.[30] Athenagoras matches Justin in his argument for resurrection from a drop of semen (*Res.* 17.2–4; Justin, *1 Apol.* 19). Both authors rely on the phrase "What is impossible with men is possible with God," a rephrasing of Matt 19:26 (*Res.* 9.2; *1 Apol.* 19). Celsus, writing about the same time as Athenagoras, claims this slogan is one Christians fall back on to promote resurrection (*Cels.* 5.14). Ultimately, authorship is less crucial than dating, since we are interested in developing attitudes about resurrection over time.

*Plea* is addressed to the emperor and his son, possibly on the occasion of their imperial tour through the eastern empire.[31] *On the Resurrection* is purportedly directed at two sets of opponents, some Christian believers and some non-Christians: "those who recognize Providence and accept the same first principles as we do, and then for some strange reason repudiate their own presuppositions," and "those who disagree on the fundamentals" (*Res.* 19.1–2). Barnard argues for three sets of hearers, probably in a public context: pagans, Christians who do not accept physical resurrection, and Christians who accept it but need help arguing their case.[32]

---

Pausanius the Travel Guide, and a Mysterious Corinthian Girl," *HTR* 85 [1992] 35–49).

[28] Grant thinks that *Res.* Is not from Athenagoras, but is a later reaction to Origen, written in the third or early fourth century ("Athenagoras or Pseudo-Athenagoras," *HTR* 47 [1954] 121–29). His view is echoed by William Schoedel, *Athenagoras: Legatio and De Resurrectione* (Oxford: Oxford University, 1972) xxv–xxxii; and Ézio Gallicet, "Athenagoras o Pseudo-Athenagoras," *Rivista di Fililogia* (1976) 420–35; idem, "Ancora sullo Pseudo-Athenagoras," *Rivista di Filiogia* (1977) 21–42.

[29] Barnard observes that, although there are few biblical quotations in either work (6 in *Plea* and 2 in *Res.*), the two quotes in *Res.* are the same as in *Plea*, which would be a striking coincidence were they not from the same author. He refutes those who argue *Res.* is a later work, written against Origen, noting that it never mentions Origen by name, nor does it cite biblical texts to support resurrection, a surprise for someone arguing against the biblicist Origen ("The Authenticity of Athenagoras' *De Resurrectione*," *StPatr* 15 [1984] 39–49). Another argument favoring authenticity appears in Bernard Pouderon, "L'Authenticité du traité *Sur la Résurrection* attribué à l'apologiste Athénagore," *VC* 40 (1986) 226–40.

[30] *Resurrection of the Body*, 28.

[31] Robert Grant, "Five Apologists and Marcus Aurelius," *VC* 42 (1988) 1–17.

[32] Barnard, "Authenticity," 44–45.

Because of the highly stylized, formal presentation in *Plea* and the multiple audiences in *Res.*, Athenagoras does not present as clear an example as Paul or Justin of "reading in" or "reading out" adherents from a community because of their stance on resurrection. Yet the polemical quality of the debate is evident in *Res.*, in its many references to "our opponents," "our disputants," and to "discord" and "confusion" in the opening chapter, and those who have been upset by the arguments for resurrection in chapter 3. *Plea* differs in that, although it refers to "informers" and "accusers," they are not talking about resurrection, but three other charges against Christians, for which resurrection forms part of the defense. Athenagoras's work is valuable because it provides a window into larger debates between pagans and Christians, and between Christians of different views, over resurrection in the second century.

An apologist steeped in Greco-Roman tradition, Athenagoras ably wields the tools of rhetoric. Schoedel illustrates his use of the same devices that appear in Menander's handbook of rhetoric for praising the king.[33] Both Grant and Schoedel argue that Athenagoras draws from a standard rhetorical tradition.[34] Because Athenagoras's goal to persuade is so clear, and the clues to social situation are so few, we turn to the method of rhetorical criticism for help. Rhetorical criticism identifies the strategies the author chooses, how they are employed, for whose ears they are intended, and what is left out. They offer clues to audience, for certain strategies will only work with some audiences.[35] Christian rhetors could turn stock themes upside down, showing what Averil Cameron calls both "the urge to appropriate" from Greco-Roman discourse and the "emphasis on the paradoxical side" of Christian belief, its roots in emotion and experience utterly different from philosophical devotion to reason.[36]

---

[33] William Schoedel, "In Praise of the King: A Rhetorical Pattern in Athenagoras," in *Disciplina Nostra. Essays in Memory of Robert F. Evans* (ed. Donald Winslow; Philadelphia: Philadelphia Patristic Foundation, 1979) 69–90.

[34] Schoedel, "In Praise of the King," 75.

[35] An example of this use of rhetorical criticism is Antoinette Clark Wire, *The Corinthian Women Prophets: A Reconstruction through Paul's Rhetoric* (Minneapolis: Augsburg Fortress, 1990). This method is critiqued as still within the historical-critical paradigm by J. D. H. Amador, *Academic Constraints in Rhetorical Criticism of the New Testament* (*JSNTSup* 174; Sheffield: Sheffield Academic, 1999). With our interest on the function of resurrection in early group self-definition, however, the approach of Wire and other suits our task.

[36] Averil Cameron, *Christianity and the Rhetoric of Empire* (Berkeley: University of California, 1991) 87.

We cannot underestimate their feat, since "Christians, the quintessential outsiders . . . talked and wrote themselves into a position where they spoke and wrote the rhetoric of empire."[37]

## Plea on Behalf of the Christians

The formal style of *Plea* does not mask the serious situation behind it. Schoedel maintains that Athenagoras, like Justin, sees himself as an ambassador for threatened Christian groups, much as Philo and Josephus delivered embassies to Rome on behalf of Jewish communities in crisis. In general, subjects throughout the empire could appeal to the emperor if they were mistreated by local officials. A mix of genres, *Plea*, says Schoedel, is "an apologetically grounded petition."[38]

Athenagoras sets out to disprove three well-known charges against Christians: atheism, cannibalism (especially Thyestean feasts), and sexual excess (especially incest). He applies many of the rhetorical strategies identified by Chaim Perelman and Lucie Olbrechts-Tyteca.[39] Part of his approach is associative, appealing to the idea that the Christians and the emperor are on the same side and agree on premises and values. He invokes the example of pagan martyrs Pythagoras, Heraclitus, and Socrates, who, like Christian martyrs, were champions of virtue persecuted for their devotion to the truth. He employs the "loci of quality" which praises the unique and uncommon,[40] against the vulgar and popular. Only the "stupid crowds" (3.3) oppose Christians, as they opposed the pagan heroes. Similarly, the Christians are, like the Stoic emperor, "servants of reason" (35.4). He further associates Christians and the emperor by noting that they are on the same side against those who believe in the exploits of the gods (32).

Resurrection comes into play in a second strategy, which comes under the category of quasi-logical arguments (so called because they imitate formal mathematical systems, but use non-formal theses),

---

[37] Cameron, *Rhetoric*, 14.

[38] William Schoedel, "Apologetic Literature and Ambassadorial Activities," *HTR* 82 (1989) 55–78.

[39] Chaim Perelman and Lucie Olbrechts-Tyteca, *The New Rhetoric* (Notre Dame: University of Notre Dame, 1969); and Chaim Perelman, *The Realm of Rhetoric* (Notre Dame: University of Notre Dame, 1982).

[40] Perelman and Olbrechts-Tyteca, *New Rhetoric*, 75.

where a thesis is disproven by showing it is incompatible with another thesis. Because Christians believe in resurrection and expect to live again, they must live impeccable lives. They cannot be guilty of the three charges against them. The charge of cannibalism is particularly absurd in light of the belief in resurrection:

> What man who believes in resurrection would offer himself as a tomb for bodies destined to arise? For it is impossible at one and the same time to believe that our bodies will arise and then eat them as though they will not arise, or to think that the earth will yield up its dead and then suppose that those whom a man had buried within himself will not reclaim their bodies (36.1).[41]

The charge of murder is refuted even more effectively because Athenagoras shows it incompatible with several facts. Christians renounce attending spectacles where people are killed, forbid abortion, and do not expose babies (*Res.* 35.4–6). The most effective way to cancel out a thesis, says Perelman, is to show it incompatible with a bundle of facts.[42]

Any kind of wrong-doing is refuted by Christian belief in resurrection (31.3–4; 33.1; 35.6; 36.1–2).

In explaining resurrection Athenagoras revises it for Stoic ears:

> . . . Since we are persuaded that when we depart this present life we shall live another life better than that here, a heavenly one, not earthly, so that we may then abide with God and with his help remain changeless and impassible (*apathēs*) in soul *as though we were not in body*, even if we have one, but heavenly spirit . . . (31.4).

Athenagoras not only invokes the Stoic virtue of *apatheia*, passionlessness, but also blurs the distinction between spiritual immortality and physical resurrection.

What is important for our study, however, is the assumption Athenagoras makes that Christian belief in resurrection is a given, something "everyone knows" about Christians. He does not need to prove it, nor does he suggest there are Christian groups out there who reject it. He understands that his accusers reject it, and in fact takes the offensive against them at many points, mounting *ad personam* attacks that condemn their morals (33.2–3; 35.4, 6). He sug-

---

[41] All translations from the edition and translation by William Schoedel, *Athenagoras: Legatio and De Resurrectione* (Oxford: Oxford University Press, 1972).

[42] Perelman, *Realm*, 24.

gests that it is their lack of belief that they will be called to account that gives them license. Resurrection here is not the subject, nor does Athenagoras set out to prove it; rather, it becomes part of his arsenal of weapons to defend Christians against their accusers, a rejoinder to other charges against them.

## On the Resurrection

The treatment of resurrection in this document differs from that in *Plea*. Here, Athenagoras (or pseudo-Athenagoras) argues vigorously for resurrection of the body against its detractors. Like *Plea*, it is an apologetic to outsiders (1.5; 11.1; 19.2). Unlike *Plea*, it is also an in-house document, written to other Christians (1.5; 19.1), some of whom reject the belief in bodily resurrection, while others accept it but need help in defending their belief. In this document, the arguments of those who reject resurrection can be heard behind Athenagoras's rejoinders. Called "our opponents" or "our disputants," these are people admired for their wisdom. Athenagoras suggests they are some kind of intelligentsia carried along by the masses: "This view [of resurrection] seems to have greatly upset some people even among those admired for their wisdom, because for some reason I cannot grasp they regarded the doubts voiced by the crowd as strong arguments" (3.3). These opponents are people affected by popular currents of thought. Athenagoras himself, Pouderon suggests, belongs to a Christian intellectual elite, a school movement independent of the churches.[43]

Athenagoras makes familiar arguments for resurrection, based on values apparent in Justin, Paul, the Pharisees, and the rabbis: God's power, ultimate justice, the unity of a human being, and the meaningfulness of life in the face of persecution. Newer and more precise arguments emerge which answer charges raised by others. The overwhelming argument for resurrection, in Athenagoras's view, is an

---

[43] Like other Hellenistic youth attaching themselves to various philosophers, young Christians would travel to study with masters like Justin in Rome, or Quadratus and Aristides in Athens. These sages and their students created an intelligentsia set apart from the less educated in the churches. See Bernard Pouderon, "Réflexions sur la formation d'une élite intellectuelle chrétienne au II siècle: Les écoles d'Athènes, de Rome, et d'Alexandrie," in Bernard Pouderon and Joseph Doré, eds., *Les Apologistes chrétiens et la culture grecque* (Paris: Beauchesne, 1998) 237–69.

argument from authority,[44] from the conviction of God's power and providence, evidenced by creation itself: ". . . as to power, the creation of our bodies shows that God's power suffices for their resurrection . . . such a power can unite what has been dissolved, can raise up what has fallen, can restore the dead to life, and can change the corruptible into incorruption" (2.3; 3.1,3). God's power also answers the problem of chain consumption: ". . . the same God and the same wisdom and power can also separate out what has been torn apart and devoured by numerous animals of every kind" (3.3; 5.1).

In fact, Athenagoras identifies the proof for God's power from creation as one of the three primary arguments that confirms resurrection, the one from which all other arguments spring: "All of our arguments [spring from the argument from creation] . . . for their principle is the origin of the first men by creation. Some arguments gain their force from the first principle itself out of which they arise . . ." (18.1). He also cites the same proof as Justin, the slogan that Celsus mocks, "What is impossible with men is possible with God" (9.2). God's power in creation is also demonstrated from natural phenomena, or as the rhetoricians put it, from the structure of reality. A model suffices to establish a rule. Athenagoras asks who, for example, could imagine that a drop of semen contains within it the beginnings of a whole person, made of flesh and bone? Who could imagine, looking at a child, the stages of development that will transform him? (17.1–2).

The second familiar argument Athenagoras makes is the argument from justice. Since justice is clearly not accomplished in this life, resurrection is necessary (18.2). Death alone cannot satisfy the thirst for ultimate justice. One death is too good for some evil-doers (19.7) and for such people insensibility would be a boon. But justice is the natural desire and goal of human life. As rational beings, humans require justice as much as they require food and offspring (14.4; 18.4).

Athenagoras seems to be answering a challenge voiced by others on the basis of both justice and logic, when he argues that humans alone of all God's creatures enjoy resurrection. He answers the obvious question, "if animals die and are no more, why should humans be different?" as well as "is it just that humans alone merit resur-

---

[44] The argument from God's authorship is the ultimate argument from authority, Perelman and Olbrechts-Tyteca, *New Rhetoric*, 305–10.

rection?" He dissociates concepts that others have joined,[45] by answering that God's gift of rationality to humans sets them apart, giving them a distinct nature (11.1; 13.1; 14.4; 15.2–5; 18.1; 24.4). They are created for different purposes than animals, and must have different ends (10.4; 24.2). Humans, as rational creatures, can contemplate God's majesty and wisdom: "The reason then, for man's creation guarantees his eternal survival, and his survival guarantees his resurrection" (13.2).

The third argument comes out of the first and second. Because God in his power creates the human as a composite, and because humans long for justice, for justice to prevail God must judge the entire human being. Justice will only happen if the body and soul are reunited. True survival means survival as a complete human being, so body and soul must both survive (13.2). Whether a person lived a life of virtue or sin, that life was lived by the body and soul together, so justice demands they be punished together (*Res.* 21–22).[46] Athenagoras asks, "Where then is justice if the soul alone is judged, when it is the body which first experiences passions and then draws the soul to participate in them and share the deeds to which the body is driven?" (21.4). To judge the composite human being, he must reunite the soul and body, so must effect resurrection (18.4).

Both this and the preceding two arguments, then, argue not only from justice, but using the rhetorical device of argument from definition, from the definition of the nature of human beings. This constitutes the rhetorical device of argument by definition. A human being is by definition both body and soul, destined by God's creation to be above the animals and to long for justice, so a human's very nature requires bodily resurrection: "A just appraiser does not assign the same destiny to beings whose nature is not the same" (10.4).

A variety of other values, problems, and pieces of argument surface in Athenagoras's works. He questions the meaningfulness of life without the hope of resurrection (19.2–3). Like Paul, he suggests that without it, people may as well abandon themselves to every excess: "... the life of beasts and wild animals is best, virtue is silly, the

---

[45] Perelman and Olbrechts-Tyteca, *The New Rhetoric*, 411.
[46] The same argument from reciprocity appears in Justin and in rabbinic literature. See *Lev. Rab.* 4.8.

threat of judgment a huge joke, the cherishing of every pleasure the greatest good, and the common doctrine and single law of all such men will be that dear to the licentious and abandoned: 'Let us eat and drink for tomorrow we die'" (19.3). He answers the question, "Why is there death at all, if humans are meant to be eternal?" Radical discontinuity, with interruptions like sleep and death, is part of God's plan for human life, and does not alter his plan that humans be permanent (16.1–4). Permanence is God's will for humanity (12.7; 13.1).

## Resurrection as Symbol and Strategy

Although Athenagoras does not explicitly "read in" or "read out" of the community on the basis of belief in resurrection, he does so implicitly by linking belief in resurrection to Christian identity. Examining both documents using rhetorical criticism yields a picture of debates over resurrection of the body in Athenagoras's time, including arguments from pagans and from other Christians. By his time, several things are apparent. First, belief in resurrection is widely recognized as part of being a Christian. In *Plea*, he does not explain it to the emperor, nor make the case for its Christian provenance. Second, belief in resurrection has drawn refutations and ridicule from the pagan world. Many of these are anticipated by Athenagoras's counter-arguments. The argument that dissociates humans from other animals and argues that humans alone merit resurrection is a response to the argument that humans no more merit resurrection than animals. The claim that the nature of humanity is body and soul is a response to those who say the soul alone is judged. Paradoxically, the quality and quantity of the arguments show that Christianity is being presented and taken seriously as a philosophy, as Cameron noted, in the process of "talking its way" into the empire. Third, the fault lines over bodily resurrection within the Christian community, visible in Paul and Justin, have deepened. A set of arguments against resurrection have grown up around the issue, so that Christians promoting resurrection need increasingly sophisticated arguments to make their case.

### Resurrection condenses a worldview

In Athenagoras's thought, resurrection serves as a shorthand for the same ideas as in our earlier materials: God's power and wisdom, ultimate justice, and the unity of the human being. The God who created the human body can also restore it, even when it is torn apart by animals, or has become food for them (*Res.* 3.3; 4.1–4; 5.1). Those who dispute it do not know God's power, acting as if he is a human potter or carpenter (*Res.* 5.1; 9.1–2). To answer those who ask, not if God can raise bodies, but why would he want to, Athenagoras demonstrates that it is a work worthy of him and willed by him (*Res.* 10.1; 11.1; 13.1; 14.4; 18.2). Justice demands resurrection to satisfy the rational human need for reward and punishment (*Res.* 10.4; 13.1; 14.5; 18.1; 19.1–7). Justice further demands that the whole person reap reward and punishment, body and soul (*Res.* 10.5; 15.1–8; 18.4; 21–23).

*Resurrection is imprecise and abstract*
Despite its distinctive Christian (and Jewish) character, Athenagoras struggles to show its compatibility with Greco-Roman ideals of truth, devotion to reason, and adherence to nature (*Res.* 17.4). Pagan martyrs to truth like Socrates and Pythagoras are likened to Christian martyrs. In *Plea* 31.4, resurrection of the body is malleable enough that Athenagoras extends it to accommodate a Stoic emperor.

*Belief in resurrection draws boundaries*
Quite unlike our other materials, the boundaries between those who believe in resurrection and those who do not are not drawn by the author. He implies they are drawn by others. Athenagoras is anxious to preserve belief in bodily resurrection, but he wants to blur or erase any boundaries it creates and he downplays differences between Christians and the larger culture. He argues that resurrection is in line with the truths to which all reasonable people give allegiance. In *Res.* 14.1, he describes a debate over resurrection, and promises to systematically make his case. He frequently refers to "our opponents" or "our disputants" (4.4; 5.1; 8.2; 9.1), saying those who argue against resurrection are ignorant of God's power and wisdom (5.1). Anyone would agree with him "who is not half-beast" (*Res.* 8.5). The opinions of unbelievers are absurd and false (*Res.* 11.1), while those who share Christian faith, but reject resurrection, ignore their own presuppositions (*Res.* 19.1–2). Athenagoras faces opposition from within and without.

In *Plea*, the boundaries are once again drawn by others. Athenagoras uses resurrection quite differently here, defending Christians who are

slandered by informers (31.1–2; 32.1) who accuse Christians of atheism, cannibalism, and incest. Belief in resurrection provides proof
that they are not guilty of these charges, since fear of judgment moti-
vates them to a disciplined, abstemious life (34.1–3) and certainly
forbids cannibalism (36.1), for how could one being destined to arise
consume another also destined to arise?

Athenagoras creates a liaison when he tries to incorporate Christians
on the same side as the emperor, the side of wisdom, "you whose
wisdom is greater than that of all the others" (31.3). Christians uphold
justice, and "the laws which you and your ancestors promulgated to
further every form of justice" (34.3). He dissociates the slanderers
from the emperor because they are adulterers, pederasts, and flouters
of justice. Athenagoras, notes Schoedel, omits some of the usual
rhetorical flourishes that would show Christians at odds with the
emperor, such as attributing divinity to the emperor or listing his
successes in war, and also limits imperial power.[47] If others must
draw boundaries, Athenagoras wants to put Christians and the emperor
on the same side.

*Belief in resurrection constructs community*
Not only pagan disputants, but also fellow Christians who disbelieve
in bodily resurrection, are a threat to the community. These people, says Athenagoras, repudiate their own principles (*Res.* 19.1). So
following Christian faith to its logical conclusion necessitates belief
in resurrection. The length and ingenuity of the arguments for resurrection in *On the Resurrection* testify to its essential place in Christian
identity. While Athenagoras's strategy of using resurrection as a
defense of Christianity seems to have been spectacularly unsuccess-
ful politically in the short term, he and the other four apologists who
petitioned Marcus Aurelius influenced their own communities in their
politics and approaches to the larger culture. They provided a rationale
for Christian theologians to accommodate Greco-Roman society, and
as Grant notes, their ideas passed into the Christian mainstream.[48]

*Resurrection is fabricated out of the tool-kit of culture*
As a Christian, Athenagoras inherits the belief in resurrection. He
uses it in traditional ways, as a shorthand for the same values it

---

[47] Schoedel, "In Praise of the King," 87–88.
[48] Robert Grant, "Five Apologists and Marcus Aurelius," *VC* 42 (1988) 1–17.

embodied in Jewish and Pauline materials: God's power, justice, the unity of the body and soul. It solves the same questions of the suffering of the righteous, and the meaningfulness of a strict life-style.

Athenagoras also draws from the wells of Greco-Roman culture, creating liaisons between it and Christianity. He quotes Plato seven times, Homer eighteen times, and numerous other lines from Greek philosophy and literature. In *Plea* 31.4, he describes bodily resurrection in a way that makes it sound like spiritual immortality, where it partakes of the Stoic virtue of ἀπάθεια: ". . . changeless and passionless in soul as thought we were not flesh, though we have it. . . ." He links Christians to the heroes of pagan culture: others who pursued virtue but were misunderstood, slandered by some, and rejected by the masses.

Similarly, he creates a liaison between two different systems, God's revelation and the dispassionate search for truth in accord with nature. He invokes "truth," saying that "it is in harmony with truth" to say "what is impossible with men is possible with God." He solves the problem of chain consumption using Galen's biology *and* belief in the providence of a powerful God. The body does not digest what is not its proper food (*Res.* 8.1–4) and God has not destined creatures to eat their own kind (5.1–2). The nature of humans created by God as rational beings requires they have a different end from other animals (13.2; 14.4; 24.2). Both God and nature are brought to bear in Athenagoras's argument.

*Resurrection solves a set of problems*

We have seen how Athenagoras uses resurrection to counter charges against Christians, attempting to solve the immediate problem of informers and others endangering Christians. More generally he faces the same problem as all the apologists. He must bridge the gap between the particularism of a group associated with Palestine and a leader executed by the Romans, and the dominant Greco-Roman culture. He turns the charges of cannibalism back on others, "Greeks and barbarians," thus aligning himself with high Roman culture (*Res.* 4.4).

Athenagoras must also soothe the problems of logic and philosophical objections to resurrection. He uses the language of philosophy, invoking truth, nature, and reason. He answers the objection raised by Celsus, that resurrection of the body is not even desirable: "If then each point of the inquiry has been demonstrated from the first natural principles, and what flows from them logically, clearly the resurrection of decomposed bodies is a work that is possible for the Creator, willed by him, and worthy of him" (*Res.* 11.1).

*Resurrection allows believers to live in the world as it is*
As in the Corinthian community, belief in resurrection provides the motive for the upright, careful lifestyle of the Christians (*Plea* 31.3; 32.1–3; 33.1–3). It answers the problem of meaninglessness. To those who deny it, he, like Paul, asks, "Is then human existence and all of life of no account whatsoever?" (*Res.* 19.2–3).

Living in the world takes on new meaning for Athenagoras's community. He does not concern himself simply with classic problems of suffering and justice, but constructs a philosophy that coincides with nature, philosophy, and the realities around him. He argues from natural phenomena like sleep, stages of development, and the creation of a human being from a drop of semen, "the chain of natural events provides confirmation of things unconfirmed by the phenomena themselves" (17.4). Reason, in seeking truth, confirms the resurrection (17.4). Christians, in their belief in it, conform to the best in Greco-Roman culture.

# CHAPTER FIVE

# PAGAN OBJECTIONS TO CHRISTIAN BELIEF IN RESURRECTION

## Celsus and Caecilius

Christian defenses of resurrection belief hint at the specific objections coming from outsiders. When Justin and Athenagoras argue at length for resurrecting the unified person as body and soul, we can guess that others argue an essential dissimilarity of body and soul. When the apologists laud God's power to create the human body as proof he can re-create, we can guess that others insist God neither could nor would re-form the body that has dissolved.

We need not settle for guesswork, however. Two pagan representatives who attack Christian belief in resurrection provide a mirror to Christian arguments. Celsus, writing in Greek around 177–180, probably in Rome or Alexandria,[1] is a staunch Platonist who is informed about Jews, Jewish complaints about Christianity, and several kinds of Christianity, including Gnosticism. Caecilius, whether a historical or a fictional character, appears as the representative of intellectual paganism in Minucius Felix' *Octavius*. Minucius Felix is a Christian jurist, probably a North African, practicing in Rome in the first half of the third century.[2] Both pagan witnesses are positioned within Christian refutations of their ideas. This itself testifies to the Christian desire to meet the pagan intellectual challenge directly: what Cameron calls their "writing and talking their way into the empire." Many of the complaints are already *topoi*, representative of entrenched pagan attitudes.

The objections to resurrection fit with general pagan slurs against Christianity. Both writers show a class snobbery that cites four interlocking characteristics. Christians are lower-class, uneducated boors.

---

[1] See Henry Chadwick, *Origen: Contra Celsum* (Cambridge: Cambridge University, 1953) xxiv–xxix. All translations of Celsus are by Chadwick.

[2] See Graham Clarke, "The Historical Setting of the *Octavius* of Minucius Felix," *Journal of Religious History* 4 (1966–67) 267–86; ibid., "The Literary Setting of the *Octavius* of Minucius Felix," *Journal of Religious History* 3 (1964–65) 195–211.

This renders them disrespectful of the civic life, religion, and the culture in which they live. They denigrate the value of life in this world. Their failure to appreciate the good life in this world in favor of the next makes them arrogant and overconfident, lacking the modesty that befits their low social status.

*Christians as Uneducated and Lower-Class*

Celsus objects, and claims even the Jews object, to belief in Jesus' resurrection as an exploitation of the simple. It rests on the unreliable testimony of "a hysterical woman" and the other beggars misled by the same sorcery (*Cels.* 2.55). The Christians, says Celsus, have mangled and misunderstood ancient traditions, invented terrors, and play flutes and music, which "with their clamor stupefy the people they wish to excite into frenzy" (*Cels.* 3.16). The doctrine of resurrection, in particular, he categorizes as too absurd to qualify as a child's bedtime story from an old woman (*Cels.* 6.34).

Celsus alternates between saying the hope of resurrection is ridiculous and saying it is nothing new, merely a misreading of the best of the Greco-Roman past. Christians claim they will go to another earth, better than this one, but do not improve on Hesiod's Islands of the blessed or Homer's Elysian Fields (*Cels.* 7.28). Similarly, they misunderstand the idea of reincarnation (*Cels.* 7.32). With their obsession with the flesh, they could not possibly tread the same path of understanding as Plato (*Cels.* 7.42) and "men of intelligence" (*Cels.* 7.45). Such doctrines were only for special people of ancient times to comprehend. Christians who cannot follow them should keep quiet and not show their lack of education (*Cels.* 7.45).

Caecilius' diatribe also links Christian lack of learning and intelligence with inferior social status. Their lack of education makes them vulnerable to old wives' superstitions (*Oct.* 13.4).[3] Untrained in arts and letters, they hold forth on the matters of the universe that even the philosophers still debate (*Oct.* 5.3–4). Even civic matters elude them, how much more so divine matters (*Oct.* 12.7). No wonder Christians are most successful with the low-class illiterates and credulous women (*Oct.* 8.4). No wonder they believe fables of a glorious afterlife (*Oct.* 5.6). Octavius the Christian's reply confirms the

---

[3] References and translations from Minucius Felix, *Octavius* (trans. G. H. Rendall; LCL).

charge by turning it around, arguing that Christians are the true philosophers (*Oct.* 17; 20.1; 34.5).

In reality Christians probably were not of uniformly low social status at this time. They served in the army by the second and third century, and were at all levels of Roman society. Even in Paul's time, some Christians possessed wealth and status. At the end of the first century Revelation seems to react to Christians who are too comfortable in the world. Beard, North, and Price show that attacks on Christians that linked them with poverty, women, and foreignness were part of conventional pagan slanders. Poverty, in particular had a positive valence for Christian piety, but was viewed negatively by Greco-Roman society.[4]

### Christians Are Antisocial

The lack of learning and breeding gives rise to the second complaint, that Christians are disrespectful of the government, customs, values, and religion of their society. Celsus says they do not appreciate the benefits of empire and high Roman culture. He links class, lack of education, and lack of patriotism. In the same breath that he denounces their unseemly attachment to the body and expectation that it will be raised, he says that it stems from their being a people who are "boorish and unclean, who are destitute of reason and suffer from the disease of sedition" (*Cels.* 8.49). Not only oblivious to the benefits of empire, they reject the gods who provide the good things of life. "Reason demands" that if Christians are going to take part in some of the pleasures of this world, such as marriage and children, they should show honor and perform rites to the gods in charge of these things (*Cels.* 8.55). Similarly, the frequent charge of "superstition" carries with it the idea of foreignness, atheism, and misanthropy.[5]

Caecilius voices the same complaint, that because Christians are uneducated and ill-mannered, they are disrespectful of the customs, values, and religion that all others value. They "band themselves against the gods," "spit upon the gods," "jeer at sacred rites" (*Oct.*

---

[4] Mary Beard, John North, and Simon Price, *Religions of Rome* (Cambridge: Cambridge University, 1998) 291–95.

[5] For these charges, see also Tacitus, *Ann.* 15.44.2–8; Suetonius, *Nero* 16; Pliny, *Letters* 10.96.1–10.

8.3–4), and "deny, reject, mock with false oaths" (*Oct.* 4.6) the very
gods that protect and aid the inhabitants of their cities. Everyone
else, "all nations," seems to recognize their importance (*Oct.* 8.1).

Robert Wilken and Robin Lane Fox stress that appeasement of
the gods was a civic responsibility. The gods were unpredictable and
easily riled, wielding great power that they could turn against mortals when they were not properly honored. In urban areas, where
most Christians lived, worship of thin-skinned but powerful deities,
whether the traditional Greek and Roman gods or the local gods
with whom they were merged, was essential to good crops, relief
from disease, and the general prosperity and well-being of the whole
area.[6] Refusal to recognize the gods' existence, bring regular offerings,
and consult their oracles, then, was not a personal matter or individual conviction, but a reckless choice that endangered the community.

Falsely, Christians ascribe to God what others ascribe to Fate (*Oct.*
11.6). Fate, the Christian Octavius retorts, is just another name for
God. Both Celsus and Caecilius resent Chrisian rejection of the con-
servative values that have so bountifully nourished the success of the
Empire, and by extension, her inhabitants. These Christians were
oddly incapable of appreciating the benefits of the empire, avoiding
games, banquets, processions, even refusing to fashion garlands of
flowers (*Oct.* 12.5–6).

## Christians Denigrate Life in this World

The third characteristic that these two pagans find particularly irk-
some grows out of the first two. The separatist sensibility and hope
for resurrection causes Christians to denigrate life in this world. They
"have no love for this life . . . offering their bodies to be tortured and
persecuted to no purpose" (*Cels.* 8.54). Lucian, also a second-century
pagan, is similarly repelled by the rejection of the good life in this
world for the hope of an afterlife, "the poor wretches have persuaded themselves as a general principle that they will be immortal
and will live for all time to come, so that they both despise death
and give themselves up of their own free will . . . they despise everything and think everything common property" (*Peregr.* 333–38).

---

[6] Robert Wilken, *The Christians as the Romans Saw Them* (New Haven: Yale, 1984)
48–67; Robin Lane Fox, *Pagans and Christians* (New York: Alfred Knopf, 1987)
38–39.

Caecilius articulates the same characteristic of the Christians. In their contempt for Roman religion and customs, despising titles and robes of honor (*Oct.* 8.4), rejecting processions, banquets, games, meat and drink offered to gods, Christians deny themselves the rightful pleasures of this world (*Oct.* 12.5). Hope for resurrection blinds them to enjoyment of this life, "poor wretches, for whom there is no life hereafter, yet who live not for today" (*Oct.* 12.6). They do not merely forego natural enjoyment of pleasures, but do not even try to avoid pain, torture, and death. They seem to seek it out. "Present tortures they despise, yet dread those of an uncertain future. Death after death they fear, but death in the meantime (present) they don't fear. For them a myth of comfort of resurrection soothes their fears" (*Oct.* 8.5). The good life provided by traditional religion and the security of the Empire is thrown away by the Christians who do not know any better.

### Christians Are Arrogant and Immodest

The fourth slur that crops up is the interpretation of Christian confidence in the resurrection of Jesus and their own resurrection as arrogance and immodesty, obnoxious traits in a people of low standing. Emblematic of their blindness to their own place in society is their blindness to their own place in the universe. Visualizing a final conflagration, they assume that "when God applies the fire (like a cook!), all the rest of mankind will be thoroughly roasted and that they alone will survive," including those of them who have already died (*Cels.* 5.14). They rate themselves higher than the stars, exclaims Caecilius, pronouncing destruction for them, but "for themselves, creatures born to perish, the promise of eternity!" (*Oct.* 11.3). Everyone else merits eternal punishment, but they expect perpetual life (*Oct.* 11.5). Only a lack of modesty and good sense propels them into pronouncing on matters even the philosophers cannot settle, "the heavenly regions, the destiny and secrets of the universe" (*Oct.* 12.7). Things that cannot be proven are better left in doubt (*Oct.* 3.4).

### Resurrection Offends Reason and Logic

Other complaints about Christian belief all come out of the claim that Christians are uneducated and simple-minded. These problems are couched as ones of intelligence and understanding. Were Christians more intellectually sophisticated, these writers imply, they would give up these notions.

Pagans did not uniformly reject the idea of an afterlife, but no consensus of views held sway. Beard, North, and Price collect a variety of documents about the afterlife from adherents of Greco-Roman religions. They range from those who deny any kind of post-mortem existence at all to those expecting a vague and shadowy existence after death, to those that predict horrific punishments.[7] While the official state cult did not concern itself with the afterlife, they argue that the emerging cults such as Mithraism and Christianity articulated death as a problem that cried out for a solution.[8] One could turn the question around, as Fox does, and use the growth of alternative cults as evidence for an increased interest in the afterlife.[9]

The doctrine of resurrection offended both writers because it offended all reason and logic. Celsus, though he seems to believe in reward and punishment after death (*Cels.* 8.49), cannot stomach the idea of the return of the body. Who has ever returned from the dead (*Cels.* 2.55) and how could the body, once dissolved, return to its original state? (*Cels.* 5.14). No one argues that the bodies of animals come back, why should human beings be any different? Since all bodies are made of matter and prone to corruption, there is no difference between the body of a bat, worm, or frog, and the body of a man (*Cels.* 4.52). The Christians contradict themselves, for their absurd stories of resurrection treat the body "as if we possessed nothing better or more precious than this," yet Christians readily submit to martyrdom, and "cast it into punishments as though it were of no value" (*Cels.* 8.49). Rather than submit to logic and reason, they fall back on the "outrageous refuge" of a slogan "anything is possible to God" (*Cels.* 5.14).

Caecilius also attacks resurrection on the grounds that it contravenes logic and is contrary to reason. He puts a riddle to the Christians, similar to the question that annoyed Paul in 1 Cor 15:35:

---

[7] Mary Beard, John North, and Simon Price, *Roman Religions: A Sourcebook* (Cambridge: Cambridge University, 1998) 235–38. They discuss the problem of epitaphs, which are usually conventions and do not necessarily reflect strongly held beliefs. See also Fox, *Pagans and Christians*, 97–98; Keith Hopkins, *Death and Renewal* (Cambridge: Cambridge University, 1983) 226–35.

[8] Beard, North, and Price, *Roman Religions*, 289–90.

[9] Fox, *Pagans and Christians*, 96.

"With what kind of body will they be raised?" If the body has been dissolved, with what kind of body can a person return? It cannot be the old body, for that has dissolved. If it is with a new body, then a new person has been created (*Oct.* 11.7–8). Like Celsus, he asks for evidence of one person who has ever come back (*Oct.* 11.8). Their arrogance allows Christians to step out of the flow of the universe and assume Nature's laws do not apply to them. Octavius's answer turns the question around, for he invokes the cycles of nature to prove re-birth (*Oct.* 34.11–12). Octavius's answer also brings reason to bear, arguing that the principle of justice is served by reward and punishment after resurrection. Like other apologists, Minucius Felix says many *hope* for annihilation to avoid giving account of their deeds (*Oct.* 34.12). He answers Caecilius's claim with the principle of material continuity, that the elements that make up a person remain in God's keeping so he may reconstruct the same person at resurrection (*Oct.* 34.9).

## *Resurrection Contradicts God's Power and Dignity*

Celsus's talk of God and what befits him is confusing only if we hold to an image of all pagans as polytheists. Robert Wilken observed some years ago that many pagan intellectuals were monotheists, critical of Christians for their claims of divine sonship and trinity.[10] A recent work argues that no sharp clash between pagan polytheists and Christian monotheists took place, but rather a widespread trend towards monotheism in late antiquity was shared by Christians and pagans.[11] Michael Frede cites Platonists, Peripatetics, and Stoics, who espouse the idea of one god who guides the universe, while accepting the existence of other gods and divine beings. He claims that little real difference existed between Christians and Plato, Aristotle, Zeno, and their followers, or the majority of philosophers in late antiquity, on this issue.[12] While others have questioned the terminology and whether "our monotheism," that is Christian, is the same as "their monotheism," pagan beliefs, the discussion helps us to understand

---

[10] Wilken, *Pagans*, 106.

[11] Polymnia Athanassiadi and Michael Frede, *Pagan Monotheism in Late Antiquity* (Oxford: Clarendon, 1999).

[12] Michael Frede, "Monotheism and Pagan Philosophy in Later Antiquity," Athanassiadi and Frede, *Pagan Monotheism*, 41–67.

Celsus's reasoning.[13] As a Platonist, he can argue about the nature of the one God, even if he knows of or participates in popular religion that pays homage to lesser or local deities. He and others explain the apparent multiplicity of gods by claiming one God has many names. Not only is the movement towards monotheism the majority view of intellectuals, say Athanassiadi and Frede, but it is a movement native to philosophy itself, not a reaction to Christianity.[14] Others have taken a less radical position, suggesting a spectrum of belief between the claim of one God's existence and true polytheism. Some Jews and Christians occupy different points on the spectrum; so too do pagans.[15] Pagans and Christians are not so far apart that they cannot talk to each other about what kinds of things God can and cannot do, nor trade barbs over who are the true monotheists.

God's power and dignity weigh against the possibility of resurrection, argue these two writers. Since the nature of the flesh is impermanence, God could not raise up a dissolved body without violating reason and the laws of the universe, namely his own nature and laws. "Neither can God do what is shameful nor does he desire what is contrary to his nature . . . for he himself is the reason of everything that exists; therefore he is not able to do anything contrary to reason or to his own character" (*Cels.* 5.14). Celsus is in sympathy with Lucian, who, in his discussion of the Genesis creation story, says that God is reason itself and cannot act contrary to it or the laws of nature without denying himself (*On the Usefulness of the Parts of the Body* 11.14).[16] Celsus's reasoning here relies on his negative assessment of the flesh, a result of his throughgoing Platonism and conviction that God is spirit.

Caecilius represents a position of skepticism about ultimate knowledge of the divine, but promotes the worship of gods of traditional cults. Frede says he is the most polytheistic of pagan writers of this period, and the most atypical. Minucius Felix attributes to Caecilius the query whether God could perform resurrection and reward the

---

[13] See review by M. J. Edwards, *JTS* 51 (2000) 339–42; Beard, North, and Price, *Roman Religion*, 286–87. Jewish monotheism is only mentioned in passing in these discussions, probably because of the lack of a large Jewish apologetic literature directed at the Greco-Roman world.

[14] Athanassiadi and Frede, *Pagan Monotheism*, 8, 20.

[15] Beard, North, and Price, *Roman Religion*, 286–87.

[16] See discussion in Wilken, *Pagans*, 83–89.

righteous, since he seems uninterested or unable to do so in this life: "Some part of you, the greater and better part of you say, suffer want, cold, toil, hunger; and yet your God permits it and seems to overlook it; he is unwilling and unable to help his own; consequently he is powerless or unjust . . . where is the God who will succour you in the next life, but in this life cannot?" (*Oct.* 12.2–4). The power of this charge explains the frequency with which Christian apologists for resurrection emphasize God's power as evidenced by creation and his justice in compelling resurrection.

### The Flesh is Impermanent and Inferior

Celsus's argument is animated by his firm convictions about the nature of the body and the inferiority of the flesh. By nature, bodies change over time and return to their original state. Since they are matter, they cannot take on permanence (*Cels.* 4.60–61). Celsus does accept some kind of afterlife, but relies on the essential dichotomy of the body and soul, or body and spirit: "The soul is God's work, but the nature of the body is different" (*Cels.* 4.58). The human being "is bound to the body, weighed down by the passions before being purified" (*Cels.* 8.53). A good Platonist, he even refers to the body as a prison. He cannot fathom the myths of the Christians that Jesus, their god, was born of a woman ("God would not thrust his spirit into vile pollution" [*Cels.* 6.73]), nor that he rose bodily from the dead, for "God would not receive back a spirit after it was defiled by the body" (*Cels.* 6.72). Nor can he accept that if Jesus had been filled with divine spirit he would have possessed a body ordinary in appearance. Even more so, he cannot understand the longing of the Christians to receive back their bodies after death (8.49). They are "bound up in the body and see nothing pure" (7.42). How strange, it strikes him, since at best the body is full of unmentionable things, but certainly after dissolution in the grave becomes even more foul. "What sort of person would want a rotted body back?" (5.14). These reactions of disgust explain why the apologists argue to such a degree for the value of the body as God's creation and a reflection of his image, and the indivisible union of body and soul in the human being.

Both pagan writers seem puzzled by the emphasis on the afterlife to the neglect of the pleasures of this world. Perkins reminds us that much of pagan religion and popular piety did not concentrate on

the afterlife.[17] Official state religion did not make much of it. Religion
was for good fortune in this life and festivals to enjoy. Whole cultures and religious systems have fared well without an elaborate sense
of the afterlife.

Pagan disgust at Christian preaching of the resurrection of the
body is propelled by two things: a set of convictions about God and
an attitude towards the body as matter. They disagree violently about
the nature of God and his involvement in human affairs. Resurrection
is utterly foreign to God because he does not violate his own laws
of nature and reason. Raising up the body, reversing the process of
death and dissolution, would violate the very laws of nature that he
has set up. The body, as matter, is by its nature and God's laws,
subject to decay and corruption. Nor would God desire to bring
back the body, since he is principally spirit, not earthly matter, and
above material things. While the belief in bodily resurrection was
hardly the only thing about Christians that riled pagans, it provides
one of the more dramatic and egregious examples of their credulity,
ignorance, arrogance, and mistaken understandings of God and nature.

The debate springs from the paradox of the body itself. On the
one hand, it is fragile and temporary, constructed to deteriorate and
dissolve. On the other hand, it is wondrous in its many functions,
its ability to go though the many stages of growth and change, to
heal itself and recover from illness. Celsus is unarguably correct, that
the body is not meant for permanence. But the apologists too are
right, that the body is remarkable evidence of God's creation.

---

[17] Perkins, *Resurrection*, 62–63.

# CHAPTER SIX

# MATERIAL EVIDENCE FOR BELIEF IN RESURRECTION

Since our literary materials give voice to the importance of belief in resurrection as an element of community self-definition, we could expect material evidence, particularly funerary inscriptions, to bear this out. References to resurrection or certain burial practices might be typical of some communities, while conspicuously absent in others. In reality, material evidence for resurrection among Jews is scarce, and is even scantier for early Christians. Of the Roman Jewish inscriptions, only 3% refer to afterlife at all.[1] For Christians, the amount of epigraphic material evidence from before the fourth century, mostly from Rome and Anatolia, rarely mentions resurrection. The earliest datable Christian epitaph, of Aberkios around 200, makes no mention of the afterlife at all.[2] Iconography tells a similar tale. If biblical typologies can be taken as evidence of belief in a generalized resurrection, then the earliest Jewish evidence appears in the depictions of Ezekiel's vision of the valley of dry bones and Elijah's raising of the widow's son from the Dura-Europas synagogue in the mid-third century. The earliest Christian examples are the images of the raising of Lazarus, which are also from the mid-third century. Jesus' resurrection does not appear until the late fourth century.[3]

We have been well-warned of the pitfalls of over-interpretation of material evidence, particularly funerary inscriptions. Many of the phrases are conventional, and may or may not reflect their original meaning.[4] Even if they are heartfelt, they could reflect the views of

---

[1] Leonard Rutgers, *The Hidden Heritage of Diaspora Judaism* (Leuven: Peeters, 1998) 159.

[2] S. Llewelyn and R. Kearsley, eds., *NewDocs* (Sydney: Macquarie University, 1992) 6:177–78.

[3] See Robin Margaret Jensen, *Understanding Early Christian Art* (London and New York: Routledge, 2000) 156–82, and Erwin R. Goodenough, *Jewish Symbols in the Greco-Roman Period* abridged, Jacob Neusner, ed. (Princeton: Princeton University Press, 1988).

[4] Pieter van der Horst provides an excellent, succinct discussion of the attendant problems in interpreting epitaphs, in *Ancient Jewish Epitaphs* (Kampen: Kok Pharos,

the deceased, the family of the deceased, or the stoneworker,[5] not all of whom necessarily belong to the same religious group. Nor is it always clear who is a Jew or a Christian, nor what religious symbols mean.[6] One scholar describes five schools of thought on the significance of a menorah alone.[7] Grave goods such as cooking vessels and personal items indicate afterlife to some, while others emphasize it indicates continued existence in the grave but not rising up from it.[8]

These cautions point to a reality: a person's deepest convictions rarely express themselves at the grave. The phrases, symbols, and customs of burial, often ambiguous or conventional, do not reflect what people are thinking, except in the very broadest ways. They often present an idealized image or elements of wishful thinking, thereby erasing controversy. They may mute polemics over identity or self-construction and show a deceptively monochromatic quality of culture.

Three kinds of material evidence come into play in searching early Jewish and Christian communities for evidence of resurrection belief. First, Jewish and Christian inscriptions in the early centuries—mostly from Rome, Beth Shearim, and Leontopolis for Jews, and Rome and Anatolia for Christians—shed some light on attitudes towards death as well as social interaction between groups. Second, the Jewish practice of secondary burial, the gathering and deposit of bones in ossuaries and a period of disintegration, has been linked by some to increased belief in bodily resurrection. Third, the presence of grave goods—items of daily life such as cooking pots, jewelry, and lamps— buried with the deceased may indicate an expectation of continued

---

1991) 11–21. See Fox, *Pagans and Christians*, 96; Beard, North and Price, *Religions of Rome* 1.235; Keith Hopkins, *Death and Renewal* (Cambridge: Cambridge University, 1983) 203–5.

[5] Gary Johnson, *Early Christian Epitaphs* (Texts and Translations 35; Atlanta: Scholars, 1995) 113.

[6] See Ross Kraemer, "On the Meaning of the Term 'Jew' in Greco-Roman Inscriptions," *HTR* 82 (1989) 35–53; idem, "Jewish Tuna and Christian Fish," *HTR* 84 (1991) 141–62; Mark Johnson, "Pagan-Christian Burial Practices of the Fourth Century: Shared Tombs?" *JECS* 5 (1997) 50.

[7] Senso Nagakubo, "Investigation into Jewish Concepts of Afterlife in the Beth Shearim Greek Inscriptions" (Ph.D. diss., Duke University, 1974) 200.

[8] Joseph Park argues that grave goods indicate continued existence in the place of the grave so do not show hope of resurrection, in *Conceptions of Afterlife in Jewish Inscriptions with Special Reference to Pauline Literature* (Tübingen: Mohr Siebeck, 2000) 41–44.

life for the deceased, whether in the grave, or in a journey to the next world.

## Inscriptions

### Explicit References to Resurrection in Jewish Sources

Jewish inscriptions, though sparse, far outnumber identifiably Christian ones. From Rome comes a poetic inscription in Latin to a Jewish woman named Regina, dead at twenty-one after only one year of marriage, from her grieving husband. The epitaph, usually dated to the third or early fourth century,[9] is frequently cited but less often discussed. It lauds Regina for her character.

> Here is buried Regina, covered by such a tomb, which her spouse set up in accordance to [his] love of her. After twice ten [years], she spent with him a year and a fourth month with eight days remaining. She will live again, return to the light again. For she can hope therefore that she may rise into the age promised for both the worthy and the pious, she, a true pledge, who deserved to have an abode in the venerable country. Your piety has achieved this for you, your chaste life, your love of your family [?] also, your observance of the Law, the merit of your marriage, whose honor was your concern. From these deeds there is future hope for you, and your grieving spouse seeks his comfort in that (*CIJ* 476).[10]

Her piety, love of her family (or people, says Leon), and observance of the Torah are the reasons that she merits the reward of an afterlife. Rutgers has observed that funerary inscriptions usually talk about customs and what the person did in this life. This one describes the ideal life of a Jewish woman, though in ambiguous phrases.[11]

Most cite this as the clearest testimony to the expectation of bodily resurrection,[12] particularly with its reference to returning to the

---

[9] See discussion in David Noy, *Jewish Inscriptions of Western Europe*, 2 vols. (Cambridge: Cambridge University, 1995) 2.86–88.

[10] Translated by Noy, *Jewish Inscriptions*, 86. See also Harry Leon, *The Jews of Ancient Rome* (Philadelphia: Jewish Publication Society, 1960; updated ed., Peabody, Mass.: Hendrickson, 1995) 335.

[11] Ross Kraemer notes the lack of specificity in this ideal picture. Observance of the Law, for example, could mean in the private sphere, the sphere usually assigned to women's piety, or in public activity in the community or synagogue. See "Non-Literary Evidence for Jewish Women in Rome and Egypt," *Helios* 13 (1986) 90.

[12] Van der Horst, *Jewish Epitaphs*, 114; Noy, *Jewish Inscriptions*, 86–87.

light again (*reditura ad lumina rursum*) and rising (*surgat*) to the age
promised to the righteous.[13] The "venerable country" (*venerandi ruris*)
she will attain has been identified as Eden, the Holy Land, or Paradise
by various scholars.[14] Yet even here, the images are not overly literal about bodily resurrection. There is nothing such as "her eyes
will see the light again" or "her feet will walk the earth again." Nor
do we possess any other inscriptions remotely similar to this in their
explicit expectation of afterlife in Jewish or Christian epigraphs. This
stands as testimony to an expectation of individual afterlife among
early Roman Jews, probably indicating bodily resurrection, but remains
singular and anomalous.

Interestingly, the most common references to resurrection in early
Jewish and Christian funerary materials do not point to the deceased
but to those who might violate the tomb. At Beth Shearim, an
inscription threatens anyone thinking of robbing or disturbing the
burial site with judgment in the next world, "Anyone who removes
this woman, the One who promises to give life to the dead, will
himself judge" (BS II 162). A Jewish inscription from Phrygia is less
explicit about resurrection but does imply a reckoning in the afterlife: "If someone inters here another body, he will have to reckon
with God Most High, and may the sickle of the curse enter his house
and leave no one alive" (CIJ 769).[15] Similarly, another inscription
from Beth Shearim that denies the tomb violator eternal life seems
to assume, Park observes, that it is the normal reward of most Jews:
"May anyone who dares to open (the grave) above us not have a
portion in the eternal life" (BS II 129).[16]

Although only the first reference clearly implies resurrection, the
second and third could include it. All three continue the characteristic connection of resurrection and afterlife with judgment. Pagans,
Jews, and Christians regularly call down a variety of punishments
on tomb violaters and their families, from fines to blindness to general ruin, usually in this world. Such inscriptions are found primarily
in Asia Minor (mainly Phrygia) in the second and third century, suggesting a particularly Anatolian concern or epigraphic commonplace.[17]

---

[13] Park, *Conceptions of Afterlife*, 167–68.
[14] See discussion in Noy, *Jewish Inscriptions*, 87.
[15] Partially reconstructed from no. 769 by van der Horst, *Jewish Epitaphs*, 57–58.
[16] Park, *Conceptions of Afterlife*, 144–45.
[17] Van der Horst, *Jewish Epitaphs*, 54–60; J. Strubbe, "Cursed be he that moves
my bones," *Magika Hiera* (ed. C. Faraone and D. Obbink; New York: Oxford

A graffito on the wall leading to a catacomb at Beth Shearim testifies to resurrection belief: "Good luck with your resurrection," or as Baruch Lifshitz translates it, "Good luck. [May you share in] the resurrection" (BS II 194).[18] Park has noted that "good luck" can imply anything from near certainty to its opposite, as one might say "lots of luck at winning the lottery." It could also be sarcasm by people who reject resurrection. In any of these cases, however, it still points to a group of people known for their belief in resurrection, whatever the writers of the graffito might believe.

## References to Resurrection that Are Suggestive

A common Jewish inscription at Rome and Beth Shearim is "Be of good courage. No one is immortal." On the face of it this is a puzzling expression since the latter half suggests no reason to be cheerful or courageous. Nor does it seem to lend itself to belief in any kind of afterlife.

Marcel Simon made the case that this phrase actually supports the idea of an afterlife, since the word θάρσει, "Be of good courage," is a formulaic way of encouraging the deceased in a dangerous journey to the next world. He cites pagan, Jewish, and Christian uses of the term in other contexts of reassurance in the face of danger, sometimes danger faced after death. The second part of the phrase he interprets as meaning death is the lot of all people, but is not without hope for an afterlife.[19] This view has been seconded by recent scholars,[20] including van der Horst, who notes one of the inscriptions at Beth Shearim that uses a form of this phrase (BS II 193) is written by the same hand that wrote BS II 194, "Good luck with your resurrection." He notes that the expression also appears in the Codex Bezae (D) version of Luke 23:43: "Be of good courage. Today you will be with me in Paradise," as well as Plato's references to immortality.[21]

University, 1991) 39. See also A. Sheppard, "Jews, Christians, and Heretics in Acmonia and Eumenia," *Anatolian Studies* 29 (1979) 169–80.

[18] Baruch Lifshitz, "Beitrage zur palästinischen Epigraphik," *ZDPV* 78 (1962) 74.

[19] Marcel Simon, "θάρσει, οὐδεὶς ἀθάνατος" *RHR* 113 (1936) 188–206; *Le christianisme antique et son contexte religieux* 1 (Tübingen: Mohr Siebeck, 1981).

[20] Kraemer, *Meanings of Death*, 63; Nagakubo, *Jewish Concepts of Afterlife*, 164–69.

[21] Van der Horst, *Jewish Epitaphs*, 121–22.

Park notes with surprise that Simon's explanation has gone largely unchallenged, except on minor points. The phrase, Park argues, can accommodate belief or non-belief in afterlife, and may simply mean to comfort with the universality of death, as it seems to in a number of pagan examples.[22] Park's argument, while a minority view, has the advantage of being the simplest reading.

### Ambiguous References that May Include Resurrection

A common epitaph on Jewish graves is "in peace her (his) sleep." In this form it can mean almost anything, but other, expanded forms of it are more suggestive. Van der Horst notes several examples of sleep "in peace with the righteous ones," possibly drawing on the image of the heavenly banquet in intertestamental and rabbinic sources.[23] Similarly, he points out the name *Anastasius/-ia*, which appears among Jewish and then Christian epigraphs, but never among pagans, points to the favor the idea of resurrection enjoyed among Jews.

Many of the inscriptions cannot be mustered to support the idea of resurrection, but refer in a vague way to an afterlife, such as those at Leontopolis that say "I await a good hope of mercy" (CIJ 1513) or "his soul (be) in the bundle of the living" (CIJ 1534) or one at Beth Shearim, "May your soul cling to immortal life" (BS II 130). The most common funerary inscription in Hebrew is the word "Shalom," which can imply a wish for a peaceful afterlife, an undisturbed tomb, or a simple farewell.

### Christian Inscriptions

Many fewer explicitly Christian inscriptions exist from this period. Most are from Rome or Asia Minor. Some imitate the Jewish and pagan threats against tomb violators. In the third and fourth centuries, the formula that the tomb violator would "reckon with God" (ἔσται αὐτῷ πρὸς τὸν θεὸν) became common around Eumenia and is called the Eumenian formula.[24] But πρὸς τὸν θεὸν could apply to any

---

[22] Park, *Conceptions of Afterlife*, 49–51.
[23] Van der Horst, *Jewish Epitaphs*, 116–17.
[24] Gary Johnson argues that this is primarily a Christian formula. Considerable discussion has circulated about whether it is primarily Jewish or Christian. Since it is found among pagans, Jews, and Christians, and the survival of ancient inscrip-

god; and the formula, or something similar to it, is found in pagan, Jewish, and Christian contexts. Whereas pagan epitaphs threatened the violator would reckon with Zeus Solymos or the katachthonic gods, Christian epitaphs predicted one would reckon with God, the Living God, or the Trinity.

A clearly Christian version is from Laodicea in the fourth century: "I, Flaouia Maria Seleukissa, set up [this monument] for my husband, Paulos, an *ordinarius* of the *campidoctorum*, in memory; and should anyone attempt to damage (it), he will reckon with the Trinity" (no. 4.11 in Johnson; *MAMA* 1 [1928] 86, no. 168).[25] In fourth-century Phrygia resurrection of the body is referred to most clearly in the epitaph of a deacon Paula: "Paula, the most beloved deacon of Christ. [cross] She built me, the tomb of her dear brother Helladius, outside the fatherland, made of stones as the protector of the body until the dreadful [cross] sound of the trumpet shall awaken the dead as God has promised" (*MAMA* 1 [1928] 120, no. 226).[26]

Others, identified as Christian by Johnson, threaten the tomb violator with final reckoning. One clearly Christian one from Salamis (not Anatolia), contains a cross and ends with the expression "Marana tha" transliterated into Greek: "[cross] Eternal home of the reader Agathon, and Euphemia, in two vaults, each one our private property. If anyone should dare to inter a body from their own family (?) here beside our two, he will give account to God and be cursed. The Lord comes" (no. 4.1 in Johnson; CIG 9303 = CIA 3.2, no. 3509). Another epitaph using the term κοιμητήριον, burial place (lit., sleeping room) which Johnson deems an exclusively Christian term, uses the same phrase "give account to God." "If anyone should violate the *koimeterion*, the lawbreaker will give account to God on Judgment Day and pay the treasury 100 denarii" (no. 2.20 in Johnson; Sahin, *Iznik* 1, no. 555). A third-century inscription on a bomos from Eumeneia threatens, "If anyone should insert another corpse, he will reckon with God both now and for all eternity and not obtain the promise of God" (formula appears twice, for father and son; no. 4.14

---

tions is serendipitous, it seems impossible to assert who used this formula more or for whom it was more characteristic. See discussion in William Tabbernee, *Montanist Inscriptons and Testimonia* (NAPSPMS 16: Mercer University Press, 1997) 144–46.

[25] Reprinted in Gary Johnson, *Christian Epitaphs*, 133.

[26] Translated and discussed in Ute Eisen, *Women Officeholders in Early Christianity* (Collegeville: Liturgical Press, 2000) 169–70.

in Johnson). Johnson suggests that the promise is salvation or resurrection.

The Eumeniean formula appears in some later epitaphs with openly
Christian expressions; for example, at Dinar towards the end of the
third century: "Christians. Kapiton . . . I made this tomb for myself
and my wife . . . and for my sister Trophime; if anyone else shall uti-
lize (this tomb) he (or she) will reckon with God." (*MAMA* 6, [1939]
87, no. 235).[27] Another inscription from Dinar, from the late third
to early fourth century, contains the chi-rho and the formula against
violation,

> "[Chi-rho] I, Aurelios Valens, son of Valens, cobbler, have prepared
> the tomb for myself and for my wife Louliana and for those who lie
> [here] with [us]; but if anyone should wish to weigh down my bones
> [by placing other bones on top of mine] that person will be answer-
> able to the One who has authority over every soul; let no one open
> [the tomb], the boundary [of which] is extensive. Whoever, at any
> time, should throw a bone out of here will reckon with God" (*MAMA*
> 6 [1939] 86, no. 234).[28]

Some inscriptions mix traditions, drawing on a stock set of metaphors
available around the Mediterranean. The lawyer Gaius, buried with
his family and mentor Roubes (whom Sheppard thinks is a Jew), has
written, "Here are the doors and the road to Hades, but the path
has no way out to the light. Indeed the righteous at all times point
the way to resurrection. This the God of Hosts. . . ."[29]

Similarly, a mix of themes appears in this inscription, "May you
claim (your due) wages in Hades or Paradise from immortal God
himself. For me it matters not. I leave behind an evil world. God
preserves the seal for me, [his] child. I, a mortal, have landed in
the immortal lap of Abraham. I am a servant of God. I live in
Paradise." Johnson and others say the seal refers to baptism, but it
could equally be the seal of circumcision.[30]

Literary materials show a mix of ideas about the afterlife and no
obvious point where one form of belief triumphed over the other.
The same is true for Jewish and Christian material evidence. M.
Johnson shows an intermingling of pagan and Christian tombs and

---

[27] Reconstruction and translation by Tabbernee, *Montanist Inscriptions*, 167.
[28] Translation, except for the final line, follows Tabbernee, *Montanist Inscriptions*,
224–25.
[29] Sheppard, "Jews, Christians, and Heretics," 178–79; Johnson, *Christian Epitaphs*,
136.
[30] Johnson, *Christian Epitaphs*, 149.

themes into the fourth century. Writing on a late third- to early fourth-century sarcophagus laments the early death of a young woman whose death is attributed to the howling Furies, servants of Pluto in the underworld, but ends with the famous formula, "Christians for Christians" (*MAMA* 10 [1993], 275).[31]

## Ossuaries

Jews practiced secondary burial, depositing their dead in hewn out *loculi* temporarily until the flesh decayed, then depositing their bones in an ossuary or bone box. This practice was prevalent around Jerusalem in the Herodian period up to 70, but some ossuaries have been found in Jericho and Beth Shearim in the Galilee, as well as one in Jordan and a few in North Africa, some as late as the third-fourth century.[32] Care was apparently taken to keep one person's body together and avoid mingling bones from others, and the bones were arranged in a certain order with the skull on top. In some cases, bones of a mother and child or husband and wife would be buried together The ossuaries themselves were typically of stone—limestone or, rarely, marble—materials that would not decompose and allow bones to mingle; though some nails and hinges that suggest some might have been wooden have also been found at Beth Shearim.

Regarding changing attitudes towards resurrection, the question is whether this custom of secondary burial and concern for the integrity of the individual's bones points to a change or amplification of belief in afterlife, especially resurrection.[33] Or is it simply a more efficient way to allow more burials in a family grave,[34] or a response to the psychological needs of the living?[35]

---

[31] Tabbernee, *Montanist Inscriptions*, 209. See Elsa Gibson, *The Christians for Christians Inscriptions of Phyrgia* (HTS 32; Missoula: Scholars Press, 1978).

[32] See L. Y. Rahmani, "Ancient Jerusalem's Funerary Customs and Tombs, Part 4," *BA* 45 (1982) 109; and Eric Meyers, *Jewish Ossuaries: Reburial and Rebirth* (Rome: Biblical Institute Press, 1971) 85, who differ somewhat on dating.

[33] Rahmani, "Ancient Jerusalem's Funerary Customs and Tombs, Part 3," *BA* 45.1 (1981) 43–53; idem, Part 4, *BA* 45.2 (1982) 109–19; Kraemer, *Meanings of Death*, 50–53.

[34] J. Park, *Conceptions of Afterlife*, 170–73. Park raises this possibility but nevertheless thinks ossuaries suggest resurrection belief.

[35] Byron McKane, "Bones of Contention? Ossuaries and Reliquaries in Early Judaism and Christianity," *SecCent* 8 (1991) 235–46.

Rabbinic references to decomposition of the flesh as a means of atonement, the well-known Pharisaic-rabbinic belief in resurrection of the body, and the emergence of the practice of ossilegium lead some scholars to conclude that the custom was motivated by an increased emphasis on resurrection of the body. Let us consider what actual information the rabbinic references contribute and what is extrapolated from them.

(1) "[When] the flesh has decomposed, they gather the bones and bury them in their place" (*m.Sanh.* 6:6). This suggests that the end of the decay of the flesh is the end of a process marked by an act of burial by the relatives.

(2) "He [Rabbi Akiba] also used to say five matters of twelve months: the judgment of the generation of the flood was twelve months; Job's judgment was twelve months; the judgment of the Egyptians was twelve months; the judgment of Gog and Magog in the future will be twelve months; *the judgment of the wicked in Gehinnom is twelve months*, as it is said 'and it shall come to pass, that from one new moon to another' [Isa 66:23]. R. Yohanan b. Nuri says; from Pesah to Atzeret, as it states 'and from one Shabbat to another'" (*m.ʿEd.* 2:10). Initial passing of judgment would be a one-time event, so this refers not to initial judgment but punishment. From this passage we may extrapolate that judgment, punishment, or atonement is completed after a period of twelve months.

(3) "The Israelites who sinned with their bodies and Gentiles who sinned with their bodies go down to Gehenna and are judged there for twelve months. And after twelve months their souls perish, their bodies are burned, Gehenna absorbs them, and they are turned into dust" (*t.Sanh.* 13.4). A period of twelve months is again associated with judgment, punishment, or atonement.

(4) In a discussion of which acts are permissible during *Hol haMoed*, "R. Meir also said: A person may gather his father's and mother's bones, as it is a joy for him" (*m.Moʿed.Qat.* 1:5). The Mishnah does not state why it is a joy, but the parallel in the Jerusalem Talmud more explicitly links gathering the bones to the end of a period of judgment or atonement: "On that day [that a man collects bones of his father the son] mourned, but later he rejoiced because his ancestors [lit. "fathers"] rested from judgment" (*y.Moʿed. Qat.* 1.5). The rabbis practiced ossilegium, and in the later Jerusalem

text, the practice apparently marks the end of a period of judgment or suffering for the deceased.

(5) Regarding the shameful burial of criminals as necessary for their forgiveness, the Talmud notes that it is not sufficient, "the decay of the flesh too is necessary for forgiveness" (*b.San.* 47b). This is a later reference, but articulates the idea that decay of the flesh brings atonement.

Combining these statements suggests that the marking of the end of decomposition is significant, probably because it ends a period of atonement. The period of one year seems significant as the end of judgment: i.e., atonement.

Putting these pieces of information together leads many to conclude that secondary burial took place after a period of a year during which the flesh decayed, effecting atonement for the deceased, perhaps preparing them for resurrection. The gathering of the bones then meant the end of expiation and a release. Such a conclusion is explicit in the tractate *Evel Rabbati*, or *Semahot*, 12.4. This tractate cannot be used with confidence, however, since it is not quoted until the Middle Ages and the current consensus is that it is gaonic.[36] Rahmani, using *Semahot*, argues decomposition effected atonement, readying the person for resurrection, and that this reflected Pharisaic dominance on religious matters.[37]

Without the later evidence, however, from *Semahot*, the Babylonian Talmud or The Jerusalem Talmud, the connections between these elements are less clear. The early rabbis do not connect ossilegium to afterlife, or say it was completed after 12 months. Furthermore, even the early evidence is later than most of the secondary burials.

The custom of ossilegium makes sense when combined with the literary evidence of growing belief in resurrection, but on its own does not prove it. Kraemer argues that some of the symbols at Beth Shearim make sense if we assume the practitioners believe in an

---

[36] Kraemer, *Meanings of Death*, 9–10. Richard Kalmin, in conversation, notes that the evidence is not strong for either early or late dating. A dissertation is presently under way on the dating of the non-canonical tractates.

[37] Rahmani, "Ancient Jerusalem's Funerary Customs and Tombs," *BA* 45 (1982) 118. He is seconded by Rachel Hachlili and Ann Killebrew, "Jewish Funerary Customs during the Second Temple Period, in Light of the Excavations at the Jericho Necropolis," *PEQ* 115 (1983) 129, and recently Park, *Conceptions of Afterlife*, 170–73.

afterlife. Some sarcophagi lids are decorated with raised projections that resemble the horns of the ancient altars in the temple. He speculates that the sarcophagi are meant to resemble ancient altars, with the dead symbolically buried beneath the altar, their decomposition viewed as an atoning sacrifice.[38] Other symbols he mentions coincide with notions of afterlife and resurrection; a horse and rider indicates a battle, the ship a journey. The ship became, among Christians, a common symbol for the resurrected body.[39] These examples might cohere with resurrection belief but are too opaque to prove its existence without support from literary materials.

Does the practice of ossilegium require a belief in afterlife, especially resurrection? Meyers makes a series of connections that are fatal to any facile connection between the practice of secondary burial and belief in resurrection. Most telling is the fact that ossilegium does not suit a highly literal understanding of resurrection, since the body is taken apart and placed in a very small container. Furthermore, it was apparently acceptable to save parts of the skeleton or pulverize the remains, which also does not suit a literalist view of resurrection that would maintain the integrity of the body at all costs. Furthermore, ossilegium and primary burial sometimes appear in the same tomb, so it was not practiced to the exclusion of primary burial.[40]

Steven Fine argues that the practice of ossilegium coincides with an influx of wealth into Jerusalem after Herod the Great. In this atmosphere a class of stonemasons arose, contributing to the production of ossuaries.[41] This explanation, while reasonable, does not clarify which was causal, the stonemason class promoting ossuaries, or the practice of ossilegium making stonemasonry more profitable. Fine and Dina Teitlebaum also argue for increased individuation in burial in general in the Greco-Roman world as a contributing factor.[42] Both seriously doubt the practice as a reflection of Pharisaic belief in resurrection, citing evidence of Sadducean use of ossuaries.

---

[38] Kraemer, *Meanings of Death*, 67–69.

[39] Bynum, *Resurrection of the Body*, 88–89.

[40] Meyers, *Jewish Ossuaries*, 85–89.

[41] Steven Fine, "A Note on Ossuary Burial and the Resurrection of the Dead in First-Century Jerusalem," *JJS* 51 (2000) 69–76.

[42] Dina Teitlebaum, "The Relationship between Ossuary Burial and the Belief in Resurrection during Late Second Temple Judaism," (Ann Arbor: University Microfilms, 1997).

An association that does seem clear is the importance of burial in the Holy Land. Although ossuaries turn up elsewhere, the majority of them are in Eretz Israel. Since resurrection will take place in the land of Israel, Isaiah Gafni suggests the transfer of bones to the land is to meant to spare the deceased the painful rolling through underground passages at the time of the resurrection.[43] A number of the ossuaries in Beth Shearim are of Jews from other parts of the Mediterranean, raising the possibility that the ossuary also had a highly practical purpose. If being interred in the Holy Land was desirable, ossuaries of clean bones would be easier to transport than whole decomposing bodies.

A set of ideas revolves around ossilegium-atonement, burial in the Holy Land, and the afterlife, especially resurrection. But the relationship of the ideas is less clear. Decomposition brings atonement whether the body is re-interred in an ossuary or not. Resurrection of the body could be held whether one practiced primary or secondary burial. Depositing bones in an ossuary may have arisen simply to acknowledge the end of the period of decomposition. Furthermore, as Meyers notes, ossilegium could accommodate either eschatological hope, immortality of the soul, or resurrection of the body.[44] What ossilegium cannot accommodate is a lack of any hope. The gathering of a loved one's bones and careful deposit in an ossuary in a way that prevents intermingling would involve a fair amount of effort and emotional strain for the survivors. It is doubtful one would go through the process if s/he believed the dead simply disappeared forever, or if it carried no meaning for the state of their deceased and merely provided a form of psychological relief.[45]

## Grave Goods

Possibly the most ambiguous evidence of all concerning afterlife is the presence of grave goods—usually personal effects like jewelry, mirrors, and coins, and things used in everyday life such as cooking

---

[43] Isaiah Gafni, "Bringing Deceased from Abroad for Burial in Eretz Israel: On the Origin of the Custom and Its Development," *Cathedra* 4 (1977) 113–20.

[44] Meyers, *Jewish Ossuaries*, 87.

[45] McKane argues that it was a family ritual primarily for the living. Yet it must have had some expected impact on the deceased for it to have a psychological effect on the survivors.

pots or utensils—buried with the deceased. Like inscriptions and ossuaries, grave goods are prone to the problems of interpretation: questions as to whether their presence is a matter of convention or deeply held belief. The range of opinions on one side includes Bloch-Smith, who deals with a much earlier period but argues that the presence of grave goods in the bench tombs of Iron Age Judea is consistent with goods in other Mediterranean cultures that clearly did believe in an afterlife.

Park offers the variety of proposed explanations for the presence of artifacts, including the idea that they were left behind by those attending the grave to being left by tomb-robbers, the latter problem attested to by many of our inscriptions.[46] Park himself believes that these goods indicate a belief that the dead survived but remained in the grave where they would need such items in their shadowy underworld. He links it to Roman customs like the Rosalia, when survivors brought food to share with the dead.

Rachel Hachlili's research suggests that some Jewish grave goods argue against afterlife or are at best inconclusive, because only broken pieces and unusable items are placed in the grave. Certain things, like gold glasses seem to have been deliberately broken leaving a disk shape.[47] *Semachot* 8.7 states personal items are placed there to arouse the grief of the mourner,[48] perhaps reminding them of the dead through their effects, or emphasizing their present state as removed from everyday life.

Similar grave goods are found in Roman burials, such as toys for children, jewelry for women, dice and drinking cups for men, but because of a similar range of attitudes towards the afterlife in Roman culture, their meaning is not always clear.[49] Hopkins does take them as suggestive of some conviction of an afterlife.

In short, grave goods seem even more opaque in their meaning than inscriptions or ossuaries, but their presence is suggestive since grave goods appear in many other cultures whose literature shows they did accept the idea of an afterlife.

---

[46] Park, *Conceptions of Afterlife*, 41–44.

[47] Rachel Hachlili, *Ancient Jewish Art and Archaeology in the Diaspora* (Leiden: Brill, 1998) 292, 303, 309–10.

[48] See Saul Lieberman, "Some Aspects of Afterlife in Early Rabbinic Literature," *American Academy of Jewish Research: Harry A. Wolfson Jubilee Volume*, 509–10. Lieberman suggests this was such a common custom the Rabbis could not uproot it, so chose to reinterpret it.

[49] Hopkins, *Death and Renewal*, 226–35.

*Conclusions*

The non-literary evidence allows us to note several things:

(1) Material evidence is generally mute on the matter of afterlife. Even funerary inscriptions generally do not attest to resurrection or afterlife in any way, and our evidence is relatively scarce compared to the written materials.

(2) Relative uniformity prevails across the Mediterranean. An inscription at Beth Shearim would not be out of place at Leontopolis or Rome. While ossuaries are more common in the land of Israel, this is probably because of the special status accorded the land, and some of the ossuaries are transported from the diaspora.

(3) Belief in immortality of the soul and in resurrection of the body exist in the same communities. In one case at Beth Shearim, inscriptions referring to both are written in the same hand. This finding, that one idea did not replace the other, is consonant with our literary findings, where resurrection was promoted as a defining characteristic of community against a backdrop of competing beliefs.

(4) Pagan, Jewish, and Christian groups share some customs, formulas, and decorations. The curse against the tomb violater, for example, appears in all three kinds of burials, differing only in who will punish the wrong-doer. Grave goods appear across the Roman world. References to Hades, the resurrection of the righteous, and the God of Hosts appear in the same inscription. In another, the Furies and Pluto in the underworld appear above the phrase "Christians for Christians." Only ossuaries seem to be a distinctively Jewish burial custom.

Our expectation that material evidence would show communities distinguished by belief in resurrection has not been fulfilled by the evidence. One kind of expression, for resurrection or against, does not typify one community over another.[50] In fact, quite the opposite happens. Social, doctrinal, and religious conflicts, so evident in written documents, are not mirrored by material evidence. Social, doctrinal, and religious conflicts are bleached out in burial inscriptions and customs. Death, if anything, seemed to obscure differences and show

---

[50] Rutgers, "Interaction"; M. Johnson, "Pagan-Christian Burial Practices."

more evidence of interaction and shared customs between groups, different kinds of Jews, Jews and Christians, Christians and pagans. As M. Johnson puts it for one instance, "the 'conflict' of pagans and Christians ended at the grave."[51] So, too, did conflicts over belief in resurrection of the body. The material evidence points us in the other direction, towards a picture of a generalized Roman culture, in the face of which certain groups felt compelled to distinguish themselves by defending, in their writing and preaching, their distinctive teaching of resurrection.

---

[51] M. Johnson, "Pagan-Christian Burial Practices," 59.

# CHAPTER SEVEN

# THE GROWTH OF RESURRECTION APOLOGETIC

## *Irenaeus*

Irenaeus, in his *Against Heresies*, articulates who his opponents are, why they have it wrong, and why resurrection of the flesh is crucial to Christian faith. Irenaeus directs his refutation primarily against the disciples of Valentinus, a leading gnostic teacher at Rome, but he also mentions Marcion and many others, claiming to refute all heresies at once (*Haer.* 2.31.1).[1] He does not limit himself to name-calling, but engages the particulars of gnostic and Marcionite belief systems.

Writing from Lyons around 180, he has become bishop after the martyrdom of the previous bishop and other Christians in 177. Martyrdom, as our other sources show, stimulates resurrection belief. His arguments are not purely situational, however, but part of a broader development of a resurrection apologetic that begins in first-century Judaism, and gathers strength in early Christian writers and apologists of the second century and early third century. He amplifies and theologizes a pre-existing resurrection apologetic, forging a response to perceived threats from heretical teachings.

Two classic themes associated with resurrection belief are profoundly nuanced by Irenaeus, the nature of God as powerful creator and the unity of the human being. He reflects on problems inherent to resurrection belief, such as change which brings death and decomposition, the connection between God and nature's laws, and the aim of history. As always, the correct interpretation of Scripture is a locus of argument. He meets the challenge of Paul's statement in 1 Cor 15:50: "flesh and blood cannot inherit the kingdom of God, nor the corruptible inherit the incorruptible."

Pagels has argued that the development of resurrection belief is part of the development of a monepiscopate that stresses apostolic

---

[1] Irenaeus relies on a lost work of Justin to refute pre-Valentinian groups, citing him in 4.6.2.

succession. Authority flows from the small group of people who saw the resurrected Jesus and its chosen successors.[2] Groups like Valentinians or others who claim direct experience of the Savior are invalid. So the stress on bodily resurrection is bound up with a closing of the ranks and development of orthodoxy.

While this view may hold for the question of Jesus' bodily resurrection, it does not necessarily follow for the belief in the eventual bodily resurrection of all believers, an event yet to occur. While bodily resurrection is a natural conclusion from the belief in Jesus' bodily resurrection, it is not a necessary one. As 1 Cor 15:3–7 shows, the earliest creedal proclamation did not contain it. Paul must make the case for the connection between Jesus' resurrection and that of believers in 15:12–13. One could hold the first idea without the second. So the stress on resurrection belief for the believer is not necessarily aimed at sidelining heterodox groups based on apostolic succession. I would argue that these groups are sidelined because their rejection of resurrection entails the rejection of a constellation of crucial beliefs.

Gérard Valée notes that Irenaeus is not uniformly threatening to those who disagree with him. He takes a relatively tolerant view of *lapsi* and Montanists. Nor does he attack the Empire or paganism directly. The gnostic groups come in for censure, he argues, because of their dualism, their two-tiered scheme rejecting the unity of God, creation, and humanity.[3] Other parts of their system, such as their emanationist scheme, are unremarkable to Irenaeus.

### Hypothesis: The Unity of God

Resurrection of the flesh, taken up in book 5, plays a role in three themes dear to Irenaeus: his ὑπόθεσις of the unity of God as powerful creator; the οἰκονομία, the economy or plan of salvation, where Irenaeus accounts for the troubling process of change; and ἀνακεφαλαίωσις recapitulation, the summing up of all history in Jesus and the participation of believers in that history.[4]

---

[2] Pagels, *Gnostic Gospels*, 10–27.
[3] Gérard Valée, *A Study in Anti-Gnostic Polemics* (Waterloo, Ontario: Wilfred Laurier, 1981) 25–30.
[4] Robert Grant identifies three rhetorical strategies that Irenaeus inherited and theologized: ὑπόθεσις, plot or structure; οἰκονομία, arrangement of plot; and ἀνακε-

Irenaeus claims to undercut the ground of all heresies in his attack on the Valentinian system. They all make the fatal error of separating God from creation (*Haer.* 2.31.1). The unity of God as creator is a major emphasis of Book 2, and, some argue, the central theme of the work.[5] Against gnostic dualism, Irenaeus argues that God is inseparable into aeons, pleromas, godheads: "It must be either that there is one Being who contains all things, and formed in his own territory all those things which have been created, according to his own will; or again, that there are numerous unlimited creators and gods, who begin from each other, and end in each other on every side" (*Haer.* 2.1.5; 2.13.3; 2.13.8; 2.28.4).[6]

The themes of God's power and goodness are embedded in the notion of God as Creator, existing above Nature, capable of creating and re-creating bodies (*Haer.* 2.29.1). Irenaeus is highly repetitive, citing throughout the book the principles of God's oneness, uniqueness, and power as creator, citing the expression "he contains all things, but he himself can be contained by no one," "enclosing, but not enclosed."[7] That God is a god of power is shown in the feat of resurrection. Yet Creation is the greater feat:

> Those men, therefore, set aside the power of God, and do not consider what the word declares, when they dwell upon the infirmity of the flesh, but do not take into consideration the power of him who raises it from the dead. For if he does not vivify what is mortal, and does not bring back the corruptible to incorruption, he is not a God of power. But that he is powerful in all these respects, we ought to perceive from our origin, inasmuch as God, taking dust from the earth, formed humans (*Haer.* 5.3.2).

---

φαλαίωσις, concluding summary. Irenaeus turns these strategies to mean the rule of truth, God's plan of salvation, and Jesus as the recapitulation of all history (*Irenaeus of Lyons* [Routledge: New York, 1997] 47–51).

[5] Richard Norris, "The Transcendance and Freedom of God: Irenaeus, the Greek Tradition, and Gnosticism," *Early Christian Literature and the Classical Intellectual Tradition*, ed. William Schoedel and Robert Wilken (Paris: Beauchesne, 1979) 88; Denis Minns, *Irenaeus* (Washington, D.C.: Georgetown University, 1994) x.

[6] Translation from Alexander Roberts and James Donaldson, eds., *The Ante-Nicene Fathers* (1885–1887. 10 vols.; repr. Grand Rapids: Eerdmans, 1985).

[7] William Schoedel shows that Irenaeus, in using the formula for God that he is "enclosing, but not enclosed" against gnostic dualism, uses a term from Xenophanes, also employed by the Valentinians: "'Enclosing, but not Enclosed:' The Early Christian Doctrine of God," in Schoedel and Wilken, *Christian Literature and Classical Tradition*, 77–81.

Irenaeus lauds the work of creation, bringing forth the familiar argument that resurrection is mere re-creation, hardly implausible in the
light of the first creation. He remarks on another now-familiar theme,
the wonder of the body in all its parts and functions, as evidence
of God's intelligence: "but those things which partake of the wisdom
and skill of God, do also partake of his power" (*Haer.* 5.3.2). He
links the argument from creation, the lauding of the body's remarkable qualities, and the assertion of God's power. He avoids the idea
that creation, or nature, *is* God.[8]

## Body, Soul, and Spirit

Irenaeus continues the line of thought apparent in Justin and
Athenagoras, that for justice to prevail, body and soul must be
reunited after death so the whole person can be judged. He moves
beyond this simple idea, however, adding dimension and depth to
the argument, and meets squarely the New Testament verse most
problematic for bodily resurrection, 1 Cor 15:50: "Flesh and blood
cannot inherit the kingdom of God, nor does the perishable inherit
the imperishable."

A certain dichotomy between body and soul is assumed in this
work. Souls can exist apart from the body, but are created by God,
not pre-existent (2.34.1–2). The perfect human is a co-mingling of
the body and soul, both receiving the spirit (5.6.1). The flesh is inferior, but can be saved and changed by the spirit. Because he believes
in change, the unfolding plan of salvation, Irenaeus argues that the
flesh will yet be irradiated by the spirit with incorruption and immortality, a notion more theologically nuanced than simply arguing body
and soul need reunification for reward and punishment:

> . . . What is strong will prevail over the weak, so that the weakness of
> the flesh will be absorbed by the strength of the Spirit . . . For when
> the infirmity of the flesh is absorbed, it exhibits the Spirit as power-
> ful; and again when the Spirit absorbs the weakness [of the flesh] it
> possesses the flesh as an inheritance in itself, and from both of these
> is formed a living man, living indeed because he partakes of the Spirit,
> but man because of the substance of flesh (5.9.2).

---

[8] Norris says that for Irenaeus, a key idea is God's freedom and authority over
nature and history. Redemption is not a matter of nature or necessity, but a result
of God's powerful actions ("Transcendence," 99).

To claim the essential dignity of the body, Irenaeus brings two power-ful proofs—Jesus' incarnation and resurrection: "Now God shall be glorified in his handiwork (body) fitting it so as to be conformable to, and modeled after his own son (5.6.1) . . . if the flesh were not in a position to be saved, the Word of God would have in no wise become flesh" (5.14.1). The disciples received their bodies back, and rose bodily, just as their master arose, so too will believers be raised up by God's power (5.31.2). Irenaeus marshals a series of proofs from Scripture for bodily resurrection, including Lazarus being raised in the flesh (5.13.1), the suffering of the martyrs in the body requir-ing their reward in the body (5.9.2; 5.32.1), Abel's blood calling out from the ground for justice (5.14.1), the more obvious cases like Isa 26:19 or Ezek 37:1, or Jesus' prediction that he would drink the blood of the new covenant in the kingdom (5.33).

To counter the obvious stumbling block of 1 Cor 15:50, he brings a string of ingenious arguments and proof-texts in 5.9–12. First, he assumes that a human being is made up of three things, flesh, soul, and spirit. The soul falls between the flesh and spirit, sometimes leaning towards the body, sometimes towards the spirit. Yet the soul is by nature superior and stronger, so it overwhelms and absorbs the flesh. Paul statement means that the flesh by itself, without the life-giving spirit, cannot inherit the kingdom (5.9.2–3). Or, he argues, the flesh does not inherit, but is inherited by the spirit (5.9.4). Alternately, Paul means if one lives as if one is *only* flesh and blood, doing the works of the flesh, he will not inherit the kingdom. Similarly, mere flesh and blood cannot inherit, but must first put on immor-tality (5.10.2). The body contains within it corruption and incor-ruption, death and life, but in Irenaeus's theology of change and the economy of salvation, corruption must give way to incorruption, death to life (5.12.1). He argues that it is not flesh and blood that cannot inherit the kingdom, but the *works* of flesh and blood: car-nality, "carnal deeds, which, perverting man to sin, deprive him of life" (5.14.4). What may inherit is the flesh made new by spirit, the body and soul of the resurrected body. He inventively uses the para-ble of the lost sheep to show that the same substance that dies must be the same substance that is raised, just as one who is lost is the same one who is found (5.12.3).

Even less predictable is the use of the olive tree analogy from Romans 11 to explain the joining of spirit and flesh. The wild olive, if successfully grafted to the "good" olive tree, produces good fruit, though its own substance as a wild olive tree does not change. Similarly, the flesh grafted onto the spirit remains flesh, but is transformed, "so also when man, is grafted in by faith and receives the Spirit of God, he certainly does not lose the substance of flesh, but changes the quality of the fruit of his works, and receives another name, showing he has become changed for the better, being now not only flesh and blood, but a spiritual man" (5.10.2). So the survival of the body is not because of its own properties, but because of God's saving actions, its nurture by God over its nature: "Our bodies are raised not from their own substance, but by the power of God" (5.6.2).

Flesh as flesh, though subordinate to the spirit, is capable of being transformed so it may inherit the kingdom. Though Irenaeus maintains the difference between the body, soul, and spirit, he retains the value of the body as God's creation, capable of being infused by the spirit as part of the divine plan.

*Economy*

Change would seem to be the ultimate victor over the flesh, propelling the body towards death and decomposition. Yet Irenaeus incorporates change into his argument against his opponents over resurrection of the body. The olive tree analogy relies on the process of growth and nurture over time. The idea that the body encompasses both corruption and incorruption, and that the former must give way to the latter, relies on transformation and change. Irenaeus promotes a divine economy, a plan of unfolding redemption, that accounts for change (1.10.2; 3.19.2; 4.33.1). All of Scripture attests to it. He argues that there are four covenants in the history of salvation with Adam, Noah, Moses, and in Jesus' incarnation, each representing progress towards perfection (3.11.8). Humans are not created perfect, but move towards perfection, just as redemption moves according to plan. Resurrection serves a purpose in this plan by demonstrating what humans are released from, and by whose power they are released:

> This, therefore, was the [object of the] long-suffering of God, that man, passing through all things, and acquiring the knowledge of moral discipline, then attaining to the resurrection from the dead, and *learning by experience what is the source of his deliverance*, may always live in a state of gratitude . . . while he also understands about God that he is

immortal and powerful to such a degree as to confer immortality on
what is mortal, and eternity on what is temporal (3.20.2).

In this way, he meets the problem of change, which stands behind
the inevitable death and decay of the body, showing that God's
actions move the plan of salvation along.

## Recapitulation

Recapitulation, the summing up of an argument in rhetoric, becomes
an expansive theological concept in *Against Heresies*, an axis of Irenaeus'
system. All things temporal and spatial, visible and invisible, are
summed up, reconciled in Christ. Temporally, all of history is
redeemed, "the whole history of salvation is resumed, so that beginning, middle, and end are brought together" (3.24.1).[9] All of scripture points to the rendering of all to immortality. From it he proves
that bodies are kept in waiting until they can be raised. The pro-
tracted ages of the patriarchs show bodily life comes from God's
will. The experiences of Enoch, Elijah, and Paul show that God can
take up his loved ones in their earthly bodies, and translate them
to immortality: "Those translated remain until the consummation [of
all things] as a prelude to immortality" (5.5.1). Irenaeus' confidence
in this process is based on God's power:

> So also now, although some, not knowing the power and promise of
> God, may oppose their own salvation, deeming it impossible for God,
> who raises up the dead; to have power to confer upon them eternal
> duration, yet the skepticism of men of this stamp shall not render the
> faithfulness of god of none effect (5.5.2).

## Summary

Irenaeus' treatment of resurrection serves his larger themes, and in
discussing it he often teases out ideas of the relationship between
body and soul, the role of the Spirit, and the emphasis on God's
unity, goodness, and power, manifest in creation. He presents a
sophisticated response to the challenge of 1 Cor 15:50, a verse
exploited by opponents, by taking the problem of change and emphasizing its role in God's plan of salvation. While recognizing a basic

---

[9] Eric Osborn, *Irenaeus of Lyons* (Cambridge: Cambridge University, 2001) 116.

dividedness of flesh and spirit, he promotes the dignity of the flesh and its participation in salvation. He is innovative in his use of verses not used in other earlier sources to defend resurrection, such as the wild olive tree analogy or the parable of the lost sheep. In part, Irenaeus is provoked by his opponents, but he also demonstrates the growing sophistication of a Christian resurrection apologetic.

For all of Irenaeus' creativity, his arguments betray the remarkable stability of certain ideas attached to resurrection, the extent to which resurrection is already part of a fixed network of ideas. He employs sources like Justin and Polycarp, amplifying some of their ideas, while ignoring others.

Most prominent is the argument for resurrection from creation, the notion that re-creation from decayed bodies is not as remarkable as the original act of creation. God is a God of power, and the proof-text is creation. This is fundamental to every text, Jewish and Christian, that we have examined. Mutatis mutandis, Irenaeus would not have disagreed with the rabbis who formed the Mishnah in *Sanhedrin 10.1* nor hesitated to affirm the *mehayyeh hametim* blessing.

Similarly, Irenaeus keeps intact the belief in the unity of the body and soul. His understanding, with the notion of a flesh enlivened by the spirit, is considerably more complex than earlier versions; but he maintains the imperative that the body and soul together represent the human person, and must, as a matter of reason and justice, be saved together.

The dignity of the flesh and a form of optimism about bodily life pervades Irenaeus. Those who despise the flesh despise God's handiwork. This idea is present in earlier works such as Justin's *On the Resurrection* and Athenagoras, representing a contrast with pagan attitudes apparent in Celsus and Minucius Felix. Here, the praise of the body is expansive, no doubt in response to claims of his "heretics."

Resurrection is proved from Scripture, and legitimacy belongs to those who interpret it correctly. Irenaeus is anxious to link it to the theme of God's oneness. Against competing views, the God who is Creator, is the God of the Hebrew Scriptures and of Jesus, is transcendant, and is the God who will raise up believers: "We at once perceive that the creator is in this passage (Ezek 37:12) represented as vivifying our dead bodies, and promising resurrection to them, and resuscitation from their sepulchers and tombs, conferring upon them immortality also (He says, 'For as the tree of life, so shall their days be' [Isa 65:22]), he is shown to be the only God who accomplishes these things, and as himself the good Father, benevolently conferring life upon those who have not life from themselves" (5.15.1). After a series of proofs of humanity's creation from earth, he declares that he has trumped the Valentinians' image of human origins: "All the followers of Valentinus, therefore, lose their case, when they say that man was not fashioned out of this earth, but from a fluid and diffused substance" (5.15.4). "Is he some unknown one and a Father who gives no commandment to anyone? Or is he the God who is proclaimed in the Scriptures, to whom we were debtors?" (5.17.1). Irenaeus presents an extensive number of passages to support resurrection, not only obvious ones like Ezekiel and Isaiah, but the man blind from birth, the wild olive tree grafted on to the good one, and the parable of the lost sheep (5.15.2). He also makes clear that only those who share the idea of the powerful Creator God who encloses all things but is not enclosed, truly understand Scripture's testimony.

### Tertullian

Resurrection apologetic found an intense advocate in the Latin West in Tertullian of Carthage. He defends the belief in three chapters at the end of *The Apology* and in a long treatise, *The Resurrection of the Dead*, a sequel to *The Flesh of Christ*. *The Apology* is officially addressed to the local officials of the Roman administration. The other two books are addressed to other Christians who deny the reality of Christ's flesh and his resurrection, and by extension reject the resurrection in the flesh of believers.

Tertullian's extended argument and use of rhetoric has invited much discussion of structure and his debt to forms of Greco-Roman rhetoric. Rhetorical criticism is a natural and useful way to look at Tertullian, and considerable work has centered on which rhetorical devices and structures he uses,[10] as well as discussions of his relative

---

[10] On the structure of *Apol.*, see Robert Sider, who argues for a thematic symmetry: "On Symmetrical Composition in Tertullian," *JTS* 24 (1973) 405–23. For a discussion of *Apol.* as a model forensic argument, as well as the place of the final three chapters, which include the discussion of resurrection, see Richard Heinze, *Tertullians Apologeticum* (Teubner: Leipzig, 1910) 281. G. Eckert sees the legal setting of *Apol.* as a fiction, and the last three chapters as the goal of the work, providing admonition to Christians facing persecution (*Orator Christianus* [Stuttgart: Steiner, 1993]). For the form of *Res.*, see Robert Sider, "Structure and Design in the 'De Resurrectione Mortuorum' of Tertullian," *VC* 23 (1969) 177–96; T. D. Barnes

debt to the Second Sophistic[11] or traditions of Latin declamation[12] and/or his attitude towards philosophy.[13] He identifies his opponents, so extended speculation on their identity seems unnecessary.

These studies have been helpful in showing Tertullian's debt to classical culture, even while he protests his distance from it. However, I am interested in the broader question of Tertullian's overall rhetorical strategies. How does he contribute to the growth of a Christian resurrection apologetic, using traditions that come to him already well-formed, while adding his own skill in classical rhetoric? How has he contributed to the development of what Foucault has called a "totalizing discourse?"[14] How has he contributed to the overall feat Cameron identifies as Christians "talking their way into Empire?"[15]

The question of why resurrection is so crucial to Tertullian is clear when we see that he invokes the same set of corollaries evident in earlier Jewish and Christian believers in bodily resurrection. The doctrine of bodily resurrection is by now a highly developed condensation symbol for a wide set of Christian ideas. Keith Hopkins suggests that faith statements were particularly useful for Christians at this stage. Their numbers have been exaggerated for this early

---

identifies rhetorical figures in *Res.*, such as a long *praemunitio* that disposes of objections and prepares his audience; a standard *confirmatio*, or bringing of proofs; an *amplificatio*, or emphasis of the topic; and *peroratio*, or summing up (*Tertullian: A Historical and Literary Study* [Oxford: Clarendon, 1971] 208–10). Robert Sider identifies Tertullian's use of received rhetorical forms, in his *Ancient Rhetoric and the Art of Tertullian* (London: Oxford University Press, 1971) 124–25.

[11] Barnes, *Tertullian*, 189, 213–16.

[12] George Kennedy argues that the Latin Fathers did not adopt much of the imitative style of the Second Sophistic, which was nostalgic about ancient Greek culture and philosophy. Tertullian is more in the tradition of Latin oratory. Rhetoric and philosophy, notes Kennedy, were often at odds with each other, rhetoric accused of pompous irrelevance and philosophy suspected of being subversive (*A New History of Classical Rhetoric* [Princeton: Princeton University 1994] 260–64). Sider points to the standard training in rhetoric of Tertullian's day, which relied on Aristotle, Cicero, and Quintilian (*Ancient Rhetoric*, 11–20).

[13] Traditionally, scholars have regarded Tertullian as opposed to philosophy, but recent scholars like Fredouille argue his affinity for philosophy. See Jean Claude Fredouille, *Tertullien et la conversion de la culture antique* (Paris: Études Augustiniennes, 1972) 337–57; Paolo Sinascalco, "Recenti studi su Tertulliano," *RSLR* 14 (1978) 396–405; and Eric Osborn, "Was Tertullian a Philosopher?" *StPatr* 31 (1997) 322–34. One who disagrees is Wendy Helleman, "Tertullian on Athens and Jerusalem," *Hellenization Revisited*, ed. Wendy Helleman (Lanham, Md.: University Press of America, 1994) 363–81.

[14] Cited in *Christianity and the Rhetoric of Empire* (Berkeley: University of California, 1991) 58.

[15] Cameron, *Christianity and Rhetoric*, 14.

period, he argues, and Christians were concentrated in small cells around the Mediterranean. Faith issues were efficient ways to encapsulate the values of the group for these small, scattered cells which had few literate members, but absorbed outsiders as new members at a rapid rate.[16] Faith statements, as opposed to learning a new life style, were useful for defining group membership and easy assimilation of newcomers.

Hopkins further notes the role of dogma as affording special status to those who could expound or defend these beliefs. This fits with another trend we have uncovered throughout our literature: the legitimacy claimed by or attributed to those who promote resurrection of the body.

### The Apology

The general tenor of *The Apology* promotes the inclusion of Christianity in the larger culture.[17] Christians are not only harmless, but compatible with the best in Roman culture. Tertullian does not introduce resurrection till the end of the work (48–50), perhaps because it sounds strangest to pagan ears. He uses the word "resurrection" infrequently here, and never uses "resurrection of the flesh" at all. Chapters 46–50 take up the case against philosophy, and depart from the standard form of argument. Whether it is a *peroratio*, or summary of the argument, or a self-standing unit,[18] Tertullian chooses to leave his hearers with the doctrine of the resurrection and its essential difference from the dictums of philosophy.

Tertullian weds classical rhetorical forms to the standard themes of resurrection apologetic, arguments from creation, God's power, the unity of body and soul, a correct interpretation of Scripture, and the legitimacy of those who teach it. In 48.5–7, he argues for the materiality of the resurrection by arguing from the creation of the individual: "You were nothing before you came into being; you become nothing when you have ceased to be; why could you not again come out of nothing into being, by the will of the very same Author whose will brought you into being out of nothing?" Along

---

[16] Keith Hopkins, "Christian Number and Its Implications," *JECS* 6 (1998) 185–226.

[17] All translations of *The Apology* from *Tertullian* (trans. T. R. Glover, LCL).

[18] Eckert, *Orator Christianus*, 178–79.

the way he seems to tweak the pagans for their common funerary inscription, "I was not [before birth], I was, I am not [now that I am dead], I don't care." Tertullian turns it around, saying, "What will be new in your experience (at resurrection)? You were not; you were made; and once again when you are not, you will be made (48.6)."

The argument from creation is part of the argument from God's power, normally the first element in earlier defenses of resurrection. Tertullian wastes no time in bringing it forward, indulging in some sarcasm at the same time, "Your doubts, I suppose, will be about the power of God? Of God, who set together the mighty frame of this universe out of what was not . . ., as if out of the deadness of emptiness and chaos, who gave it the breath of life by that spirit, which gives life to all lives, who sealed it to be itself a testimony for you, a type of human resurrection" (48.7). After accomplishing the creation of the individual and the universe, the re-creation of a person is comparatively easy. No pagan who accepts the notion of one God would argue against his power.[19] Celsus, for example, argues it is beneath God's dignity or willingness to concern himself with fleshly matters or go against his own laws, but not beneath his power.

Tertullian's famous question, "What has Athens to do with Jerusalem?" (*Praesc. Haer.* 7.10) suggests he views revelation and reason as utterly at odds with each other. Yet in this chapter, he argues first for resurrection from the standpoint of revelation, but then moves to the argument from reason. He cites nature as proof of resurrection: the cycle of night and day, the cycle of the seasons, the seed which is dissolved in order to grow into a plant (48.8). He invokes the dictum of Pythia, the Delphic priestess, to understand oneself.

Tertullian privileges the knowledge that comes from revelation, but shows he can compete in the arena of reason. He wants to maintain difference and, at the same time, use the proof-texts of the natural world and reason. His rhetoric and knowledge of Greco-Roman ways of thinking are tools he uses ultimately against the culture, both proving his point about resurrection; but he also asserts the superiority of arguments from faith. He uses but defuses pagan ways. Cameron suggests this is typical of the earliest Christian rhetoric, from Paul to Augustine, that "deploys every technique of the art of

---

[19] See the discussion of pagan monotheism in the chapter on pagan objections to Christian preaching of the resurrection.

eloquence, even while concluding that the conditions for truth must lie elsewhere."[20]

In his arrangement of arguments, Tertullian implies the argument from nature and reason is secondary to the argument from God's power in creation. He begins here to imply quietly what he will proclaim loudly at the end: the essential difference between Christian faith and philosophy and, by extension, the value-system of the empire. His final statement makes the point: "There is a rivalry between God's ways and humanity's; we are condemned by you, we are absolved by God" (50.16).

The underscoring of difference, says Cameron, was a useful rhetorical device, that accomplished two things. It allowed thinkers like Tertullian to compete with the best of classical culture, while not being swallowed up by it. Christianity could be argued as the ideal philosophy, but at the same time not just one more philosophy to be folded into the public milieu.

Tertullian further unfolds the theme of difference in 48.14–15, where, having just argued that resurrection is apparent to all in the workings of the universe, he insists that in matters of reward and punishment, there is a distinction between truths apparent on the surface and hidden truths:

> The philosophers know the distinction between mysterious and common fire. The fire that serves humanity's use is one thing; the fire that ministers to the judgment of God is another, whether flashing the thunderbolts from heaven, or rushing up from the earth through the mountain-tops . . . he who is touched by fire from heaven, is safe—no fire will turn him to ashes. Take this as evidence for fire eternal, this as a type of endless judgment with punishment ever renewing. The mountains burn and endure. What of the guilty, what of God's enemies?

This example serves to show another rhetorical device of Christian discourse particularly congenial to Tertullian: the love of paradox. Using paradox allowed writers to wrest virtue and glory for the faith from their unpopularity, persecution, and suspect quality. Tertullian recounts the suffering of Christians at the hands of the vulgar crowds (49.4, 6). Like Athenagoras, he implies only the vulgar rabble dislike and hound Christians, a patently untrue statement. But the difference between the apparent and the hidden shows that the power is really in the hands of the Christians. The paradox is that Christians

---

[20] Cameron, *Christianity and Rhetoric*, 35.

control the situation, deciding if they choose to be condemned or not: "You can only condemn me if I wish to be condemned. When your power is thus against me, only at my will, it is no power at all (so) your power depends on my will, not on power in you. Similarly, the joy of the rabble in our persecution is not a real joy; the joy they count theirs is ours, who prefer to be condemned rather than to fall from God" (49.5–6). Tertullian's statements would apply to any political dissident, who chooses dissent knowing the possible consequences.

Tertullian further underscores the defeat that is really a victory by bringing out language and symbols of Roman military victory and claiming them for the Christians—the robe with the palm[21] and the triumphal chariot. Similarly, he invokes martyrs of the Greco-Roman world, whose suffering is recalled as their glory (50.5–9, 14). Tertullian goes back to claiming the heroes of the surrounding culture, while arguing Christian distance from its values. He further makes a virtue of paradox in his well-known statement that trying to wipe out Christians by torture and death accomplishes the opposite and wins more to the faith: "We multiply whenever we are mown down by you; the blood of Christians is seed" (50.13).

The final paradox is that pagans too try to give their martyr-heroes a kind of resurrection in casting statues of them or carving inscriptions of their achievements. Christians hope for a genuine resurrection from God and are counted fools for it (50.11). Tertullian offers a fairly shaky comparison here, since keeping up the memory and bodily resurrection are hardly the same; but this comparison is another example of his claiming superiority to paganism on its own plane, while emphasizing fundamental difference. He again exploits the difference between the apparent and the hidden, the apparent immortality of pagan martyrs in public memory versus the hidden future resurrection cherished by Christians.

## The Resurrection of the Dead

The sequel to *The Flesh of Christ*, which answered those who denied the bodily incarnation and resurrection of Jesus, *The Resurrection of the Dead* answers those who deny the bodily resurrection of believers. While the rhetorical forms of *The Apology* are relatively clear,

---

[21] See Livy, 10.7; 30.15 for the *tunica palmata* as a robe of triumph.

more ambiguity about rhetorical forms exists here. Tertullian's argument is choppy and full of asides. His inheritance of well-developed themes of resurrection apologetic may intrude on the neat structures of rhetoric that he knows well. Moreover, giving too much attention to specific rhetorical devices distracts from the overall rhetorical effect. As Kennedy notes, declaimers often veered from formal argumentation and substituted ethos, pathos, and general hyperbole,[22] techniques liberally applied by Tertullian.

Because Tertullian engages in an extremely extended discourse in this work, I have chosen only three chapters (3, 16, and 22) to elucidate his rhetorical strategy. He refers to opponents and heretics early in the work; and in both this and *Carn. Christ.*, names Marcion, Apelles, Basilides, and Valentinus, as well as their followers, as his targets.[23]

As in *The Apology*, Tertullian uses the strategy of proving his case from popular ideas—what most would call "common sense"—from nature, and from philosophy: "Now it is possible even on the basis of popular ideas to be knowledgeable in the things of God, though for evidence of the truth, not in support of falsehood, to establish what is in accordance with the divine ordinance, not what is opposed to it. For some things are known even by nature, as is the immortality of the soul among many people and as is our God among all. Consequently I shall use the pronouncement of one Plato who declares, 'All soul (or every person) is immortal'" (*Res.* 3.1–2; CCSL 2.924).[24]

In other words, he can prove resurrection of the flesh from ideas and forms held dear by the Roman world, but the conditions for truth lie elsewhere. He strains for congruence, since Plato's dictum surely refers to spiritual immortality. But to the extent that popular or philosophical ideas support resurrection, he will use them. Yet they are minor supports. He uses, then defuses them, turning against them because of their vulgar origins, "the heart of the world is reckoned by God as ashes, and the very wisdom of the world is declared foolishness" (*Res.* 3.3; CCSL 2. 924).

As earlier, Tertullian claims the wisdom of the pagan world, but then asserts the superiority of Christian truth. He emphasizes fundamental difference; Christians are by nature unlike the rest of the

---

[22] Kennedy, *History of Rhetoric*, 170.
[23] See appendix on the Nag Hammadi documents.
[24] Edition and translation of *The Resurrection of the Dead* by Ernest Evans (London: SPCK, 1960). He, like some others, refers to it as *The Resurrection of the Flesh*.

world. Addressing a "heretic," he argues, "So long as you regard yourself as a Christian, you are a different man from the Gentile; give him back his own ideas, for neither does he equip himself with yours (3.3)." A series of metaphors follow: for example, why would one who sees lean on a blind guide, one who has put on Christ take clothing from one who is naked, one armed by the apostle use another man's shield? "Rather let that man learn from you to confess the resurrection of the flesh than you from him to discredit it."

Heretics, he argues, have borrowed ideas from non-Christians and been led astray by them. To be a Christian is to believe in resurrection, "thus one cannot be a Christian who denies that which Christians confess (resurrection), and denies it by arguments that non-Christians use" (3.5). By this point, the wisdom of the world, *vulgi ignorantia*, is antithetical to a Christians's own knowledge, *sua scientia*. In 1.1 he claims resurrection of the flesh draws a line between insiders and outsiders. Without it, one is not a Christian: "The resurrection of the dead is the confidence of Christians. By it we are believers" (*Res.* 1.1; CCSL 2.921).

Proofs from Scripture trump all other forms of argument. If one took away from the heretics all their "Gentile" arguments and forced them to argue from Scripture alone, he claims, they would be unable to make their case against resurrection of the flesh (3.6). So difference is expounded via resurrection, to assert the final superiority of scripture over other forms of knowledge.

He rejects the popular or common by asserting the paradox between truth that is apparent to all and the superior truth that is hidden. Some ideas are popular because they are simple, congenial, familiar, and seem to work on the superficial level: "They define things that are exposed and open and generally recognized; divine reason is in the marrow, not on the surface, and often rivals things as they appear" (3.6). As he did in *The Apology*, Tertullian has moved from an argument of congruence, maintaining that elements of worldly wisdom such as nature, philosophy, and common knowledge attest to resurrection, to an argument of antithesis. Hidden, divine truth is opposed to the truths that appear on the surface. The paradoxical nature of resurrection, its lack of empirical support, is in fact its strength. Belief in resurrection is for Tertullian the marker for a genuine Christian and a guarantee against heresy. It expresses the profound and hidden element of difference, that by which Christians identify themselves and hold the empire and its modes of thought at arm's length.

In chapter 16, Tertullian turns his attention to the unity of body and soul in resurrection. Others argue that the flesh is not even the servant of the soul, since even a servant has free choice and is held responsible for his actions. Rather, they argue, the flesh is like a receptacle (16.1–2; CCSL 2.939). No one judges a cup guilty because someone put poison in it, or a sword because someone committed robbery with it. Similarly, the flesh is innocent of any wrongdoing which the soul made it perform (16.4–5; CCSL 2.939).

The assertion of the unity of body and soul for judgment is, we have seen in earlier sources, an essential component of the belief in resurrection and early Christian resurrection apologetic.[25] In the style of Roman declamation, with its love of speech and inventiveness, Tertullian takes the opponents' metaphors and turns them to his own advantage. He argues, for example, that a vessel does share guilt by association. No one would want a cup used for divination, for example: "... as for the cup, one tainted with the breath of a witch, or a sodomite or a gladiator or a hangman—I wonder if you would condemn it any less than those people's kisses? ... as for the sword that is drunken with murders, is there anyone who will not expel it from his whole house?" (16.6–7; CCSL 2.939). "A cup with a good conscience" carefully taken care of, or a sword that won battles, on the other hand, is made holy by use. Tertullian strains the metaphor here, perhaps loosely employing Hermagoras' stasis theory on legal questions, which examines who commits a crime, how, and under whose jurisdiction it falls.[26] He no doubt is responding to the critics of bodily resurrection, and shows the orator's inventive use of language. He invokes selected verses from Paul to prove the flesh's deserving of reward and punishment. No doubt Paul was the favorite of Tertullian's opponents, since he says flesh and blood cannot inherit the kingdom of God (1 Cor 15:50), and has a negative assessment of the flesh in Romans 7–8.

---

[25] The Rabbis worried about the same problem as Tertullian, at about the same time, and came to the same conclusion. For the question of the relative culpability of body and soul, see *Lev. Rab.* 4.8, discussed in Burton Visotzky, "The Priest's Daughter and the Thief in the Orchard," in Wiles, Brown, and Snyder, *Putting Body and Soul Together*, 165–71.

[26] Kennedy, *History of Rhetoric*, 97–101.

Cameron discusses the figural quality of earliest Christian writing. As often as not, writers communicated by way of symbols and signs as argumentation. I have argued throughout this work that resurrection functioned as a classic symbol, embodying a whole set of ideals and values. Writers further communicated by way of story, "providing a plot by which Christians could live out their lives." In chapter 22, Tertullian uses resurrection to fill out this plot, building an alternative universe in which a drama is presently unfolding. As Todd Klutz has put it, the power of the discourse of the earliest Christians was not so much their "capacity to explain the past accurately, but rather their ability to redescribe it persuasively."[27]

Tertullian's immediate problem is to answer those who argue that resurrection is already accomplished by virtue of becoming a Christian or those who argue that it happens immediately after death. He does so by weaving together biblical verses and proposing a sacred history, a history that is hidden from sight. This chronology trades on the difference between the apparent and the secret, providing an alternative plot to the outward success of the empire. He even uses the outward success of empire to prove his point, that Christian history has yet to finish its task.

Tertullian employs the parable of the fig tree in Luke 21:29–31, which says the kingdom is near but has not yet arrived, combined with Luke 21:31 and 21:36, which predicts one will stand before the Son of Man to prove resurrection: "When you have seen all these things come to pass, know that the kingdom of God is near. Watch at every season that you may be able to escape those things that will happen, and stand before the Son of Man—evidently by means of the resurrection, when all those things have previously been accomplished. This though in the acknowledgement of the pledge it comes to bud, yet it comes to flower and fruit at the Lord's actual presence" (22.8; CCSL 2.948). None of the many biblical predictions of the end of history have come to pass: the coming of Elijah, the fight from the Antichrist, the defeat of the enemies of Christ. It cannot be, says Tertullian, when the populace still cries out "Christians to the lions!" Those Christians who claim to have already experienced (spiritual) resurrection still suffer the pains of the body, and "wrestle with the rulers of this world" (22.11; CCSL 2.949).

---

[27] Todd Klutz, "The Rhetoric of Science in *The Rise of Christianity*: A Response to Rodney Stark's Sociological Account of Christianization," *JECS* 6 (1998) 184.

The knowledge of resurrection, he says is an oath, or pledge (*sacramentum*) which begins to bud, but will only come to full flower at the Lord's return. While the metaphors are mixed, we know what he means. The final culmination of history is yet to come and is hidden from the world.

In these three chapters are examples of Tertullian's broad rhetorical strategy. He uses the tools of formal rhetoric to present and further his resurrection apologetic. He exploits difference: between Christian and pagan, the knowledgeable few and the vulgar many, the hidden and the apparent, truth and heresy. He provides an alternative sacred chronology to replace what is apparent to the casual observer: that Christians are politically weak, small in number, and suffering from sporadic persecution. Resurrection is at the heart of his rhetorical strategy, the essence of this hidden, non-worldly wisdom known only to the few, carrying with it the essential elements of the Christian system. He can argue that it determines who is a genuine Christian and how one may be recognized.

CHAPTER EIGHT

CONCLUSIONS

While the roots of resurrection belief go back to Pharisaism, and ultimately to the Hebrew Bible, belief in resurrection of the body grows rapidly in the second century; it burgeons into an articulate resurrection apologetic among early Christians that presents an intellectually respectable front to the Greco-Roman world, but helps maintain a separate, distinctive identity. At the same time, a remarkable stability in the concepts associated with resurrection endures across Jewish and Christian works, from the Pharisees to Tertullian. Resurrection is more than a single, curious belief; it functions as a shorthand for an interlocking web of values, a condensation symbol that helps to construct community.

*Development of Resurrection Belief*

In the introduction to this book, I have argued that resurrection of the body has its roots in the Hebrew Bible in the implications of God's creation of the world and the human body, hints of afterlife belief in language and practices, and the uses of resurrection as figurative in Ezekiel, the Isaian apocalypse, and Daniel. Several scholars offer reasons for suppression of a more explicit concept of the afterlife and resurrection in ancient Israel.[1]

Martyrdom is a stimulus to resurrection belief in Judaism in its encounter with Hellenism, where the belief in the body's being raised up appears explicitly as a response to its destruction in 2 Maccabees 7 and 12.[2] But martyrdom is neither its single nor primary cause. It appears among the Pharisees as a preaching that distinguishes them from other sects. In Josephus's works and Acts, it resonates with the people and is linked to their popularity. Yet the Pharisees were no more physically threatened than other sects. The rabbis use

---

[1] See pp. 6–10.
[2] Van Henten, *Maccabean Martyrs*.

it in the Mishnah to distinguish who is faithful to the rabbinic program. In Jewish liturgy, it functions similarly as a public declaration of who belongs and who does not. Both seem aimed at threat to belief from within the community, not outside threats of execution. So in early Judaism, resurrection is useful primarily as a distinguishing marker between Jewish groups, promoting the movements that preached it, not simply as reassurance in the face of threat.

Paul uses it as the rabbis do, to define legitimacy within the group. Polycarp's *Letter to the Philippians, 2 Clement,* and scattered remarks in Ignatius's letters hint at its increasing significance as a boundary-marking concept. Furthermore, in Paul's use is the beginning of what will become a major Christian use of the doctrine. It is an answer to the encroachment of the larger society, a rejection of the values and power structure of empire. Christianity inherits the belief in resurrection and presents it in an intensified, apocalyptic form, amplifying its subversive quality.

A ramping up in intensity in the defense of resurrection occurs with the apologists, the flowering of a full-blown resurrection apologetic. Although Polycarp, Clement and Ignatius talk about resurrection and about flesh, Justin is the first to use the term "resurrection of the flesh." With Justin and Athenagoras, both the numbers of arguments and their levels of sophistication increase. These apologists confront the pagan intellectual challenge to resurrection belief, attempting to carve out a place in the larger society by importing its martyrs, rhetoric, and forms of argument. They answer political charges of atheism, incest, and cannibalism, as well as philosophical objections leveled by people like the pagan Celsus and the pagan interlocutor in Minucius Felix' *Octavius.* At the same time, these apologists maintain the uniqueness of Christian identity, its fundamental distance from the culture with which it competes. Tertullian similarly applies wholesale forms of rhetoric that defuse arguments against resurrection of the body, proving the belief in the arenas of reason and natural law, while denigrating the ultimate value of those forms of proof.

*Resurrection's Subversive Message*

While resurrection is not merely a response to persecution and martyrdom, nor is it a concept ever promoted by a group that is entirely at ease in society, or that wields absolute power. It is linked to nationalist aspirations as early as Ezekiel. Its first explicit appearance in 2 Maccabees is, as van Henten has shown, part of the drama of religio-political restoration of a Jewish way of life. While Josephus implies strong Pharisaic influence on the Hasmoneans, after 63 the Pharisees and their successors were under Roman occupation and subject to the vagaries of imperial patronage. Irenaeus, often cited as the architect of orthodoxy, takes up as bishop of Lyons after the martyrdom of the previous bishop and other Christians. Paul, Justin, Athenagoras, and Tertullian are openly at odds with the societies in which they live, despite their skill in using the rhetorical and philosophical tools of those societies.

The preaching of resurrection often goes hand in hand with a political agenda that resists the more powerful forces in the Roman world. The Pharisees, according to Josephus, and by implication, Acts, garnered popularity with the urban Jewish folk by preaching resurrection, situating themselves between the people and the local Roman bureaucrats, as what Saldarini has called "a literate retainer class."

Paul's preaching of resurrection is more openly resistant. Using the work of Horsley, Elliot, and others, I have placed resurrection within his preaching of an anti-imperial polemic. He overturns the conventional pyramid of power, placing the crucified criminal at the top instead of the emperor. The blessings normally bestowed by the emperor will soon flow from God to his believers. If Paul and his hearers now live in the beginning of the last act of history, resurrection of the body will be the final evidence that the power of Rome is broken.

Because the nature of apologetic literature prevents the two early apologists, Justin and Athenagoras, from open antagonism to Rome, they make the case for their essentially alien and subversive system to fit into the larger culture. Energetic, expansive, and imaginative, they use language and rhetoric congenial to paganism, arguments from reason and nature, and the values and heroes of the broader culture. Sporadic actions against Christians in Asia, Gaul, and North Africa in the following decades show their lack of success in the short term. They illustrate that apologetic literature is more compelling for insiders than outsiders.

Tertullian, in his *Apology*, like the apologists before him, employs the tools of classical rhetoric to argue that Christianity can compete with the best in Greco-Roman culture but poses no threat to it. Ultimately truth belongs to a different order and proof proceeds from revelation. Like Paul, he argues an essential difference between Christian faith and philosophy, and by extension, the values of empire. Like Paul, he uses symbols of Roman military might—the robe, the palm, and the triumphal chariot—and claims them for Christians. He exploits the difference between the apparent and the hidden, making a virtue of the paradox of Christianity's essential appropriateness in the culture, while claiming distance from it. Resurrection is the test case of the superiority of revelation over reason, Christian hope over philosophy.

The Christian documents we have considered show an elaborate, wholesale use of rhetoric to defend resurrection that is not in the Jewish materials. Josephus recommends the Pharisees as the most popular Jewish sect and packages their resurrection belief as compatible with Greco-Roman ideas of immortality; yet, with the exception of the anomalous *Against Apion*, Judaism is missing a self-conscious apologetic.[3] Language alone bars the Mishnah's pronouncements and liturgy from outsiders. Jews making a case with the Gentile world in mind, like Paul, Josephus, Matthew, and Philo, write in Greek. Similarly, the legal form of the Mishnah makes it irrelevant to non-Jews. Any heroes they cite come out of the Pharisaic and rabbinic tradition. Liturgy is by nature for insiders. Jews are an older, more recognizably distinct people than Christians with a particularist lifestyle. The rabbis, to the extent that they consider the outside world, generally highlight difference.[4] Christians, especially the apologists, highlight sameness as a strategy of arguing their political harmlessness. Despite the different directions they went in using resurrection belief, both early Jews and Christians are poised between the need to assert a separate, distinctive identity and the need to accommodate the surrounding society.

---

[3] The topic of Jewish apologetic is a source of debate between John J. Collins and Erich Gruen. See Collins, *Between Athens and Jerusalem* (2nd. ed.; Grand Rapids: Eerdmans, 1999) 14–16. Both agree that *Against Apion* is exceptional, but Collins points to the number of Jewish materials that promote Judaism to a larger society, even if they do not fit the formal category of apologetic. See also Gruen's "Greeks and Jews: Mutual Misperceptions in Josephus's *Conta Apionem*" in Carol Bakhos, ed., *Judaism in its Hellenistic Context*, *JSJSup*; Leiden: Brill (forthcoming).

[4] An example of this highlighting of difference is the early rabbinic attack on Epicureanism. See my article, "'Talking their Way into Empire': Pagans, Jews, and Christians Debate Resurrection of the Body," in Carol Bakhos, ed., *Judaism in its Hellenistic Context*, *JSJSup*; Leiden: Brill (forthcoming).

*Rhetorical Uses and Defenses of Resurrection*

Christian writers use the tools of rhetoric to argue for their belonging in the larger culture, while undermining its value at the same time. First, they appropriate the symbols of the dominant culture and, in a series of symbolic reversals, withdraw their value. In Paul's image of the victory procession in 1 Corinthians and his reversal of the pyramid of power, weakness becomes strength and martyrdom becomes victory. Justin argues the superiority of Moses to Homer; the value of the fleshly body not as the despised partner to the soul, but as God's handiwork; death as not blessed insensibility and the liberation from the body, but the initiating of a process of reward and punishment. Tertullian also imports symbols of the dominant culture. He employs military imagery, cribs from the Delphic priestess and Plato, mentions the custom of erecting statues to pagan martyr-heros and refers to the common pagan funerary inscription, and argues from reason and natural law. Then he declares their insignificance. Reason and natural law are inferior to revelation. Statues to heroes vainly mimic genuine resurrection. The common funerary inscription ("I was not, I was, I am not, I do not care") is turned on its head to proclaim its opposite, that one was made once and will be made again.

Christian apologists use other forms of argument beyond symbolic reversals, untroubled by their contradicting earlier arguments. Some use the device of association, incorporating themselves on the same side as the best of Greco-Roman culture. Athenagoras puts himself in league with the emperor, declaring them both to be servants of reason, and invokes the pagan martyrs as the same as the Christian ones, both martyrs to truth. Tertullian and others sometimes argue from congruence, that resurrection matches elements of worldly wisdom, such as nature, philosophy, and common practice.

These writers argue equally vigorously by antithesis. Divine truth is hidden, opposed to truths that appear on the surface. Both Athenagoras and Tertullian dissociate themselves from the vulgar masses, Athenagoras claiming only the "stupid crowds" oppose Christians, and Tertullian contrasting the *vulgi ignorantia*, the ignorance of the masses, with Christian understanding, *sua scientia*.

Irenaeus employs three common rhetorical strategies, using them to fashion an alternative, sacred history. *Hypothesis*, plot or structure in public rhetoric, becomes the rule of truth in Irenaeus' theology;

*oikonomia*, the arrangement of plot, becomes God's plan of salvation; and *anakephalaiôsis*, a concluding summary, becomes Jesus as the recapitulation of all history.

Through the appropriation of symbols from the Greco-Roman world, symbolic reversals of their hierarchy of values, and employment of standard rhetorical devices, these early Christian writers underscore fundamental differences and assert the ultimate, separate truth of Christian faith. A prime example of the process of undermining the culture while using its devices exists in the preaching of resurrection of the body, a concept that seems ridiculous and offensive to outsiders.

The discussion of our material evidence pointed to a generalized Roman culture in which both Jews and Christians participated. For our writers to accommodate it was essential, yet so, too, was the careful delineation of themselves from that culture, holding the Empire and its hierarchy at arm's length.

## *The Utility of Resurrection Belief*

The rapid growth in resurrection apologetic and increasing specificity in language, from "resurrection" to "resurrection of the body" to "resurrection of the flesh" in Christian circles, can be attributed to its greater utility for a growing church. Christians were a much smaller minority than Jews in the Mediterranean world,[5] existing in a network of small groups. Paul makes clear a lack of uniformity in practice and belief across churches in his time, and Justin, 100 years later, also alludes to differing forms of practice and belief. Hopkins makes the point that for Christians, absorbing new converts from a variety of backgrounds at a rapid rate, a set of faith statements serves as a helpful précis of group values and marker for who belongs in the group. Learning a new lifestyle, as the convert to Judaism must, takes relatively more time and acculturation. In time, Christians too were recognized by their lifestyle, particularly their refusal to sacrifice to the emperor or the gods. Resurrection functions as a shorthand

---

[5] No one claims much certainty about numbers of Jews or Christians in the first few centuries. For some estimates, see Stephen Wilson, *Related Strangers* 21–25 and Hopkins article, "Christian Number."

or condensation symbol for the basic values of both Jews and Christians; but the need to consolidate values into a brief statement is more pressing for a smaller, more diffuse, rapidly growing group like the Christians than for the more ancient, recognizably distinct Jews.

While the uses of resurrection change and expand, certain key ideas coalesce around the belief, showing constancy across time and place. They become more explicitly articulated as circumstances demand. The doctrine carries several ideas in its wake: the power of God, the composite quality of a human as a unity of body and soul, the demand for ultimate justice, the testimony from Scripture, and the legitimacy of those who preach resurrection.

### The Power and Providence of God

This fundamental belief is evident in some way in virtually every source we have looked at. As early as 2 Macc 7:22–23, the mother encourages her son to martyrdom, saying it was not she who gave him life, but the creator of the universe who will give him back life and breath. The Pharisees are differentiated from the Sadducees, says Josephus, because they attribute all things to Fate and God, while the latter removes God from human affairs (*J. W.* 2.162–65). Sadducees are dismissed in the New Testament as people who reject resurrection because they do not know God's power or the Scriptures (Mark 12:24–27 and its Matthean parallel; Acts 4:1–2). In the *Shemoneh Esreh*, the central prayer of Jewish liturgy, the *mehayeh hametim* bless-ing of God who raises the dead, appears in the *gevurah* ("might") sec-tion as an aspect of God's power. In the Mishnah, those who reject resurrection are joined with Epicureans, who reject God's providence in the world, as two of three groups who are read out of the next world, a privilege that extends to all Israel.

In 1 Corinthians, Paul's reversal of the categories of worldly wis-dom and power results in talk of weakness, foolishness, and the folly of the cross. But in Paul's understanding of the unfolding apocalyptic drama, these categories project God's power and the beginning of the process that will overthrow the existing order. The final act in the drama and sign of the overcoming of the world will be the res-urrection of bodies.

For Justin and Athenagoras, the primary proof text for resurrec-tion is the reality of creation, especially of human bodies: "As to power, the creation of our bodies shows that God's power suffices for their resurrection" (Athenagoras, *Res.* 2.3; 3.1–3). Both marvel at the idea that a drop of semen could contain the beginnings of a whole person, and the way the stages of growth transform the body (Justin, *1 Apol.* 19; *Res.* 5.7; Athenagoras, *Res.* 17.1–2). Those who dispute resurrection dispute God's power, thinking he is like a human potter or carpenter who cannot remake his creation (Athenagoras, *Res.* 5.1; 9.1–2).

Irenaeus echoes the early apologists, arguing that creation is a greater feat than resurrection, "for if he does not vivify what is mortal, does not bring the corruptible to incorruption, he is not a God of power. But that he is powerful in all these respects, we ought to perceive from our origins, inasmuch as God, taking dust from the earth, formed humans" (*Haer.* 5.3.2). Tertullian says as much, but with a certain amount of sarcasm: ". . . your doubts, I suppose, will be about the power of God? of God, who set together the mighty frame of the universe out of what was not, as if out of the deadness of emptiness and chaos, who gave it the breath of life by that spirit, which gives life to all lives, who sealed it to be itself a testimony for you, a type of human resurrection" (*Apol.* 48.6–7).

All of our sources answer the question "could God raise the dead?" with a resounding yes. The apologists face a more difficult one, particularly from the pagans: "Why would he raise the dead, thus seeming to violate his own laws of nature?" They argue from the demands of justice and from the identity of the human being as a composite of body and soul.

### The Unity of Body and Soul

Our early Jewish sources do not contain discussions of the relation of body and soul, partially because of the nature of the sources as law and liturgy, but also because it is assumed. The earliest Jewish anthropology sees a distinction between body and soul as a soft distinction only. The two aspects of the human being only function as a unit. As Alon Goshen Gottstein offers, body and soul are like a gadget and its power source.[6] While many of our sources, Jewish and Christian, recognize a distinction between body and soul, and

---

[6] Alon Goshen Gottstein, "The Body as Image of God in Rabbinic Literature," *HTR* 87 (1994) 176–77.

some, like Irenaeus, even a subordination of the body to the soul, they reject an absolute dualism. A human being is, by definition, both body and soul, so must be restored as both.

Paul is the most difficult to characterize, since he insists on resurrection and looks forward to the resurrection of the body (σῶμα), but proclaims that flesh (σάρξ) and blood cannot inherit the kingdom. Martin explains Paul as seeing the body as a "heirachy of essence," a combination of elements that occur on the spectrum between matter (ὕλη) and spirit (πνεῦμα). Wright reflects Irenaeus in arguing only flesh that belongs to the realm of ordinary life will not inherit, not that infused with God's spirit. According to either view, Paul reverses the normal hierarchy and argues the spirit must submit to the body, not seek to be freed from it.

In *2 Clement* and Polycarp's *Letter to the Philippians*, there is more talk of resurrection in conjunction with talk of the flesh. But Justin first uses the term "resurrection of the flesh." Belief in it is the sign of the "straight-thinking Christian" (*Dial.* 80.5). God values the flesh as his creation, the site of Jesus' miracles, and the locus of Jesus' resurrection, so it cannot be discounted. Nor does the flesh or body sin alone, but is inextricably joined to the soul like a pair of oxen (*Res.* 7.12).

Similarly, Athenagoras argues that humans are a composite, so for justice to prevail, body and soul must be raised for God to judge the entire human being. Life is lived by body and soul so they must be punished together (*Res.* 18.4; 21.4). Irenaeus continues the same theme, that resurrection reunites body and soul as essential for judgment and justice. He takes on the most difficult verse for this view, 1 Cor 15:50: "I tell you this, brothers, flesh and blood cannot inherit the kingdom of God, nor does the imperishable inherit the imperishable." Irenaeus accepts a dichotomy of body and soul, but says they are mingled and both may be infused with spirit. The soul stands midway between flesh and spirit. The body is inferior to the soul, but both are in the process of change and both may be infused with spirit and move towards salvation. In a series of arguments, he argues that only flesh that has not been transformed will not inherit the kingdom. Irenaeus accounts for change, the seeming enemy of the body, by putting forth God's economy of salvation. God's plan, through change and action by the spirit, will bring the body from corruption to incorruption (1.10.2; 3.19.2; 4.33.1). Its essential dignity and possibility is proved by Jesus' incarnation and resurrection.

Tertullian also argues that flesh must be restored for purposes of judgment. Against resurrection's detractors, who argue that a vessel is not responsible for what it contains, he shows how even a receptacle can share guilt by association (*Res.* 16.6–7). Who, for example, would want to use a diviner's cup?

## *Justice*

As these sources show, the restoration of body and soul is required for reward and punishment, so that justice may prevail, something Athenagoras says humans need as much as they need food and offspring (*Res.* 14.4; 18.4). Even the earliest explicit references in 2 Maccabees cite the bodily resurrection of the martyr as recompense. Resurrection solves the problem of the apparent triumph of injustice in this world. Death by itself is no solution, as Justin and Athenagoras say, since it is meted out to all, and would be a boon for the wicked if no judgment followed (Justin, *1 Apol.* 18.1; Athenagoras, *Res.* 19.7). Irenaeus predicts the reuniting of body, soul, and spirit to carry out justice.

Several authors make clear that justice will be a public event. Paul coopts the image of imperial procession, but puts the crucified criminal over the worldly powers. The system of power and patronage all around him is beginning to be dismantled and an alternative society, the ἐκκλησία of believers, put in its place. Both Justin and Tertullian visualize a public spectacle of eternal punishment for the wicked (Justin, *Dial.* 130.2). Tertullian savors the notion of an unending conflagration: "The mountains burn and endure. What of the guilty, what of God's enemies?" (*Apol.* 48.14–15).

## *Resurrection is Proved by Scripture*

In spite of the lack of explicit references to resurrection in the Hebrew Bible, Scripture is regularly invoked as the ultimate proof for it. The Sadducees deny it because they do not understand Scripture, while the Pharisees, as expert interpreters, preach resurrection (Mark 12:24–27; Luke 16:31; 20:37; Acts 24:14–15; 26:22–23). In the Mishnah and Tosefta, those who deny resurrection are linked to those who deny the Torah's divine origin, both undercutting the rabbis as its authoritative interpreters.

In Justin's work, resurrection of the flesh is proven by Ezekiel and Daniel. Those who deny resurrection blaspheme the God of Abraham, Isaac, and Jacob (*Dial.* 80.4–5). When resurrection takes place, it will settle once and for all who really understands Scripture, a major concern for Justin in his dispute with Jews and Judaism. Irenaeus brings a string of ingenious biblical proofs, from Abel's blood crying out from the ground in Genesis, to the raising of Lazarus in John. Tertullian similarly employs an array of scriptural proofs. Any prediction that has yet to come to pass he explains as requiring resurrection. In the parable of the fig tree in Luke 21:29–31, 36, for example, Jesus predicts the coming of the kingdom and that some will soon stand before the Son of Man. These will only happen at the culmination of history when resurrection takes place. Like Paul, Justin, and Irenaeus, he visualizes an alternative, sacred history beyond the visible one that is pointed to by Scripture. While reason, nature, custom, and argument may support the idea, resurrection is primarily proven by an appeal to Scripture. Its authority vanquishes all other arguments.

## The Legitimacy of those who Preach Resurrection

By extension of the idea that Scripture proves resurrection, only those who properly interpret Scripture are legitimate authorities. The Marcan passage dismissed the Sadducees as failing to understand the Scriptures, whereas the Pharisees in Acts are the most authentic representatives of Judaism and the preachers of resurrection. The liturgical placement of the blessing that God raises the dead by its nature as public prayer fixes the concept as normative for the community. The mishnaic pronouncement against the three groups who deny resurrection, the Torah's divine origin, and presumably, God's providence, are pronounced by the rabbis not as sinners, but as no longer Israel, since they do not merit the privilege of the next world, in which all Israel has a share. It assumes that the rabbis have the authority to judge these matters.

Paul hinges his own and his co-workers' legitimacy as preachers on the truth of resurrection (1 Cor 15:12–19). If he is wrong that believers will be raised, Christ's own resurrection did not happen (v. 13); then his preaching and the dangers he faces daily are absurd

(vv. 19, 32). The authority of Paul's mission and his hearers' acceptance of his word rests on it.

Justin says only he and others who understand that resurrection was preached by the prophets deserve the name Christian. Turning around Jesus' complaint against the Pharisaic παράδοσις in Mark 7, Justin says the resurrection believers follow God's teaching, not human invention. Irenaeus cites four biblical covenants between God and Adam, Noah, Moses, and Jesus as God's plan of salvation, moving towards perfection that can only be realized in resurrection (*Haer.* 3.11.8). One who rejects the notion rejects God's promises (*Haer.* 5.5.2). Tertullian says one who argues against resurrection is a non-Christian (*Res.* 1.1), for "the resurrection of the dead is the confidence of Christians. By it we are believers" (*Res.* 3.5).

Because these ideas are so firmly embedded in the concept of resurrection of the body, it functioned as a symbol that could conveniently condense them into a single, recognizable article of belief. Belief in resurrection could draw boundaries between insiders and outsiders, solve problems of injustice and suffering, and underscore the legitimacy of those who preached and taught it.

Our sources have provided more than a glimpse of large groups of people who do not hold a view of the body's resurrection. The view of the deniers was no doubt the more widely held, quite understandable, and more congenial to modern sensibilities. These deniers were a threat, however, because they undermined the authority of the preachers, and threatened to dismantle the bulwark of some communities. They blurred the symbolic boundaries that some Christians had carefully constructed, boundaries that maintained a sense of distinctive self, able to absorb others into the group, while accommodating a larger society that fluctuated between interest, indifference, and hostility. These resurrection-believers successfully avoided being bleached out by the appealing Greco-Roman culture around them or destroyed by the powerful Roman state; and in time, they overtook both.

# APPENDIX

*Resurrection in Selected Nag Hammadi Documents*

We cannot talk about groups haggling over resurrection of the body without acknowledging the many documents from Nag Hammadi and elsewhere that feature groups who are opposed to the idea, or are simply functioning quite successfully without it. The materials discovered at Nag Hammadi in 1945, as well as some cognate materials found elsewhere, indicate Christians of a spiritual bent who did not long for resurrection of the physical body and, in many cases, found it repellent.

Scholars now question the appropriateness of talking about "Gnosticism" as a distinctly identifiable religious movement.[1] "Gnostic" is not a self-designation, and the term is used by heresiologists in different ways, though normally in a negative sense, perhaps along the lines of "know-it-alls."[2] No one can articulate a list of attributes, such as dualism, anti-world, anti-flesh attitudes, and a distinctive cosmogony, that are present in every gnostic work; and many of the proposed attributes are evident in orthodox works as well.[3] King diagnoses the problem with understandings of gnosticism: "a rhetorical term has been confused with a historical entity."[4] Early heresiologists saw gnosticism as a unified movement to be defeated, and nineteenth- and twentieth-century scholars have incorporated the idea of a recognizable heterodox group with a fixed set of beliefs. Stressing difference, these constructions ignore shared ideas with emerging orthodoxy.

A label traditionally applied to these groups is a general rejection of the material world and an accompanying hatred of the body that leads to utter renunciation of the body via ascetic practice or liber-

---

[1] For a discussion of nineteenth and twentieth century uses of gnosticism, see Karen King, *What is Gnosticism?* (Cambridge, Mass.: Harvard University, 2003) 55–110. See also Michael Allen Williams, *Rethinking Gnosticism* (Princeton: Princeton University, 1996).

[2] Elaine Pagels, *Beyond Belief* (New York: Random House, 2003) 33.

[3] See Williams, *Rethinking Gnosticism*, 116–38.

[4] King, *What is Gnosticism?*, 1.

tinism. Williams has shown this to be a worn cliché that fails to reflect the evidence. While negative references to the body as a prison for the soul and the like abound, similar things appear in writers later deemed orthodox. Some other statements see the form of the body as divine, "the best visible trace of the divine in the material world."[5] For some writers, the substance of the body as matter may be impure, but the form of it is divine, made in God's image.[6] Furthermore, Williams cites examples where the bodies of the savior and special persons occur as models.[7]

Where does this leave us in our discussion of resurrection of the body as a tool in the symbolic construction of community? It would be wrong to think of a separate group of Christian heretics professing an anti-resurrection stance while orthodox Christians battled on behalf of bodily resurrection. Some notions of spiritual resurrection and self-knowledge were more congenial to most in the Greco-Roman world than bodily resurrection. These texts do demonstrate a wide horizon of people professing Christianity and entertaining different understandings of life after death. Clues to actual controversies and evidence of a view of the afterlife as definitive for community are less clear, probably because some gnostic attitudes did not distinguish them from the rest of Greco-Roman society as such; and the mythic quality or isolated sayings of many of these texts leaves fewer traces of community realities. Few references to opponents, where their position is identified, or caricatured, then refuted, appear.

To illustrate the milieu of varied interpretive choices, we will look at three sets of documents: literature associated with Thomas, *Treatise on the Resurrection*, and *The Gospel of Philip*.

### The Thomas Traditions

Three works that invoke the figure of the apostle Thomas treat the physical body as a negative and its resurrection as undesirable. While these three works—*The Gospel of Thomas, The Book of Thomas the Contender*, and *The Acts of Thomas*—span two centuries, they represent a

---

[5] Williams, *Rethinking Gnosticism*, 117.
[6] Williams, *Rethinking Gnosticism*, 118–20.
[7] Williams, *Rethinking Gnosticism*, 124–27.

stream of tradition associated with Syriac Christianity, and show a trajectory that is anti-world, anti-body, and anti-resurrection.[8]

*The Gospel of Thomas*[9]

*Gos. Thom.* shows a form of realized eschatology: "The dead are not alive, and the living will not die" (11.2). Rather than looking to the future in apocalyptic expectation, the believer recognizes and regains primordial perfection by withdrawing or "seeing through" the evil and errors of the world (18:1–3).[10]

A world-foreignness combines with a distaste for the physical body, which is at odds with the soul, and is associated with death and the world:[11]

> Jesus said, "If the flesh came into being because of a spirit, it is a wonder. But if spirit came into being because of the body, it is a wonder of wonders. Indeed I am amazed at how this great wealth has made its home in this poverty" (29).
>
> Jesus said, "He who has recognized the world has found the body, but he who has found the body is superior to the world" (80.1).
>
> Jesus said, "Wretched is the body that depends on a body. And wretched is the soul that depends on these two" (87.1–2).
>
> Jesus said, "Woe to the flesh that depends on a soul; woe to the soul that depends on the flesh" (112).

Given the negative quality of the body, we would not expect this text to be positive about its resurrection. Two sayings may refer to death as the happy shedding of the body, but the meaning of these sayings is not transparent:

---

[8] See Gregory Riley, *Resurrection Reconsidered: Thomas and John in Controversy* (Minneapolis: Fortress, 1995) 127–75; A. F. J. Klijn, "Christianity in Edessa and the Gospel of Thomas," *NovT* 14 (1972) 70–77; Hans Drijvers, "Facts and Problems in Early Syriac Speaking Christianity," *SecCent* 2 (1982) 157–75; John D. Turner, *The Book of Thomas the Contender from Codex II of the Cairo Gnostic library from Nag Hammadi* (*SBLDS* 23; Missoula: Scholars, 1975); Philip Sellew, "Death, the Body, and the World in the Gospel of Thomas," *StPatr* 31 (1997) 530–35; ibid., "Thomas Christianity: Scholars in Quest of Community," *The Apocryphal Acts of Thomas*, ed. Jan Bremmer (Leuven: Peeters, 2001) 11–35.

[9] Translations by Thomas O. Lambdin, *The Nag Hammadi Library in English*.

[10] Karen King explains how the language of kingdom is used non-apocalyptically, linked to wisdom, in "Kingdom in the Gospel of Thomas," *Forum* 3 (1987) 48–97.

[11] Sellew's article demonstrates the consistent association of the body and the world with death in the gospel ("Death, the Body, and the World").

Mary said to Jesus, "Whom are your disciples like?" He said, "They are like children who have settled in a field that is not theirs. When the owners of the field come, they will say, 'Let us have back our field.' They (will) undress in their presence in order to let them have back their field and to give it back to them . . ." (21)

   Jesus said, "When you disrobe without being ashamed and take up your garments and place them under your feet like little children and tread on them, then (will you see) the son of the living one, and you will not be afraid." (37)

While Wright argues that "undressing" means the divestment of the physical body at death,[12] April De Connick suggests it refers to renouncing sexuality and returning to a primordial state in preparation for the ascent to heaven and vision of God.[13] Jonathan Smith argues that both these sayings refer to baptismal practice rather than dispensing with the body at death.[14]

Another sign associated with those of understanding is their "rest." In sayings 49 and 50, the solitary and elect find the kingdom and return to its light, but the evidence of their status is their "rest."

Jesus said, "If they say to you, 'Where did you come from?' say to them, 'We came from the light, the place where the light came into being on its own accord and established [itself] and became manifest through their image.' If they say to you 'Is it you?' say 'We are its children, and we are the elect of the living father.' If they ask you, 'What is the sign of your father in you?' say to them, 'It is movement and repose.'"

"Repose" or "rest" has a special significance in gnostic literature, explains Judith Wray, where it is not a state achieved after death but is already available to the elect.[15] The idea of rest or refreshment also appears in canonical works such as Matt 11:28–29 and Rev 14:13. Repose or rest is realized in this world. Waiting for death will be too late: "His disciples said to him, 'When will the repose of the dead come about, and when will the new world come? He

---

[12] Wright, *Resurrection*, 535.

[13] De Connick, *Seek to See Him* (Leiden: Brill, 1996) 143–47.

[14] Smith argues that the four elements in 37—nakedness, lack of shame, being like little children, and treading on garments—are found together only in baptismal rituals and homilies ("The Garments of Shame," *HR* 5 [1965–66] 217–38).

[15] For a survey of the theme of rest in Nag Hammadi literature see Judith Hoch Wray, *Rest as a Theological Metaphor in the Epistle to the Hebrews and the Gospel of Truth* (*SBLDS* 166; Atlanta: Scholars, 1997) 36–43. See also Jon Laansma, *"I Will Give You Rest": The Rest Motif in the New Testament with Special Reference to Mt 11 and Heb 3–4* (*WUNT* 2/98; Tübingen: Mohr Siebeck, 1997).

said to them, 'What you look forward to has already come, but you do not recognize it'" (51), or "Take heed of the living one while you are alive, lest you die and seek to see him and be unable to do so" (59). Once achieved, this rest means one has overcome death, "Had (Adam) been worthy (he would) not (have experienced) death" (85) or "And the one who lives from the living one will not see death" (111).

Riley interprets two difficult verses as rejection of physical resurrection. In saying 71 "Jesus said, 'I shall (destroy this) house, and no one will be able to build it . . .'" "House," argues Riley, is a term for the body (here substituted for temple), and this verse denies Jesus' resurrection.[16] Similarly, the parable of overcoming the strong man is, Riley maintains, about the soul overcoming the body. Since "house" means body, he says, putting the sword through the wall of the house means slaying the body to overcome it, "Jesus said, 'The kingdom of the father is like a certain man who wanted to kill a powerful man. In his own house he drew his sword and stuck it into the wall in order to find out whether his hand could carry through. Then he slew the powerful man" (98). While Riley's interpretation has not won consensus, it is compatible with the gospel's general attitudes towards the physical body and the flesh.

These sayings share certain themes: world-foreignness, a dichotomy of body and soul, rest, the saving power of knowledge, recognition of wisdom, self-understanding, realized eschatology, and the idea that with proper understanding, one will not taste death at all. It offers no notions of sin and atonement, nor expectations of salvation after death, nor linear movement to an apocalyptic climax.

## The Book of Thomas the Contender

Dated by J. D. Turner to the first half of the third century, *Thom. Cont.* shows some evidence of knowledge of *Gos. Thom.* Turner argues that it is midway in time and theme between the gospel and *The Acts of Thomas*, and that the three works reflect Syrian ascetic tradi-

---

[16] Riley, *Resurrection*, 147–56. Some question Riley's thesis of a conflict between Thomasine and Johannine communities over resurrection. Ismo Dunderberg claims that Thomas' doubt in John's gospel is over identifying Jesus, not physical resurrection, and no outright controversy between the two groups is evident, "John and Thomas in Conflict?" *The Nag Hammadi Library after Fifty Years*, ed. John Turner and Anne McGuire (Leiden: Brill, 1997) 360–80.

tions that coalesce around the figure of Thomas the twin (derived from John 11:16; 21:2).[17] The Book of Thomas the Contender amplifies ascetic themes of the separation of body and soul, a fear of the body, and a rejection of sexuality. It also shares with gnostic works like *The Gospel of Philip*, *The Apocryphon of James*, and *The Dialogue of the Savior* themes of bondage of the body, rest, and the metaphor of the garment.

The work contains lurid descriptions of punishment by fire and being thrown into the abyss. As in *Gos. Thom.* and other Nag Hammadi works, salvation must be realized before death: "Nor does he find the way to the east so as to flee there and be saved, for he did not find it in the day he was in the body, so that he might find it in the day of judgment." As Riley notes, the east is the traditional way to the underworld.[18]

A clear denial of resurrection appears in 143.10–15:

> Then the savior continued, saying, "Woe to you godless ones, who have no hope, who rely on things that will not happen! Woe to you who hope in the flesh and in the prison that will perish! How long will you be oblivious? And how long will you suppose that the imperishables will perish too?[19] Your hope is set upon the world, and your god is this life! You are corrupting your souls!"

A series of woes follow, condemning those in error, who have intercourse with women, and are "in the grip of the powers of the body" (144).

Thomas is told that it is beneficial to rest among one's own. For the vessel of the flesh will dissolve, and return to the world (as shades) to suffer. Visible things will dissolve, "for the vessel of the flesh will dissolve . . . they will be gathered back to what is visible . . . in the midst of the tombs they will forever dwell upon the corpses in pain and corruption of soul" (141.13–19). Even in the absence of bodies,

---

[17] J. D. Turner, *Thomas the Contender*. Turner identifies two sources. Source A is the dialogue of the risen savior with his twin brother Thomas. See also Sellew, "Thomas Christianity," and Hans-Martin Schenke, who argues it is a Christianized Jewish work of Wisdom literature, "*The Book of Thomas* (*NHC* II 7): A Revision of a Pseudepigraphic Letter of Jacob the Contender," in *New Testament and Gnosis* (Edinburgh: T. & T. Clark, 1983) 213–28.

[18] Riley, *Resurrection*, 160.

[19] Riley emends this difficult text to "and as for the things which perish (how long) will you think that they will not perish?" *Resurrection*, 164. Translation by Thomas O. Lambdin, *The Nag Hammadi Library in English*.

there will be recompense for the wicked. The problem of justice is not a problem, since it is accomplished apart from the body.

This work carves out a place for its ideas by invoking the authority of Thomas and Jesus. Images of error, darkness, death, body, burning, and sexuality oppose images of the elect, light, knowledge, and salvation that is realized before death. Those in error live in the world of flesh and assert its survival. Flesh by nature is linked to the world and suffering:

> Watch and pray that you not come to be in the flesh, but rather that you come forth from the bondage of the bitterness of this life. And as you pray, you will find rest, for you have left behind the suffering and the disgrace. For when you come forth from the sufferings and passions of the body, you will receive rest from the good one, and you will reign with the king, you joined with him and he with you, from now on, forever and ever. Amen (145.9–16).

## The Acts of Thomas

Similar signs of an ascetic Syrian theology appear in the third century work, *The Acts of Thomas*. It contains the earmarks of a romance, elaborate stories woven together, including that of the king's son, as well as the Hymn of the Pearl, which shows the theme of the garment and bridal clothing. Sellew states that it "exemplifies the Christian sector of popular literature in late antiquity, the 'early Christian fiction' compared so aptly in recent years to the Greek novels of the Roman imperial period."[20] It reflects the same anti-world, anti-body, anti-sexuality stance of the other documents bearing Thomas' name.[21]

Klijn notes that *Acts Thom.* is "dominated by the contrast between the corruptible and the incorruptible. The body is an inconvenience in the relation with God, but it can be conquered by an ascetic way of life."[22] A believer can be united with Christ while still in the body (12, 14, 61, 98, 158). The work is more ambiguous on the subject of resurrection and contains references on both sides of the ques-

---

[20] Sellew, "Thomas Christianity," 23–24.
[21] This document is not from Nag Hammadi, however, and not everyone links it to the Thomas traditions. See Hans Drijvers, "East of Antioch: Forces and Structures in the Development of Early Syriac Theology," *East of Antioch: Studies in Early Syriac Christianity* (London: 1984) 1–27.
[22] A. F. J. Klijn, *The Acts of Thomas: Introduction, Text, and Commentary* (Leiden: Brill, 1962) 35–36.

tion. Riley suggests that some "orthodox" revision of the work has taken place in the light of controversy over resurrection.[23]

Riley summarizes the references to the body in *Acts Thom.*,[24] but may be too inclusive. He is certainly right that the work stresses the body's temporary nature. It will wear out and its beauty vanish (37, 88). The soul is not fundamentally at home in the body: "The Savior is nourisher, preserving and giving rest in alien bodies, the savior of our souls" (39). Souls alone are saved (157). Death is "not death, but deliverance and release from the body" (160–63). The body is a garment of the soul (37, 66, 126, 147). The saved acquire rest while still in the body. The soul is saved, the body is not raised. Jesus abides forever, along with "the souls which hope in him" (117).

But I am not certain that the Hymn of the Pearl (108–13) is about bodies, even if it does refer to the soul reawakening to its heavenly nature. The prince suddenly awakens and remembers his origins and identity: "Of a sudden, when I received it, the garment seemed to me to become like a mirror of myself. I saw it all in all, and I too received all in it, for we were two in distinction-and yet again one in one likeness" (112.76–78). Klijn describes it as the soul, which forgot its heavenly origins, receiving a "letter" from God in the form of the garment and finding its way back.[25] Yet the garment is not the body, but the vehicle of sudden understanding. If not, then "discarding the garments of Egypt" (109.29) would not mean leaving aside the body. Nor is the "dirty and unclean garment" necessarily a reference to the body (111.62–63). Sebastian Brock is emphatic that Syriac tradition did not go the direction of understanding Gen 3:21 as putting on bodies (as Origen did) or the body as the garment of the soul.[26] The hymn, says Brock, draws on a basic myth of salvation history where Adam and Eve are clothed in "robes of light" (a pun on the words for skin and light). At Jesus' incarnation, God puts on a body, and in his descent into the Jordan at baptism he deposits a "robe of glory" that is available to believers at baptism. So baptism is the recovery of primordial glory: "God puts on

---

[23] Riley, *Resurrection*, 167–70.
[24] Riley, *Resurrection*, 173–74.
[25] Klijn, *Acts*, 281.
[26] Sebastian Brock, "Clothing Metaphors as a Means of Theological Expression in Syriac Tradition," in M. Schmidt and C. Geyer, *Typus, Symbole, Allegorie bei den ostlichen Vatern und ihren Parallelen in Mittelalter* (Regensburg: Friedrich Pustet, 1982) 11–38.

Adam/Man in order that Adam/Man may put on God."[27] The hymn, then, is not about discarding the body, but about recovering one's former godly nature.

*The Acts of Thomas* does not polemicise against resurrection of the body, but provides a lyric set of descriptions of the soul's heavenly origin, while denigrating the body and this world. It shows us writers and readers enlivened by an image of the soul that survives without the body, self-recognition as salvation, an alienation from the world, and a longing for re-integration and return to a heavenly home.

### Treatise on the Resurrection (Letter to Rheginos)

Written in the second or third century in the form of a response on the subject of resurrection, many elements in this treatise echo a negative attitude toward the material world and the body. The metaphor of the savior who destroys death points to spiritual immortality: "The Savior swallowed up death—(of this) you are not reckoned as being ignorant—for he put aside the world which is perishing. He transformed [himself] into an imperishable Aeon and raised himself up, having swallowed the visible by the invisible, and he gave us the way of our immortality" (45.14–24).[28] While in this world, we wear the world like a garment, but at death are drawn up to the savior in heaven, like rays going back to the sun (45.29–36). "This is a resurrection of the spirit, which swallows resurrection of the soul along with resurrection of the body" (45.40–46.1). The body is something to be released from (49.32). Resurrection is the overcoming of the state of dispersion and body and can be accomplished in this life (49.20–24). It uncovers the elements in the self that have already arisen (47.38). Bentley Layton understands this treatise as participating in the Platonic atmosphere of its time that regarded the sojourn in the physical world as a state of bondage, but interpreting it by way of the myth of the pre-existent Pleroma, now dispersed in the world and moving towards reintegration.[29]

---

[27] Brock, "Clothing Metaphors," 16.

[28] Translations by Malcolm Peel, *Nag Hammadi Codex I (The Jung Codex)*, ed. Harold Attridge (Leiden: Brill, 1985) 139–55.

[29] Layton, *The Gnostic Treatise on the Resurrection from Nag Hammadi* (Missoula, Mont.: Scholars, 1979) 3–4.

Yet one passage seems to entertain the idea of resurrection of the body:

> For if you were not existing in flesh, you received flesh when you entered this world. Why will you not receive flesh when you ascend into the Aeon? That which is better than the flesh is that for which is for it (the) cause of life. That which came into being on your account, is it not yours? Does not that which is yours exist with you? Yet, while you are in this world, what is it that you lack? This is what you have been making every effort to learn (47.4–16).

Some commentators have argued that the use of the term "flesh" here requires us to see a form of bodily resurrection. Stephen Shoemaker, drawing on Malcolm Peel's arguments, suggests that it refers to the raising of a transformed body, similar to Paul's "resurrection body" that some see in 1 Corinthians.[30] Peel sees the letter as a combination of Valentinian ideas and Pauline concepts, and both works do share a notion that resurrection is already realized in some way in this world. Peel argues that the proof that the treatise does not foresee a purely spiritual resurrection is the use of the appearance of Moses and Elijah at the transfiguration as an example of those who have been raised (48.6–13). A spiritual resurrection would not retain their recognizable characteristics.[31] Yet Peel may be too literal here in his understanding of the transfiguration. Both Peel and Shoemaker require a certain understanding of Paul to make their case. Furthermore, Wright argues, this work parts company with Paul on the value of creation. Whatever his ambiguities, Paul does not argue for a spiritual resurrection, as this work does, but for one of bodies.

The source of disagreement on this passage is the rhetorical question and its implied answer. The question "why would you think you might ascend without your flesh?" can imply a positive answer, as in "of course you will not ascend without your flesh. You came into the world with it, why would you leave the world without it?" Or we can assume a negative answer, as for an interpretation incorporated by Layton's into his translation. He answers "you might

[30] Stephen Shoemaker, *Ancient Traditions of the Virgin Mary's Dormition and Assumption* (New York: Oxford, 2002) 244–46. See also Kurt Rudolph, *Gnosis* (trans. R. McLachlan Wilson; Edinburgh: T. & T. Clark, 1983) 189–94.

[31] Malcolm Peel, "The Treatise on the Resurrection," *Nag Hammadi Codex I (The Jung Codex)* (ed. Harold Attridge; Leiden: Brill, 1985) vol. 1, 136–37.

wrongly think you ascend with your flesh because you came into the world with it, but this is incorrect." Here is Layton's translation.

> Now [you might wrongly suppose][32] granted you did not preexist in the flesh—indeed you took on flesh when you entered this world— why will you not take your flesh with you when you return to the realm of eternity? It is the element superior to the flesh that imparts vitality to it; [furthermore you might suppose] does not whatever comes into being for your sake [viz. the flesh] belong to you? So may we not conclude that whatever is yours will coexist with you?

Given the generally negative tenor of the letter towards the body and the world, this second approach seems more probable. It also makes sense with the passage that follows that underscores the negative valence of the physical body, "The afterbirth of the body is old age and you exist in corruption" (47:19–20). While ambiguous, this work leans much more towards a realized rebirth of the spirit that involves ascent and reintegration with the pleroma, than towards any form of bodily resurrection.

## The Gospel of Philip

The *Gospel of Philip*, another Valentinian work, contains statements that mentions "the flesh" in the context of some form of resurrection, situated within a passage that is ambiguous about the body and the world:

> Some are afraid lest they rise naked. Because of this they wish to rise in the flesh, and [they] do not know that it is those who wear the [flesh] who are naked. [It is] those who [. . .] to unclothe themselves who are not naked. "Flesh [and blood shall] not inherit the kingdom [of God]" (1 Cor 15:50). What is this which will not inherit? That which is on us. But what is this, too, which will inherit? It is that which belongs to Jesus and his blood. Because of this he said, "he who shall not eat my flesh and drink my blood has not life in him" (John 6:53). What is it? His flesh is the word, and his blood is the holy spirit. He who has received these has food and he has drink and clothing. I find fault with the others who say that it will not rise. Then both of them are at fault. You (sg.) say that the flesh will not rise. But tell me what will rise, that we may honor you (sg.). You (sg.) say the spirit in the flesh, and it is also this light in the flesh. (But) this

---

[32] The words in brackets are added by Layton.

too is a matter which is in the flesh, for whatever you (sg.) shall say, you (sg.) say nothing outside the flesh. It is necessary to rise in this flesh, since everything exists in it. In this world those who put on garments are better than the garments. In the kingdom of heaven the garments are better than those who have put them on (56.29–57.21).[33]

This passage seems to contain two contradictory formulas, one promoting the resurrection of the flesh and the other denying it. Schenke suggests two sources with opposing views joined by a gloss at line 10: "then both of them are at fault."[34]

Van Eijk has proposed a solution that does not require redaction criticism. He links the crucial formula about flesh and blood in 1 Cor 15:50, that it will not inherit the kingdom, with the formula about flesh and blood in John 6:53–56, that one who eats the flesh and drinks the blood of Christ attains eternal life and will be raised up on the last day. This gospel, van Eijk argues, espouses a view not far from Clement of Alexandria or Irenaeus that the flesh that will rise and inherit the kingdom is flesh that has been transformed by receiving the Eucharist.[35]

The image of putting on garments by receiving the body and blood of Christ and rising in this transformed way incorporates the image of line 29 and maintains a form of resurrection of the body. Yet it satisfies 1 Cor 15:50 in that not all flesh and blood is raised, but only that which has been transformed. In this, notes van Eijk, the author is not far from Irenaeus or Clement who struggle with Paul's verse while arguing a bodily resurrection.

Shoemaker makes the case for a form of spiritual resurrection here in the heavenly realm, "the spiritual body that will clothe the elect after their restoration to the heavenly realm."[36] The references to garments seem to necessitate the raising of some kind of body. Lines 19–20 imply a change in ascent to a heavenly realm where one is reclothed, "In this world those who put on garments are better than the garments. In the kingdom of heaven the garments are better than those who have put them on."

---

[33] *Nag Hammadi Codex II*, 2–7, v. 1, ed. B. Layton (Leiden: Brill, 1989) 152–55.

[34] Hans-Martin Schenke, "Auferstehung und Gnosis," *ZNW* 59 (1968) 124.

[35] A. H. C. van Eijk, "The Gospel of Philip and Clement of Alexandria: Gnostic and Ecclesiastical Theology on the Resurrection and the Eucharist," *VC* 25 (1971) 94–120.

[36] Shoemaker, *Dormition and Assumption*, 245.

Both *Treatise on the Resurrection* and *Gospel of Philip* present an ambigu-ous picture, which most scholars have explained via a certain under-standing of Paul's "resurrection body" in First Corinthians. Without that model of a transformed body that is raised but is not literally flesh and blood, statements in these texts are contradictory. Yet this argument for a "spiritual body" in Paul contains its own problems, nor do we know that these other authors thought along Pauline lines.

These texts show that the idea of resurrection of the body was so powerful that it criss-crossed community boundaries and made its way into groups, orthodox and not, who also showed negative atti-tudes towards the body. Furthermore, some texts do not allow a simple yes-or-no answer to the question of resurrection of the body. Despite positive affirmations about the body in many Christian thinkers, their views are complicated by 1 Cor 15:50, which must be reconciled with bodily resurrection.

# BIBLIOGRAPHY

Athanassiadi, Polymnia, and Michael Frede. *Pagan Monotheism in Late Antiquity*. Oxford: Clarendon, 1999.
Avery-Peck, Alan, and Jacob Neusner. *Judaism in Late Antiquity Part 4. Death, Life-after-Death, Resurrection and the World-to-Come in the Judaisms of Antiquity*. Leiden: Brill, 2000.
Barkay, Gabriel. *Ketef Hinnom: A Treasure Facing Jerusalem's Walls*. Jerusalem: The Israel Museum, 1986.
Barnard, L. W. "The Authenticity of Athenagoras' *De Resurrectione*." *StPatr* 15 (1984) 39–49.
Barnes, T. D. *Tertullian. A Historical and Literary Study*. Oxford: Clarendon, 1971.
Barth, Gerhard. "Zur Frage nach der in 1 Korinther bekämpten Auferstehungsleugnung." *ZNW* 83 (1992) 187–201.
Barth, Karl. *The Resurrection of the Dead*. Translated by H. J. Stenning. New York: Revell, 1933.
Baumgarten, Albert. *The Flourishing of Sects in the Maccabean Era: An Interpretation*. Leiden: Brill, 1997.
—— "Qumran and Jewish Sectarianism during the Second Temple Period." Pages 139–51 in *Megillot Midbar-Yehudah: Arba'im Shenot Mehkar* (Heb.). Edited by Magen Broshi, Sara Japhet, and Shemaryahu Talmon. Jerusalem: Mosad Bialik, 1992.
—— "The Pharisaic *Paradosis*." *HTR* 80 (1987) 63–77.
Beard, Mary, John North, and Simon Price. *Religions of Rome*. Cambridge: Cambridge University Press, 1998.
—— *Roman Religions: A Sourcebook*. Cambridge: Cambridge University Press, 1998.
Bloch-Smith, Elizabeth. *Judahite Burial Practices and Beliefs about the Dead*. *JSOTSup* 123. Sheffield: Sheffield Academic Press, 1992.
Boyce, Mary. *Zoroastrians*. London: Routledge, 1979.
Brawley, Robert. *Luke-Acts and the Jews*. Society of Biblical Literature Monograph Series 33. Atlanta: Scholars, 1987.
Brichto, Herbert C. "Kin, Cult, and Afterlife." *HUCA* 44 (1973) 1–54.
Brock, Sebastian. "Clothing Metaphors as a Means of Theological Expression in Syriac Tradition." Pages 11–38 in *Typus, Symbole, Allegorie bei den ostlichen Vatern und ihren Parallelen in Mittelalter*. Edited by M. Schmidt and C. Geyer. Regensburg: Friedrich Pustet, 1982.
Brodeur, Scott. *The Holy Spirit's Agency in the Resurrection of the Dead*. Rome: Gregorian University Press, 1996.
Broshi, Magen, Sara Japhet, and Shemaryahu Talmon. *The Scrolls of the Judean Desert: Forty Years of Research*. Jerusalem: Mosad Bialik, 1992.
Bynum, Caroline Walker. *The Resurrection of the Body in Western Christianity 200–1336*. New York: Columbia University Press, 1995.
—— "Why All the Fuss about the Body?" *Critical Inquiry* 22 (1995) 1–33.
Cadbury, Henry J. "Intimations of Immortality in the Thought of Jesus." Pages 115–49 in *Immortality and Resurrection*. Edited by Krister Stendahl. New York: Macmillan, 1965.
Cameron, Averil. *Christianity and the Rhetoric of Empire*. Berkeley: University of California Press, 1991.
Carroll, John, and Joel Green, eds. *The Resurrection of Jesus in Early Christianity*. Peabody: Hendrickson, forthcoming.

Cassirer, Ernst. *An Essay on Man.* New Haven: Yale University Press, 1944.

Cavallin, Hans. *Life After Death.* Gleerup: CWK, 1974.

Charlesworth, James, ed. *The OTP.* 2 vols. Garden City: Doubleday, 1983.

Chilton, Bruce. "Resurrection in the Gospels." Pages 215–39 in *Judaism in Late Antiquity, Part Four: Death, Life After Death, Resurrection, and the World to Come in the Judaisms of Antiquity.* Edited by Alan Avery-Peck and Jacob Neusner. Leiden: Brill, 2000.

Chow, John K. "Patronage in Roman Corinth." Pages 104–25 in *Paul and Empire.* Edited by Richard Horsley. Harrisburg: Trinity, 1997.

Clarke, Graham. "The Historical Setting of the *Octavius* of Minucius Felix." *JRH* 4 (1966–67) 267–86.

—— "The Literary Setting of the *Octavius* of Minucius Felix." *Journal of Religious History* 3 (1964–65) 195–211.

Cohen, Anthony. *The Symbolic Construction of Community.* London and New York: Tavistock, 1985.

Cohen, Shaye J. D. *From the Maccabees to the Mishnah.* Philadelphia: Westminster, 1987.

Collins, John J. "The Afterlife in Apocalyptic Literature." Pages 119–39 in *Judaism in Late Antiquity, Part Four: Death, Life After Death, Resurrection, and the World to Come in the Judaisms of Antiquity.* Edited by Alan Avery-Peck and Jacob Neusner. Leiden: Brill, 2000.

—— *Between Athens and Jerusalem.* 2nd. ed.; Grand Rapids: Eerdmans, 1999.

Cooper, J. "The Fate of Mankind: Death and Afterlife in Ancient Mesopotamia." Pages 19–33 in *Death and Afterlife: Perspectives of World Religions.* Edited by Hiroshi Obayashi. New York: Greenwood, 1992.

Cullmann, Oscar. *Christ and Time.* Philadelphia: Westminster, 1950.

—— "Immortality of the Soul or Resurrection of the Dead?" Pages 9–53 in *Immortality and Resurrection.* Edited by Krister Stendahl. New York: Macmillan, 1965.

Darr, John. *On Character Building.* Louisville: Westminster John Knox, 1992.

Davies, Jon. *Death, Reburial, and Rebirth in Religions of Antiquity.* New York: Routledge, 1999.

Davies, Philip. "Death, Resurrection and Life after Death in the Qumran Scrolls." Pages 189–211 in *Judaism in Late Antiquity, Part Four: Death, Life After Death, Resurrection, and the World to Come in the Judaisms of Antiquity.* Edited by Alan Avery-Peck and Jacob Neusner. Leiden: Brill, 2000.

Davis, J. "Factors Leading to the Emergence of Belief in Resurrection of the Flesh." *NTS* 23 (1972) 448–55.

De Boer, Martin. *The Defeat of Death.* *JSNTSup* 22. Sheffield: Journal for the Study of the New Testament, 1998.

De Connick, April. *Seek to See Him.* Leiden: Brill, 1996.

De Maris, Richard. "Corinthian Religion and Baptism for the Dead (1 Cor 15:29): Insights from Archaeology and Anthropology." *JBL* 114 (1995) 661–82.

Donahue, Paul J. *Jewish-Christian Controversy in the Second Century.* Ann Arbor: UMI, 1990.

Douglas, Mary. *Natural Symbols.* New York: Vintage, 1973.

Douglass, Frederick. *My Bondage and My Freedom.* New York: Arno Press and the New York Times, 1969.

Drijvers, Hans. "East of Antioch: Forces and Structures in the Development of Early Syriac Christianity." Pages 1–27 in *East of Antioch: Studies in Early Syriac Christianity.* London: Variorum, 1984.

—— "Facts and Problems in Early Syriac Speaking Christianity." *SecCent* 2 (1982) 157–75.

Duff, Paul. *Honor or Shame: The Language of Processions and Perception in 2 Cor 2:14–6:13; 7:2–4.* Ph.D. diss., University of Chicago, 1988.

Dunderberg, Ismo. "John and Thomas in Conflict?" Pages 360–80 in *The Nag Hammadi Library after Fifty Years.* Edited by John Turner and Anne McGuire. Leiden: Brill, 1997.

Eckert, G. *Orator Christianus.* Stuttgart: Steiner, 1993.

Edwards, M. J., M. D. Goodman, and S. R. F. Price. *Apologetics in the Roman Empire.* Oxford: Oxford University, 1999.

Eisen, Ute. *Women Officeholders in Early Christianity.* Collegeville: Liturgical Press, 2000.

Eisenbaum, Pamela. "A Speech Act of Faith: The Early Proclamation of the Resurrection of Jesus." Pages 24–45 in *Putting Body and Soul Together: Essays in Honor of Robin Scroggs.* Edited by Virginia Wiles, Alexandra Brown, and Graydon Snyder. Valley Forge: Trinity, 1997.

Eisenstadt, Samuel N. "Religious Organizations and Political Process in Centralized Empires." *The Journal of Asian Studies* 21 (1962) 271–94.

Elbogen, Ismar. *Jewish Liturgy.* Translated by Raymond Scheindlin. Philadelphia: Jewish Publication Society, 1993.

Elliott, Neil. "The Anti-Imperial Message of the Cross." Pages 167–83 in *Paul and Empire.* Edited by Richard Horsley. Harrisburg: Trinity, 1997.

——— *Liberating Paul.* Maryknoll: Orbis, 1994.

Evans, Craig F. *Resurrection and the New Testament.* Studies in Biblical Theology 2.12. Napier: Allenson, 1970.

Ferguson, John. "Epicureanism under the Roman Empire." *ANRW* II 36.4:2257–327.

Fine, Steven. "A Note on Ossuary Burial and the Resurrection of the Dead in First-Century Jerusalem." *JJS* 51 (2000) 69–76.

Finkelstein, Louis. "The Develoment of the Amidah." *JQR* n.s. 16 (1925/26) 1–43.

Fischel, Henry A. *Rabbinic Literature and Greco-Roman Literature.* Leiden: Brill, 1973.

Fitzmyer, Joseph. *The Acts of the Apostles.* Anchor Bible 31. New York: Doubleday, 1998.

Fleischer, Ezra. "On the Beginnings of Obligatory Jewish Prayer (Heb.)." *Tarbiz* 59 (1990) 397–404.

Flesher, Paul. "The Resurrection of the Dead and the Sources of the Palestinian Targums to the Pentateuch." Pages 311–31 in *Judaism in Late Antiquity, Part Four: Death, Life After Death, Resurrection, and the World to Come in the Judaisms of Antiquity.* Edited by Alan Avery-Peck and Jacob Neusner. Leiden: Brill, 2000.

Fox, Robin Lane. *Pagans and Christians.* New York: Alfred Knopf, 1987.

Frede, Michael. "Monotheism and Pagan Philosophy in Later Antiquity." Pages 41–67 in *Pagan Monotheism in Late Antiquity.* Edited by Polymnia Athanassiadi and Michael Frede. Oxford: Clarendon, 1999.

Fredouille, Jean Claude. *Tertullien et la conversion de la culture antique.* Paris: Etudes Augustiniennes, 1972.

Friedman, Richard Elliott, and Shawna Dolansky Overton. "Death and Afterlife: The Biblical Silence." Pages 35–59 in *Judaism in Late Antiquity, Part Four: Death, Life After Death, Resurrection, and the World to Come in the Judaisms of Antiquity.* Edited by Alan Avery-Peck and Jacob Neusner. Leiden: Brill, 2000.

Gafni, Isaiah. "Bringing Deceased from Abroad for Burial in Eretz Israel-on the Origin of the Custom and its Development." *Cathedra* 4 (1977) 113–20.

Gager, John. "Body Symbols and Social Reality: Resurrection, Incarnation, and Asceticism in Early Christianity." *Religion* 12 (1982) 345–63.

Gallicet, Ezio. "Ancora sullo Pseudo-Athenagoras." *Rivista di Filologia* (1977) 21–42.

——— "Athenagoras o Pseudo-Athenagoras." *Rivista di Filologia* (1976) 420–35.

Geertz, Clifford. "Religion as a Cultural System." Pages 87–125 in *The Interpretation of Cultures.* New York: Basic Books, 1973.

Georgi, Dieter. *The Opponents of Paul in Second Corinthians.* Philadelphia: Fortress, 1986.

Gibson, Elsa. *The Christians for Christians Inscriptions of Phrygia.* Harvard Theological Studies 32. Missoula: Scholars, 1978.

Gillman, Neil. *The Death of Death.* Woodstock: Jewish Lights, 1997.

Goldenberg, Robert. "Bound Up in the Bond of Life: Death and Afterlife in Jewish Tradition." Pages 97–108 in *Death and Afterlife: Perspectives of World Religions.* Edited by Hiroshi Obayashi. New York: Greenwood, 1992.

Goldin, Judah. "A Philosophical Session in a Tannaitic Academy." Pages 366–86 in *Essays in Greco-Roman and Related Talmudic Literature.* New York: Ktav, 1977.

Gordon, Richard. "The Veil of Power." Pages 126–37 in *Paul and Empire.* Edited by Richard Horsley. Harrisburg: Trinity, 1997.

Goshen Gottstein, Alon. "The Body as Image of God in Rabbinic Literature." *HTR* 87 (1994) 171–95.

Grant, Robert. *Irenaeus of Lyons.* Routledge: New York, 1997.

—— "Five Apologists and Marcus Aurelius." *VC* 42 (1988) 1–17.

—— *Greek Apologists of the Second Century.* Philadelphia: Westminster, 1988.

—— "Athenagoras or Pseudo-Athenagoras." *HTR* 47 (1954) 121–29.

—— "The Resurrection of the Body." *JR* 28 (1948) 120–30, 188–208.

Green, William Scott. "Messiah in Judaism: Rethinking the Question." Pages 1–13 in *Judaisms and their Messiahs.* Edited by Jacob Neusner, William Scott Green, and Ernest Frerichs. Cambridge: Cambridge University Press, 1987.

Gruen, Erich. "Greeks and Jews: Mutual Misperceptions in Josephus's *Contra Apionem* in *Judaism in its Hellenistic Context.* Edited by Carol Bakhos. *JSJSup* Leiden: Brill, forthcoming.

Hachlili, Rachel. *Ancient Jewish Art and Archaeology in the Diaspora.* Leiden: Brill, 1998.

Hachlili, Rachel, and Ann Killebrew. "Jewish Funerary Customs during the Second Temple Period, in Light of the Excavations at the Jericho Necropolis." *PEQ* 115 (1983) 109–32.

Hafemann, Scott. *Suffering and Spirit: An Exegetical Study of 2 Cor 2:14–3:3 within the Context of the Corinthian Correspondence.* Tübingen: Mohr Siebeck, 1986.

Hays, Richard. *First Corinthians.* Louisville: John Knox, 1997.

Fleischer, Ezra. "On the Beginnings of Obligatory Jewish Prayer." (Heb.) *Tarbiz* 59 (1990) 397–44.

Goodenough, Erwin R. *Jewish Symbols in the Greco-Roman Period* Abridged and Edited by Jacob Neusner. Princeton: Princeton University Press, 1988.

Heinemann, Yitzhak. *Prayer in the Talmud.* Translated by Richard Sarason. Berlin and New York: De Gruyter, 1977.

Heinze, R. "'Tertullians Apologeticum." Bericht über die Verhandlungen d. Kon. sächs Ges.d. Wiss. Zu Leipzig, Phil-hist' Kl. 62 (1910)

Helleman, Wendy. "Tertullian on Athens and Jerusalem." Pages 363–81 in *Hellenization Revisited.* Edited by Wendy Helleman. Lanham: University Press of America, 1994.

Hengel, Martin. *Crucifixion.* Translated by J. Bowden. London: SCM, 1977.

Hoffman, Lawrence. *The Canonization of the Synagogue Service.* Notre Dame: University of Notre Dame Press, 1979.

—— *Beyond the Text.* Bloomington: Indiana University Press, 1987.

Holleman, Joost. *Resurrection and Parousia.* Leiden: Brill, 1996.

Hopkins, Keith. *Death and Renewal.* Cambridge: Cambridge University Press, 1983.

—— "Christian Number and Its Implications." *JECS* 6 (1998) 185–226.

Horner, Timothy. *Listening to Trypho.* Leuven: Peeters, 2001.

Horsley, Richard A. "1 Corinthians: A Case Study of Paul's Assembly as an Alternative Society." Pages 242–52 in *Paul and Empire.* Edited by Richard Horsley. Harrisburg: Trinity, 1997.

—— *Sociology and the Jesus Movement.* New York: Crossroad, 1989.

——, ed. *Paul and Empire.* Harrisburg: Trinity, 1997.

—— "How Can Some of You Say 'There is No Resurrection of the Dead?' Spiritual Elitism at Corinth." *NovT* 20 (1978) 203–31.

—— "*Pneumatikos* vs. *Psychikos*: Distinctions of Status Among the Corinthians." *HTR* 69 (1976) 269–88.

Horst, Pieter van der. *Ancient Jewish Epitaphs*. Kampen: Kok Pharos, 1991.

—— *The Sentences of Pseudo-Phocylides*. Leiden: Brill, 1978.

Jensen, Robin Margaret. *Understanding Early Christian Art*. London and New York: Routledge, 2000.

Jaeger, Walter. "The Greek Ideas of Immortality." Pages 97–114 in *Immortality and Resurrection*. Edited by Krister Stendahl. New York: Macmillian, 1965.

Johnson, Gary. *Early Christian Epitaphs From Anatolia*. Texts and Translations 35. Early Christian Literature Series 8. Atlanta: Scholars, 1995.

Johnson, Mark. "Pagan-Christian Burial Practices of the Fourth Century: Shared Tombs?" *JECS* 5 (1997) 37–59.

Keck, Leander. "Death and Afterlife in the New Testament." Pages 83–96 in *Death and Afterlife: Perspectives of World Religions*. Edited by Hiroshi Obayashi. New York: Greenwood, 1992.

Kennedy, George. *A New History of Classical Rhetoric*. Princeton: Princeton University Press, 1994.

Kimelman, Reuven. "*Birkat ha Minim* and the Lack of Evidence for an Anti-Christian Jewish Prayer in Late Antiquity." Pages 226–44 in vol. 2 of *Jewish and Christian Self-Definition*. Edited by E. P. Sanders, Albert Baumgarten, and Alan Mendelson. Philadelphia: Fortress, 1981.

King, Karen. *What is Gnosticism?*. Cambridge: Harvard University Press, 2003.

—— "Kingdom in the Gospel of Thomas." *Forum* 3 (1987) 48–97.

Klijn, A. F. J. "Christianity in Edessa and in the Gospel of Thomas." *NovT* 14 (1972) 70–77.

Klutz, Todd. "The Rhetoric of Science in *The Rise of Christianity*: A Response to Rodney Stark's Sociological Account of Christianization." *JECS* 6 (1998) 162–84.

Koester, Helmut. "Imperial Ideology and Paul's Eschatology in 1 Thessalonians." Pages 158–66 in *Paul and Empire*. Edited by Richard Horsley. Harrisburg: Trinity, 1997.

Kovacs, Judith. "The Archons, the Spirit, and the Death of Christ: Do We Need the Hypothesis of Gnostic Opponents to Explain 1 Corinthians 2:6–16?" Pages 217–36 in *Apocalyptic in the New Testament: Essays in Honor of J. Louis Martyn*. Edited by Joel Marcus and Marion Lloyd Soards. *JSNTSup* 24. Sheffield: Journal for the Study of the New Testament, 1989.

Kraemer, David. *The Meanings of Death in Rabbinic Judaism*. London and New York: Routledge, 2000.

Kraemer, Ross. "Jewish Tuna and Christian Fish." *HTR* 84 (1991) 141–62.

—— "Non-Literary Evidence for Jewish Women in Rome and Egypt." *Helios* 13 (1986) 85–101.

—— "On the Meaning of the Term 'Jew' in Greco-Roman Inscriptions." *HTR* 82 (1989) 35–53.

Laansma, Jon. *"I Will Give You Rest": The Rest Motif in the New Testament with Special Reference to Mt 11 and Heb 3–4*. Wissenschaftliche Untersuchungen zum Neuen Testament 2/98. Tübingen: Mohr Siebeck, 1997.

Lang, Bernhard. "Afterlife: Ancient Israel's Changing Vision of the World Beyond." *BRev* 4 (1988) 12–23.

Leon, Harry. *The Jews of Ancient Rome*. Philadelphia: Jewish Publication Society. Repr. Peabody. Hendrickson, 1995.

Lieberman, Saul. "Some Aspects of Afterlife in Early Rabbinic Literature." Pages 495–532 in vol. 2 of *Harry Austyn Wolfson Jubilee Volume on the Occasion of his Seventy-fifth Birthday*. Edited by the American Academy of Jewish Research. Jerusalem: American Academy of Jewish Research, 1965.

Lifshitz, Baruch. "Beitrage zur palästinischen Epigraphik." *ZDPV* 78 (1962) 64–88.
Lifshitz, Baruch, and Moshe Schwabe. *Beth Shearim*. Jerusalem: Israel Exploration Society, 1967.
Llewelyn, S., and R. Kearsley, eds. *New Documents Illustrating Early Christianity*. Ancient History Documentary Centre. Sydney: Macquarie University, 1992.
Luedemann, Gerd. *The Resurrection of Jesus*. Minneapolis: Fortress, 1994.
Marshall, Peter. "A Metaphor of Social Shame: *Thriambeuein* in 2 Cor 2:14." *NovT* 25 (1983) 302–17.
Martin, Dale. *The Corinthian Body*. New Haven: Yale, 1995.
Martin-Achard, Robert. *From Death to Life*. Edinburgh: Oliver and Boyd, 1960.
Martyn, J. Louis. *Galatians*. Anchor Bible 33A. New York: Doubleday, 1997.
Mason, Steve. "Chief Priests, Sadducees, Pharisees, and Sanhedrin in Acts." Pages 115–77 in *The Book of Acts in Its Palestinian Setting*. Edited by Richard Bauckham. Vol. 4 of *The Book of Acts in Its First Century Setting*. Edited by Bruce Winter. Grand Rapids: Eerdmans, 1995.
—— "Pharisaic Dominance before 70 C.E. and the Gospels' Hypocrisy Charge (Matt 23:2–3)." *HTR* 83 (1990) 363–81.
—— *Flavius Josephus on the Pharisees*. Leiden: Brill, 1991.
—— "Was Josephus a Pharisee? A Reexamination of *Life* 10–12." *JJS* 40 (1989) 30–45.
McKane, Byron. "Bones of Contention? Ossuaries and Reliquaries in Early Judaism and Christianity." *SecCent* 8 (1991) 235–46.
Meier, John. "The Debate on the Resurrection of the Dead: An Incident from the Ministry of the Historical Jesus?" *JSNT* 77 (2000) 3–24.
Mendenhall, George. "From Witchcraft to Justice: Death and Afterlife in the Old Testament." Pages 67–81 in *Death and Afterlife: Perspectives of World Religions*. Edited by Hiroshi Obayashi. New York: Greenwood, 1992.
Meyers, Eric. *Jewish Ossuaries: Reburial and Rebirth*. Rome: Biblical Institute Press, 1971.
Millar, William. *Isaiah 24:27 and the Origin of Apocalyptic*. Harvard Semitic Monograph Series 11. Missoula: Scholars, 1976.
Minns, Dennis. *Irenaeus*. Washington: Georgetown University Press, 1994.
Mitchell, Margaret. *Paul and the Rhetoric of Reconciliation*. Louisville: Westminster John Knox, 1992.
Moltmann, Jürgen. *Is There Life after Death?* Milwaukee. Marquette University Press, 1998.
Murnane, William "Taking it With You: The Problem of Death and Afterlife in Ancient Egypt." Pages 35–48 in *Death and Afterlife: Perspectives of World Religions*. Edited by Hiroshi Obayashi. New York: Greenwood, 1992.
Nagakubo, Senso. "Investigation into Jewish Concepts of Afterlife in the Beth Shearim Greek Inscriptions." Ph.D. diss., Duke University, 1974.
Neusner, Jacob. *From Politics to Piety*. 2nd ed. New York: Ktav, 1979.
—— "Josephus's Pharisees." Pages 224–53 in *Ex Orbe Religionum: Studia Geo Widengren*. Leiden: Brill, 1972.
—— *Rabbinic Traditions about the Pharisees Before 70*. Leiden: Brill, 1971.
—— *The Pharisees: Rabbinic Perspectives*. Leiden: Brill, 1973.
Nickelsburg, George. "Judgment, Life after Death and Resurrection in the Apocrypha and Non-Apocalyptic Pseudepigrapha." Pages 141–62 in *Judaism in Late Antiquity, Part Four: Death, Life After Death, Resurrection, and the World to Come in the Judaisms of Antiquity*. Edited by Alan Avery-Peck and Jacob Neusner. Leiden: Brill, 2000.
—— *Resurrection, Immortality, and Eternal Life in Intertestamental Judaism*. Harvard Theological Series 26. Cambridge: Harvard University Press, 1972.
Nikolainen, Aimo. *Der Auferstehungsglaube in der Bibel und ihrer Umwelt*. 2 vols. AASI B 49/3, 59/3. Helsinki, 1944–46.

Norris, Richard. "The Transcendance and Freedom of God: Irenaeus, the Greek Tradition, and Gnosticism." Pages 87–100 in *Early Christian Literature and the Classical Intellectual Tradition*. Edited by William Schoedel and Robert Wilken. Paris: Beauchesne, 1979.

North, Helen. "Death and Afterlife in Greco-Roman Tragedy and Plato." Pages 49–64 in *Death and Afterlife: Perspectives of World Religions*. Edited by Hiroshi Obayashi. New York: Greenwood, 1992.

Noy, David. *Jewish Inscriptions of Western Europe*. Cambridge: Cambridge University Press, 1995.

Obayashi, Hiroshi, ed. *Death and Afterlife: Perspectives of World Religions*. New York: Greenwood, 1992.

Osborn, Eric. *Irenaeus of Lyons*. Cambridge: Cambridge University Press, 2001.

—— "Was Tertullian a Philosopher?" *StPatr* 31 (1997)

Pagels, Elaine. *Beyond Belief*. New York: Random House, 2003.

—— *The Gnostic Gospels*. New York: Random House, 1979.

Park, Joseph. *Conceptions of Afterlife in Jewish Inscriptions with Special Reference to Pauline Literature*. Tübingen: Mohr Siebeck, 2000.

Pearson, Birger. *The Pneumatikos/Psychikos Terminology of 1 Corinthians: A Study in the Theology of the Corinthian Opponents of Paul and its Relation to Gnosticism*. Missoula: Scholars Press, 1973.

Perelman, Chaim. *The Realm of Rhetoric*. Notre Dame: University of Notre Dame Press, 1982.

Perelman, Chaim, and Lucie Olbrechts-Tyteca. *The New Rhetoric*. Notre Dame: University of Notre Dame Press, 1969.

Perkins, Pheme. *Resurrection*. Garden City: Doubleday, 1984.

Peuch, Emile. *La croyance des Ésseniens en la vie future: immortalité, resurrection, vie éternelle?* Etudes Bibliques Nouvelle 22. Paris: Gabalda, 1993.

Pouderon, Bernard. "Réflexions sur la Formation d'une Élite intellectuelle chrétienne au II Siècle: Les Écoles d'Athènes, de Rome, et d'Alexandrie." Pages 237–69 in *Les Apologistes Chrétiens et la Culture Grecque*. Edited by Bernard Pouderon and Joseph Doré. Paris: Beauchesne, 1998.

—— "Le contexte polémique du *De Resurrectione* attribué à Justin: destinataires et adversaires." *StPatr* 31 (1997) 143–66.

—— "L'Authenticité du Traité *Sur la Résurrection* Attribué à l'Apologiste Athénagore." *VC* 40 (1986) 226–40.

Powell, Mark Allan. "Do and Keep What Moses Says (Matthew 23:2–7)." *JBL* 114 (1995) 419–35.

Prigent, Pierre. *Justin et l'ancien Testament*. Paris: Gabalda, 1964.

Rahmani, L. Y. "Ancient Jerusalem's Funerary Customs and Tombs, Part 4." *Biblical Archaeologist* 45.2 (1982) 109–19.

—— "Ancient Jerusalem's Funerary Customs and Tombs, Part 3." *Biblical Archaeologist* 45.1 (1981) 43–53.

Rajak, Tessa. "Talking at Trypho: Christian Apologetic as Anti-Judaism in Justin's *Dialogue with Trypho the Jew*." Pages 59–80 in *Apologetics in the Roman Empire*. Edited by M. J. Edwards, M. D. Goodman, and S. R. F. Price. Oxford: Oxford University Press, 1999.

Raphael, Simcha. *Jewish Views of the Afterlife*. Northvale and London: Jason Aronson, 1994.

Riley, Gregory. *Resurrection Reconsidered: Thomas and John in Controversy*. Minneapolis: Fortress, 1995.

Rivkin, Ellis. *A Hidden Revolution*. Nashville: Abingdon, 1978.

—— "Defining the Pharisees: The Tannaitic Sources." *HUCA* 40–41 (1969–70) 205–49.

Roetzel, Calvin. "'As Dying, and Behold We Live' Death and Resurrection in Paul's Theology." *Int* 46 (1992) 5–18.

Rubin, Nissan. *Kets ha-Hayim* (Heb.). Tel Aviv: Ha-Kibuts ha-Me'uhad, 1997.

—— "The Sages Conception of Body and Soul." Pages 47–103 in *Essays in the Social Scientific Study of Judaism.* Edited by Simcha Fishbane and Jack Lightstone. Montreal: Concordia University Press, 1990.

Rudolph, Kurt. *Gnosis.* Translated by Robert McLachlan Wilson. Edinburgh: T. & T. Clark, 1983.

Ruprecht, Louis. "Athenagoras the Christian, Pausanius the Travel Guide, and a Mysterious Corinthian Girl." *HTR* 85 (1992).

Rutgers, Leonard. *The Hidden Heritage of Diaspora Judaism.* Leuven: Peeters, 1998.

Saldarini, Anthony. *Pharisees, Scribes, and Sadducees in Palestinian Society.* Wilmington: Michael Glazier, 1988. Repr. Grand Rapids: Eerdmans, 2001.

Schenke, Hans-Martin. "*The Book of Thomas.* (*NHC* II.7): A Revision of a Pseudepigraphic Letter of Jacob the Contender." Pages 213–28 in *New Testament and Gnosis.* Edinburgh: T. & T. Clark, 1983.

—— "Auferstehung und Gnosis." *ZNW* 59 (1968) 123–26.

Schmidt, Brian. "Memory as Immortality: Countering the Dreaded 'Death after Death' in Ancient Israelite Society." Pages 87–100 in *Judaism in Late Antiquity, Part Four: Death, Life After Death, Resurrection, and the World to Come in the Judaisms of Antiquity.* Edited by Alan Avery-Peck and Jacob Neusner. Leiden: Brill, 2000.

—— *Israel's Beneficent Dead.* Tübingen: Mohr Siebeck, 1994.

Schoedel, William. *Athenagoras: Legatio and De Resurrectione.* Oxford: Oxford University Press, 1972.

Schoedel, William. "Apologetic Literature and Ambassadorial Activities." *HTR* 82 (1989) 55–78.

—— "In Praise of the King: A Rhetorical Pattern in Athenagoras." Pages 69–90 in *Disciplina Nostra: Essays in Memory of Robert F. Evans.* Edited by Donald Winslow. Philadelphia: Philadelphia Patristic Foundation, 1979.

—— "Enclosing, Not Enclosed: The Early Christian Doctrine of God." Pages 75–86 in *Early Christian Literature and the Classical Intellectual Tradition.* Edited by William Schoedel and Robert Wilken. Paris: Beauchesne, 1979.

Schwartz, Seth. *Imperialism and Jewish Society.* Princeton: Princeton University Press, 2001.

Scott, James. *Domination and the Arts of Resistance.* New Haven: Yale University Press, 1990.

Scurlock, J. A. "Death and Afterlife in Ancient Mesopotamian Thought." Pages 1883–93 in vol. 4 of *Civilizations of the Ancient Near East.* Edited by Jack Sasson. New York: Scribners, 1995.

Segal, Alan. *Life After Death: A History of the Afterlife in Western Religion.* New York: Doubleday, 2004.

—— "Life after Death: The Social Sources." Pages 90–125 in *The Resurrection.* Edited by Stephen Davis, Daniel Kendall, and Gerald O'Collins. Oxford and New York: Oxford University Press, 1997.

Sellew, Philip. "Thomas Christianity: Scholars in Quest of Community." Pages 11–35 in *The Apocryphal Acts of Thomas.* Edited by Jan Bremmer. Leuven: Peeters, 2001.

—— "Death, the Body, and the World in the Gospel of Thomas." *StPatr* 31 (1997) 530–35.

Sellin, Gerhard. *Der Streit um die Auferstehung der Toten.* Forschungen zur Religion und Literatur des Alten und Neuen Testaments 138. Göttingen: Vandenhoeck und Ruprecht, 1986.

Setzer, Claudia. "Resurrection of the Dead as Symbol and Strategy." *JAAR* 69 (2001) 65–101.

—— "Talking their Way into Empire: Pagans, Jews, and Christians debate Resurrection of the Body" in *Judaism in its Hellenistic Context, JSJSup.* Edited by Carol Bakhos. Leiden: Brill (forthcoming).

—— *Jewish Responses to Early Christians.* Minneapolis: Fortress, 1994.

Sheppard, A. R. R. "Jews, Christians, and Heretics in Acmonia and Eumenia." Pages 169–80 in *Anatolian Studies* 29 (1979).

Shoemaker, Stephen. *Ancient Traditions of the Virgin Mary's Dormition and Assumption.* New York: Oxford, 2002.

Sider, Robert. "On Symmetrical Composition in Tertullian." *JTS* 24 (1973) 405–23.

—— *Ancient Rhetoric and the Art of Tertullian.* London: Oxford University Press, 1971.

—— "Structure and Design in the 'De Resurrectione Mortuorum' of Tertullian." *VC* 23 (1969) 177–96.

Sievers, Joseph. "Josephus on the Afterlife." Pages 20–34 in *Understanding Josephus.* Edited by Steve Mason. *JSPSup* 32. Sheffield: Sheffield Academic Press, 1998.

Simon, Marcel. "θάρσει, οὐδεὶς ἀθάνατος" *RHR* 113 (1936) 188–206.

—— *Le christianisme antique et son contexte religieux.* Tübingen: Mohr Siebeck, 1981,

Sinascalco, Paolo. "Recenti studi su Tertulliano." *RSLR* 14 (1978) 396–405.

Skarsaune, Oskar. *The Proof from Prophecy. NovTSup* 56. Leiden: Brill, 1987.

Smith, Jonathan Z. "The Garments of Shame." *HR* 5 (1965–66) 217–38.

Smith, Martin Ferguson, ed., *Diogenes of Oinoanda: The Epicurean Inscription.* Naples: Bibliopolis, 1993.

Smith, Morton. "What is Implied by the Variety of Messianic Figures?" *JBL* 78 (1959) 66–72.

—— "Palestinian Judaism in the First Century." Pages 67–81 in *Israel: Its Role in Civilization.* Edited by Moshe Davis. New York: The Jewish Theological Seminary, 1956.

Soards, Marion Lloyd. *The Speeches in Acts: Their Content, Context, and Concern.* Westminster: John Knox, 1994.

Stemberger, Gunther. *Pharisees, Sadducees, Essenes.* Minneapolis: Fortress, 1995.

Stendahl, Krister, ed. *Immortality and Resurrection.* New York: Macmillan, 1965.

Stowers, Stanley. "The Social Sciences and the Study of Early Christianity." Pages 149–81 in *Approaches to Ancient Judaism.* Edited by William Scott Green. Brown Judaic Series 32. Atlanta: Scholars, 1985.

Strubbe, J. H. M. "'Cursed be he that moves my bones.'" Pages 33–59 in *Magika Hiera.* Edited by C. Faraone and D. Obbink. New York: Oxford University Press, 1991.

Swidler, Ann. "Culture in Action: Symbols and Strategies." *American Sociological Review* 51 (1986) 273–86.

Tabbernee, William. *Montanist Inscriptions and Testimonia.* North American Patristic Society Monograph Series 16. Atlanta: Mercer University Press.

Teitelbaum, Dina. "The Relationship between Ossuary Burial and the Belief in Resurrection during Late Second Temple Judaism." M.A. diss., Carleton University, CA, 1997. UMI: Ann Arbor, 1997.

Tuckett, Christopher M. "The Corinthians Who Say 'There is No Resurrection of the Dead.'" Pages 247–75 in *The Corinthian Correspondence.* Edited by R. Bieringer. Leuven: Peeters, 1996.

Valée, Gérard. *A Study in Anti-Gnostic Polemics.* Waterloo, CA: Wilfred Laurier, 1981.

Van Eijk, A. H. C. "The Gospel of Philip and Clement of Alexandria: Gnostic and Ecclesiastical Theology on the Resurrection and the Eucharist." *VC* 25 (1971) 94–120.

—— "'Only that can rise which has previously fallen': The History of a Formula." NTS n.s. 22 (1971) 517–29.

Van Eijk, Ton H. C. *La resurrection des Morts chez les Pères Apostolique.* Paris: Beauchesne, 1974.

Van Henten, Jan Willem. *The Maccabean Martyrs as Saviours of the Jewish People. JSJSup* 57. Leiden: Brill, 1997.

Vielhauer, Philipp. "On the Paulinism of Acts." Pages 33–50 in *Studies in Luke-Acts.* Edited by Leander Keck and J. Louis Martyn. Nashville: Abingdon, 1966.

Visotzky, Burton. "The Priest's Daughter and the Thief in the Orchard." Pages 165–71 in *Putting Body and Soul Together. Essays in Honor of Robin Scroggs*. Edited by Virginia Wiles, Alexandra Brown, and Graydon Snyder. Valley Forge: Trinity, 1997.

Wartelle, André. "Le Traité *De la Résurrection* de Saint Justin ou Le destin d'une Œuvre." Pages 3–10 in *Histoire et Culture Chrétienne*. Edited by Yves Ledure. Paris: Beauchesne, 1992.

Wedderburn, A. J. M. *Baptism and Resurrection*. Wissenschaftliche Untersuchungen zum Neuen Testament. Tübingen: Mohr Siebeck, 1987.

Weinstein, S. *Rabbinic Criticism of Self-Imposed Religious Stringency*. Ann Arbor: University Microfilms, 1995.

Wilken, Robert. *The Christians as the Romans Saw Them*. New Haven: Yale University Press, 1984.

Williams, Michael Allen. *Rethinking Gnosticism*. Princeton: Princeton University Press, 1996.

Wilson, Stephen. *Related Strangers*. Minneapolis: Fortress, 1995.

Wire, Antoinette Clark. *The Corinthian Women Prophets: A Reconstruction Through Paul's Rhetoric*. Minneapolis: Augsburg Fortress, 1990.

Witherington, Ben. *Conflict and Community in Corinth*. Grand Rapids: Eerdmans, 1995.

Wray, Judith Hoch. *Rest as a Theological Metaphor in the Epistle to the Hebrews and the Gospel of Truth*. Society of Biblical Literature Dissertation Series 166. Atlanta: Scholars, 1997.

Wright, N. T. *The Resurrection of the Son of God*. Minneapolis: Fortress, 2003.

Yamauchi, Edwin. "Life, Death, and Afterlife in the Ancient Near East." Pages 21–50 in *Life in the Face of Death*. Edited by Richard Longenecker. Grands Rapids: Eerdmans, 1998.

Young, Frances. "Greek Apologists of the Second Century." Pages 81–104 in *Apologetics in the Roman Empire*. Edited by M. J. Edwards, M. D. Goodman, and S.R.F. Price. Oxford: Oxford University Press, 1999.

Young, M. O. "Justin Martyr and the Death of Souls." *StPatr* 16 (1985) 209–15.

# INDEX OF MODERN AUTHORS

# INDEX OF PRIMARY SOURCES

APOCRYPHA AND PSEUDEPIGRAPHA

## APOLOGISTS AND CHURCH FATHERS

### JUSTIN

### ATHENAGORAS